Confluence of Policy and Leadership in Academic Health Science Centers

A PROFESSIONAL AND PERSONAL GUIDE

Edited by
STEVEN A. WARTMAN
Editor
President/CEO
Association of Academic Health Centers

Foreword by
ANDREW M. IBRAHIM AND M. ROY WILSON

CULTURE, CONTEXT AND QUALITY IN HEALTH SCIENCES
RESEARCH, EDUCATION, LEADERSHIP AND PATIENT CARE
Series Editors
THOMAS S. INUI AND RICHARD M. FRANKEL

Radcliffe Publishing
London • New York

Radcliffe Publishing Ltd
33–41 Dallington Street
London
EC1V 0BB
United Kingdom

www.radcliffehealth.com

British Library Cataloguing in Publication Data

A catalogue record for this book is available from the British Library.

ISBN-13: 978 184619 525 9

The paper used for the text pages of this book
is FSC® certified. FSC (The Forest Stewardship
Council®) is an international network to promote
responsible management of the world's forests.

Typeset by Darkriver Design, Auckland, New Zealand
Printed and bound by TJ International Ltd, Padstow, Cornwall, UK

Contents

Contents

Foreword

To cope with increasing change and uncertainty, Academic Health Centers (AHCs), collectively and individually, must be able to learn quickly and act expeditiously. This will require changes in institutional culture that increase openness, teamwork, commitment to learning, continuous improvement, accountability, and patient centeredness. Transforming the culture of AHCs is likely to be a lengthy and complex process.
—Commonwealth Fund Task Force on Academic Health Centers[1]

ALTHOUGH SLIGHT VARIATIONS EXIST IN THE DEFINITION OF AN academic health science center (AHSC), all share a common thread: the alignment of an academic entity with a clinical one. The Association of Academic Health Centers defines an academic health science center as "an educational institution that includes a medical school and at least one additional health professions school (e.g. nursing, dentistry, pharmacy, allied health, public health, veterinary medicine, graduate school in biomedical sciences), and either owns or is affiliated with a teaching hospital or health system."[2] The development of these entities has become an increasingly common partial answer to the growing complexity of problems surrounding health care. AHSCs are characterized by a symbiotic relationship between scientific research, medical education, and clinical care. They are thus uniquely positioned to maintain and advance health care in the twenty-first century within the United States and around the world. In fact, as noted in the Institute of Medicine's *Academic Health Centers: Leading Change in the 21st Century* report,[3] AHSCs have a *responsibility* to reform medical education, develop new paradigms for patient care, and translate scientific discoveries into improved population outcomes. Doing so will require AHSCs to creatively connect previously independent institutions to create synergistic relationships. Such transformations will require AHSCs to recruit and develop strong leaders who can orient, organize, and finance AHSCs to meet societal needs.

Because these are among the most complex of institutions, *policy and leadership* are important organizational tools for AHSCs. These elements affect all persons in an institution and serve as the foundation for its success. Policy can serve as an important leadership tool, as detailed by Joséph Michelli in *Prescription for Excellence: Leadership Lessons for Creating a World-Class Customer Experience from UCLA Health System.*[4] Mitchell traces how in just 3 years a health system was able to move from the 36th percentile in patient satisfaction to the 99th percentile. Underlying this dramatic improvement were new institutional policies that focused on patient care. Their development engaged a broad range of stakeholders to create clear expectations for employees while tracking agreed-upon measurable outcomes. More than simple policy changes, the described transformation used policy creation as a tool to change the institutional culture. Under strong leadership, multiple components across various parts of the system were engaged to consistently contribute to the formulation of institutional policies and a shared mission. In this way, it was both a "top-down" and a "bottom-up" transformation to focus resources and policies toward improving patient care.

This volume on the important intersection of policy and leadership consists of 12 chapters written by leaders with substantial experience in AHSCs. They cover a range of topics essential to the creation and future success of these complex institutions. How AHSCs foster relationships from the micro level of its own members and components, through to legislative and regulatory bodies, and beyond to international duty and collaborations, is described.

Chapter 1 has Wartman and Gabel setting the stage by discussing the components of leadership that are fundamental to the success of AHSCs. Successful leadership is viewed through a transformational as opposed to a transactional lens. In the latter, the traditional "carrot and stick" approach is implemented through a system of reward and punishment. Transformational leadership, on the other hand, places institutional values and principles at its core and leads by both example and inspiration. The authors also describe the career paths to leadership of these major institutions and strongly suggest the need for the "demystification" of academic administration with the development of leadership training and succession planning.

In Chapter 2, Robillard describes the "Academic Health Science Center in a New World Order" and the compelling need to align goals of patient care with the academic programs of teaching and research. In tracing the recent history of AHSCs, he describes the variation in governing structures that have developed over time, ranging from a "single fiduciary, one executive leader model" to the "multiple fiduciary, multiple executive leaders model." Regardless of governing structure, Robillard offers 10 principles to guide high-performance AHSCs, including the need for accountability and transparency and centering on a single, core mission. It is important to note, however, "*that the success or failure of a model is predominantly a function of who holds leadership positions. The 'right people' can make most any system work (although poor structures make it harder and may discourage the best people), but the right structure will never make the 'wrong people' successful."*

The formation of an AHSC does not lend itself to an easy road map, as it must align two distinctly separate areas (patient care and academics) under leadership with a common set of goals. In Chapter 3, Grossman and Berne give a candid account of the structural changes that occurred between the hospital, medical school, and university, when their hospital merged and then subsequently demerged with another hospital from another university. Balancing both theoretical and pragmatic philosophies, they ultimately were able to make data-driven decisions. For example, average length of stay (ALOS) is a common quality metric for many AHSCs. Going a step further to understand the drivers of ALOS – physician treatment, hospital resources, nursing care, family/social situation – can help inform where resources can be reallocated to decrease ALOS and ultimately improve patient care. However, to simply "state that 'good data' are an essential ingredient for quality and financial stability is to proclaim the obvious, yet it is clear that many institutions neither have 'good data' nor the desire to fundamentally use data to change processes or operations."

In Chapter 4 Balser and colleagues explain important financial management considerations specific to the AHSC enterprise. The components that come together to create an AHSC may have previously held contrasting financial models, relied on different sources of funding, and had conflicting priorities for spending. Explaining how these can be reconciled, the authors discuss how a shared mission for clinical care, research, and education can be realized through "cross-subsidies." In applying this principle, profits generated from one component of the AHSC (often clinical care) are directed toward another (usually education or research), with the guiding principle to serve all the components of the mission. "Balancing these competing priorities is not only the challenge," the authors explain, "but also the real substance of AHSC financial management. For an AHSC to be successful, particularly in the future, the approach to these negotiations would ideally reflect a cohesive strategic vision that is shared by key leaders responsible for managing all three (clinical, research, and education) mission areas."

Hutchinson and colleagues in Chapter 5 describe challenges to AHSCs in building relationships with private industry. While there is sensible overlap with the goals of the biomedical industry and the research and clinical missions of AHSCs, these relationships have inevitable conflicts of interest at the individual and institutional level. Tight definitions, broad consensus, and policies promoting transparency of these interactions can facilitate the protection of patient well-being, the primary consideration. Within the AHSC, the authors point out, "no matter how sophisticated our information technology systems and no matter how tightly wound the regulations, AHSCs will still depend on personal professional integrity to guide the vast majority of personal and financial interactions."

In Chapter 6 Boyd and Goodman describe the challenges for AHSCs in regulation, accreditation, and compliance. To address an upsurge in health-care fraud and concerns over patient safety, payers and regulators in the last two decades have required unprecedented levels of documentation and oversight. While these external regulations provide a guide, the onus remains on institutions to establish working relationships with the various regulatory bodies and proactively engage them. The authors suggest that the institution benefits most when the institutional culture encourages "developing a habit of self-reporting and calling the appropriate agency for questions even when the call reveals an area of concern."

Paz and colleagues examine policies that promote the recruitment and retention of personnel within an AHSC in Chapter 7. Doing both effectively requires administrators to seek continual input from employees to create an environment that allows personal and professional growth. "Both an institutional culture and specific human resource policies aimed at responding to generational differences, including differences in attitudes toward such issues as work-life balance, telecommuting, and flexible scheduling, will be essential if AHSCs are to succeed in attracting and retaining talented and diverse faculty and staff."

Yet, developing policies are only useful so much as they reflect the true sense of how the institution does business. In Chapter 8, Bishop and Linville Jr. explore the essential elements of trainee and student policies within AHSCs. The policies are influenced by numerous organizations and accrediting bodies (e.g., Liaison Committee on Medical Education, Professional Societies) and cross many domains including academics, safety, and professionalism. The authors systematically trace 10 steps to developing a policy, beginning with recognition of a need and solicitation of broad input. As each policy is implemented, it should be consistently applied, revised, and updated.

In Chapter 9, Smith and Davies use their experience in Europe to explain the complexity of accountability within AHSCs. The Head of such an institution (and the leaders of each component) find themselves accountable to numerous groups including clinical providers, care-seeking patients, researching scientists, private industry, nonprofit donors, regulating bodies, professional societies, tuition-paying students, and others. Part of this responsibility requires creating an environment in which unique relationships across these groups can be fostered. Initiating and maintaining these connections are challenging tasks, but the effort can contribute synergistically to the overall success of the AHSC's vision.

An overarching theme underlying all policy decisions is the importance of effective communication within and from AHSCs. In Chapter 10, Owen Jr. and Miller outline principles to manage communication between the AHSC and the faculty, students, employees, alumni, local community, press, government agencies, and other stakeholders. Individual members of the AHSC should be encouraged to speak freely about their work. Although personal opinions can be offered, care must be exercised in distinguishing when they are speaking on behalf of the AHSC or as individuals. Ultimately, speech cannot be "censored," but only "managed," and this is done most effectively by assuring that all participants are knowledgeable of and engaged in the mission and vision of the AHSC.

AHSCs are inevitably tied to the communities they serve and need to build meaningful and reciprocal relationships with them. In Chapter 11, Atkinson and colleagues describe their experience in a state-supported AHSC. In their model, community support was facilitated by an Advancement Board – initially a group of 20 community leaders (and later more than 80 members) actively contributing to and advocating for the goals of the AHSC. In building robust community support, the AHSC was able to expand state, federal, and private sources of funding and promote important legislation that directly affect the AHSC.

In the final chapter, Chapter 12, Ackerly and colleagues describe the connection of AHSCs in an era of globalization. Given significant disparities in health-care access, variation in evidence-based practice, and workforce shortages across the world, AHSCs are uniquely qualified to address all three challenges through clinical care, research, and education. By leveraging their myriad strengths through strategic partnerships, "AHSCs can amplify the impact of their mission-based activities and reduce health disparities both at home and abroad."

Taken together, this volume focuses on policy considerations that provide the foundation for AHSCs to thrive. While the legislation, challenges, and strategies will change over time, the need for strong policy to influence and guide organizational and individual behavior will not. AHSCs are complex organizations that must continue to evolve to face the multifactorial nature of health-care problems. How they do so will depend to a great extent not only on having appropriate policies in place but also on their success in translating these policies into effective implementation.

Andrew M. Ibrahim
M. Roy Wilson
July 2012

References

1. Commonwealth Fund Task Force on Academic Health Centers. *Envisioning the Future of Academic Health Centers: final report of the Commonwealth Fund Task Force on academic health centers.* Commonwealth Fund; 2003.
2. www.aahcdc.org
3. Committee on the Roles of Academic Health Centers in the 21st Century; for Institute of

Medicine. *Academic Health Centers: leading change in the 21st century.* Kohn LT, editor. Washington, DC: National Academies Press; 2003.

4. Michelli, JA. *Prescription for Excellence: leadership lessons creating a world-class customer experience from UCLA Health System.* New York, NY: McGraw-Hill; 2011.

Preface

THIS IS A BOOK ABOUT THE LEADERSHIP AND MANAGEMENT OF institutions that have profound effects on the knowledge economy, the workforce, infrastructure development, and – ultimately and most importantly – health and well-being. Academic health science centers are the part of universities that educate the next generation of health professionals, conduct leading biomedical and clinical research that leads to new treatments and diagnostic breakthroughs, and deliver comprehensive patient care from the basic to the most advanced level. They range in size from moderate to among the largest employers in their regions. Because they have both *academic* (teaching and research) and *clinical* (patient care) roles, they represent a unique hybrid of business and academic functions. These institutions have many different structures but, in a time of disruptive change, have in common the difficult goal of aligning their education, research, and clinical programs – not only to survive but also to achieve excellence.

The leaders of these complex institutions carry an array of titles: vice president for health affairs, principal, dean, chancellor, among others. In many regards, those who attain these positions represent the highest levels of academic medical administration. The path to their appointments as leaders of academic health science centers varies, but generally they are highly successful medical professionals who have achieved distinction in research and leadership. Many have served as department chairs, institute directors, or deans. As a result, their training and preparation for the effective leadership of academic health science centers is highly variable. In not a few cases, some are characterized as "accidental leaders," who achieve their position not as a result of a longtime career ambition, but rather as part of a selection process that came along at the right time in their professional lives.

This book is an effort to describe and depict, on both personal and professional levels, what effective leadership of these complex institutions entails. These leaders have enormous responsibilities, beginning with the core responsibility of delivering optimal, affordable health care, and extending to the management of students, faculty, and staff, compliance with a large number of regulations, financial stewardship, fundraising, invention, management of intellectual property, internal and external communications, community relations, and strategic leadership and decision making. As such, the book is a primer for the faculty and staff of academic health science centers and their current and future leaders. At the same time, it should be standard reading for both those enrolled in faculty leadership development courses and the broad audience interested in the future of health care. It is written in the spirit of collaboration that leads to the sharing of best practices and insights.

Steven A. Wartman, MD, PhD, MACP
Editor
President/CEO
Association of Academic Health Centers
July 2012

Author's note: All cost figures are in U.S. dollars unless otherwise specified.

About the Authors

Foreword

Dr. Andrew M. Ibrahim

Andrew M. Ibrahim, MD, completed his undergraduate work at Case Western Reserve University and obtained his medical degree from the same university in 2012. He is the recipient of the Doris Duke Fellowship within the Department of Surgery at Johns Hopkins University and has also completed course work at University College London in Social Anthropology. Dr. Ibrahim has published numerous peer-reviewed articles, editorials, and book chapters related to surgical outcomes and patient safety.

Dr. M. Roy Wilson

M. Roy Wilson, MD, MS, is Deputy Director, Strategic Scientific Planning and Program Coordination, National Institute on Minority Health and Health Disparities, the National Institutes of Health (NIH). As Deputy Director, Dr. Wilson provides leadership and direction for strategic planning and oversees the development and implementation of an integrated system for coordinating the NIH minority health and health disparities research portfolio, working in collaboration with the NIH Institutes and Centers. Prior to joining the National Institute on Minority Health and Health Disparities, Dr. Wilson served as chancellor of the University of Colorado, Denver; president of the Texas Tech University Health Sciences Center, Amarillo; and dean of the Creighton University School of Medicine, Omaha, Nebraska. Most recently, Dr. Wilson chaired the board of trustees at Charles R. Drew University of Medicine and Science, Los Angeles, serving as acting president from 2010 to 2011. Under Dr. Wilson's leadership, the university regained full institutional accreditation and stabilized its finances.

Dr. Wilson's major scientific contributions have been in bridging the fields of epidemiology and ophthalmology. He has delivered more than 200 invited lectures, many of these internationally, and has published more than 300 articles, book chapters, and abstracts. The recipient of numerous honors and awards, Dr.

Wilson has served on many governing advisory councils and boards including that of the Association of Academic Health Centers.

Chapter 1

Dr. Steven A. Wartman

Steven A. Wartman, MD, PhD, MACP, is the President and Chief Executive Officer of the Association of Academic Health Centers, a nonprofit association based in Washington, DC, that seeks to advance health and well-being through the vigorous leadership of academic health science centers. Prior to assuming this position in 2005, he was Executive Vice President for Academic and Health Affairs and Dean of the School of Medicine at the University of Texas Health Science Center in San Antonio. Dr. Wartman's more than 25-year career in academic medicine includes chairing a department of medicine at two institutions and being the founding director of a division of general internal medicine.

A board-certified internist and a sociologist, Dr. Wartman is recognized internationally for his work in the organization and management of academic health centers, where he has taken the lead on critical issues such as the need for alignment between an institution's clinical, research, and education functions. In 2008 he founded the Association of Academic Health Centers International, a global organization dedicated to improving health and well-being worldwide. Dr. Wartman is the author of numerous publications and the recipient of many awards and honorary degrees.

Dr. Stewart Gabel

Stewart Gabel, MD, is the Medical Director for the Division of Children and Family Services in the New York State Office of Mental Health, and coordinates a seminar series for senior level psychiatrists working in the public sector throughout New York State. He has held several leadership positions in health and mental health programs and previously served as the Chair, Department of Psychiatry and Behavioral Sciences, Children's Hospital, Denver, and Professor of Psychiatry and Pediatrics, University of Colorado Health Sciences Center from 1992 to 2002. While at Children's Hospital, Denver, he also provided organizational consulting services.

A general, child, and adolescent psychiatrist and a pediatrician, Dr. Gabel has authored or edited numerous books and articles that address issues in child and adolescent psychiatry, pediatrics, and leadership and organizational change.

Chapter 2
• • • • • • • • • • • • •

Dr. Jean E. Robillard

Jean E. Robillard, MD, is Vice President for medical affairs at the University of Iowa and is charged with integrating planning and operations for UI Health Care, which comprises University of Iowa Hospitals and Clinics; the Carver College of Medicine; and University of Iowa Physicians, the state's largest multispecialty physician group practice. He served 4 years as Dean of the Carver College of Medicine and prior to his appointment as dean, Dr. Robillard served as chair and professor of the Department of Pediatrics at the University of Michigan Medical School and physician-in-chief at C.S. Mott Children's Hospital.

Dr. Robillard is a pediatric nephrologist whose work focuses on the developmental physiology of the kidney. He has published numerous scientific papers during his career, many of which have contributed to advances in the field. He is a Fellow of the American Association for the Advancement of Science, and in 2006 served as Chair of the Board of Directors of the American Board of Pediatrics. He is also a member of the American Clinical and Climatological Association, the Iowa Business Council, and Rotary International.

Chapter 3
• • • • • • • • • • • • •

Dr. Robert I. Grossman

Robert I. Grossman, MD, is the Saul J. Farber Dean and Chief Executive Officer of New York University Langone Medical Center. Dr. Grossman leads both the NYU School of Medicine and NYU Hospitals Center, the latter comprising Tisch Hospital, the Rusk Institute of Rehabilitation Medicine, and the Hospital for Joint Diseases. He assumed these responsibilities in 2007. Dr. Grossman joined New York University in 2001 as the Louis Marx Professor of Radiology, chairman of the Department of Radiology, and professor of neurology, neurosurgery, and physiology and neuroscience. In his previous position at the Hospital of the University of Pennsylvania, he had been professor of radiology, neurosurgery, and neurology; chief of neuroradiology; and associate chairman of radiology.

Board certified in radiology and neuroradiology, Dr. Grossman has pioneered research in magnetic resonance in medicine and biology and received many distinguished awards, including the Javits Neuroscience Investigator Award by the National Institutes of Health in 1999 for his work on multiple sclerosis. Alongside his award-winning research, Dr. Grossman has been a passionate educator and widely published scholar. He has trained over 100 fellows, many of whom occupy prominent positions worldwide, and has authored numerous publications and five books, including *Neuroradiology: The Requisites*, a best-selling textbook in neuroradiology.

Dr. Robert Berne

Robert Berne, PhD, is the Executive Vice President for Health at New York University (NYU). He is responsible for working with deans, university leadership, and boards on long-term academic, financial, and operational strategies for the wide range of health activities at NYU. Dr. Berne is involved in various strategic issues at the NYU Langone Medical Center and the NYU College of Dentistry and College of Nursing including academic direction, governance, long-term financial and academic performance, and organizational linkages. Dr. Berne has led the development of NYU's Masters in Global Public Health degree, a unique six-school collaboration that has enrolled its second class, and he has overseen NYU's Center on Catastrophe Preparedness and Response, which draws on faculty from all of NYU's schools to address the complex issues related to natural and man-made disasters.

Dr. Berne previously held the positions of Senior Vice President for Health, Vice President for Academic and Health Affairs, and Vice President for Academic Development. He has also served as dean of NYU's Robert F. Wagner Graduate School of Public Service. A scholar of public education policy and financing, Dr. Berne has authored multiple books and studies and was a founder and codirector of NYU's Institute for Education and Social Policy.

Chapter 4

Dr. Jeffrey R. Balser

Jeffrey R. Balser, MD, PhD, is Vice Chancellor for Health Affairs at Vanderbilt University, overseeing all health-related programs. He also has served as Dean of the School of Medicine since his appointment in 2008. Prior to this he held the position of Chief Research Officer for the Vanderbilt Medical Center, heading a period of significant expansion that moved Vanderbilt into tenth place among US medical schools in National Institutes of Health (NIH) funding. In 2001, he was appointed the Gwathmey Professor and Chair of Anesthesiology when, under his leadership, Vanderbilt's clinical services supporting surgery and intensive care medicine grew by 25%.

Dr. Balser is trained in anesthesiology and critical care medicine; his clinical work has primarily involved the care of postoperative cardiac surgery patients in intensive care unit settings. When he joined Vanderbilt in 1998 he established an intramural mentoring program for junior faculty physician scientists that has been a national model for centralized management of physician scientist career development, and is supported by the NIH. Dr. Balser is a member of the Institute of Medicine of the National Academy of Sciences, the American Society of Clinical

Investigation, the Association of American Physicians, and has chaired the NIH Director's Pioneer Awards Committee.

Edward R. Marx

Edward R. Marx, MBA, is Director of the Strategic Analytics department at Vanderbilt University Medical Center, which conducts complex analytics in order to drive better strategic decisions. In this capacity, he works with leaders across the Medical Center to help them frame their opportunities and questions, design the analytics that will most effectively answer their questions, and present the results of the analytics and potential implications of their decisions. Prior to joining Vanderbilt, he worked for McKinsey and Company where he focused on helping providers with their strategic and finance questions, while also working on operational, purchasing, and quality initiatives. During his time there, he helped create the McKinsey Hospital Institute (now Objective Health), focused toward community providers enabling them to capture bottom-line impact and build capabilities through proprietary analytics, web-based performance tools, and benchmarking/expertise.

Combined with an MBA from Harvard Business School, Mr. Marx has used his expertise to assist in the creation and delivery of finance, operations, and strategy performance assessments. He has also led the development of client solutions including a cost allocation model, physician utilization analyses, and lean training/implementation. Marx is a member of the External Advisory Board for the Schreyer Honors College at The Pennsylvania State University.

Dr. John F. Manning

John Manning, PhD, MBA, is the Chief Administrative Officer and Associate Vice Chancellor for Health Affairs for Vanderbilt University Medical Center, and the Senior Associate Dean for Operations and Administration for the School of Medicine at Vanderbilt University, where he applies his business and budgetary background as an analyst and administrator to develop and utilize technology and connect a variety of disciplines across the institution, integrating business plans with rational budgets. Prior to this position, Dr. Manning served as Director of Research Resources in the Office of Research and as Vice President for Research Operations at Vanderbilt where he put his research experience and business know-how to work to strengthen the Medical Center's research resources.

Manning has also served on the faculty at the University of Alabama-Birmingham School of Public Health before joining Argonne National Laboratory as the head of a research group focused on bioremediation. Dr. Manning has coauthored numerous publications focused on research in the area of hazardous waste environmental decontamination.

Chapter 5
••••••••••••

Dr. Raymond J. Hutchinson

Raymond J. Hutchinson, MS, MD, serves as the Associate Dean for Regulatory Affairs at the University of Michigan Medical School. In this role, he oversees the outside interest disclosure process for Medical School faculty, staff, trainees, and students and serves as the chairperson of the Medical School Conflict of Interest Board. He also oversees the medical institutional review boards and chairs, works with the university's institutional review board council to assure regulatory compliance, oversees noncompliance remediation, and collaborates with other institutional entities responsible for oversight of and education regarding clinical and translational research regulations.

Dr. Hutchinson is also a Professor in the Department of Pediatrics and Communicable Diseases at the University of Michigan Medical School. In addition to his work at the academic health center, he is a member of the Steering Committee for the Association of American Medical Colleges' Forum on Conflict of Interest in Academe. He also served on the task force that authored the Association of American Medical Colleges publication *In the Interest of Patients: Recommendations for Physician Financial Relationships and Clinical Decision Making*, published in 2010.

Dr. Sanjay Saint

Sanjay Saint, MD, MPH, a Professor of Internal Medicine at the University of Michigan, is the Director of the VA/University of Michigan Patient Safety Enhancement Program and the Associate Chief of Medicine at the Ann Arbor VA Medical Center. His research focuses on enhancing patient safety by preventing health-care-associated infection and translating research findings into practice. He has authored approximately 200 peer-reviewed papers with over 60 appearing in the *New England Journal of Medicine*, *JAMA*, or the *Annals of Internal Medicine*.

In addition to his current position at the University of Michigan, he was a visiting scholar at the University of Florence during the 2007–2008 academic year, where he studied diffusion of innovation and hand hygiene practices in Italian hospitals. He has been a visiting professor at over 30 universities and hospitals in the United States, Europe, and Japan. He has received several major teaching awards while at the University of Michigan, including the Kaiser Permanente Award for Excellence in Clinical Teaching.

Dr. James O. Woolliscroft

James O. Woolliscroft, MD, serves as Dean and the Lyle C. Roll Professor of Medicine at the University of Michigan Medical School. He is an internationally recognized scholar and medical educator and has played major roles in medical student, resident, and fellow education at the University of Michigan and nationally. Previous administrative roles at the University of Michigan include Associate Chair in the Department of Internal Medicine, Chief of Staff of the University of Michigan Hospitals, Associate Dean and Director of Graduate Medical Education, and the Executive Associate Dean of the University of Michigan Medical School.

He has authored numerous publications, and his research interests in medical education resulted in invited presentations, and visiting professorships across the United States and internationally. Dr. Woolliscroft was selected as the first Josiah Macy Jr. Professor of Medical Education, an endowed professorship awarded through a national competition. Additionally, he is the recipient of numerous awards recognizing his achievements in medical education.

Chapter 6
• • • • • • • • • • • • •

Dr. Cynthia E. Boyd
Cynthia Boyd, MD, MBA, is Associate Vice President and Chief Compliance Officer at Rush University Medical Center. In this position she provides direction and oversight of the Compliance Program including Health Insurance Portability and Accountability Act of 1996 privacy and security. She is responsible for identifying and assessing areas of compliance risk for Rush University Medical Center and communicating the importance of the Compliance Program to executive management and the board of trustees. Dr. Boyd also provides oversight of all research compliance-related activities at Rush, the Research Compliance Office, and also insures the implementation and operation of the Corporate Compliance Program at Rush's subsidiaries.

Boyd is also nationally recognized in the compliance arena and academic medical institutions for her expertise and knowledge of clinical trial billing compliance. She is a distinguished speaker and has published numerous articles on compliance-related topics. Dr. Boyd is Associate Professor of Medicine at Rush Medical College and serves as Director of Medical Staff Operations. She is board certified in internal medicine and a Fellow of the American College of Physicians. She has served on the Board of Directors of the Health Care Compliance Association and as the Chair of the Governance and Ethics Committee of the Health Care Compliance Association. She is also past Chair of the Forum on Regulation of the Association of Academic Health Centers.

Dr. Larry J. Goodman
Larry J. Goodman, MD, is the chief executive officer of Rush University Medical

Center. He also serves as president of Rush University, president of the Rush System for Health, and principal officer of the Rush Board of Trustees. Goodman was president and chief executive officer of Rush from 2002 until September 2010. Prior to being named president and chief executive officer, Goodman was Senior Vice President for Medical Affairs at Rush and the Henry R. Russe Dean of Rush Medical College. He is also a professor of medicine. Before accepting the position of Senior Vice President in 1998, he was Medical Director of Cook County Hospital, a position he had held since 1996. During his tenure, Rush has attained national recognition in quality outcomes, ranking consistently in the top statistical group of all academic health centers in the University Health Systems Quality and Accountability analysis.

A highly respected clinician, researcher, and medical educator, Goodman has published in such prestigious publications as the *Journal of the American Medical Association* and the *Journal of Infectious Diseases*. His research has focused particularly on gastrointestinal infections in HIV-positive patients. Dr. Goodman serves on the board of the CORE Foundation of Cook County, and on the national level, Goodman has served as a site survey team member for the Liaison Committee on Medical Education, which accredits medical schools.

Chapter 7

Dr. Harold L. Paz

Harold L. Paz, MD, MS, has served as Chief Executive Officer of the Milton S. Hershey Medical Center, The Pennsylvania State University's (Penn State) Senior Vice President for Health Affairs and dean of its College of Medicine since April 2006. With almost 9000 employees and a combined budget of over $1.2 billion, the Medical Center and College serve the citizens of Pennsylvania. During his tenure at Penn State, Dr. Paz has initiated the formation of the Penn State Hershey Health System, which includes four hospitals, 54 ambulatory care practices, and eight affiliated hospitals and has overseen a major three-quarter million square foot expansion of the Penn State Milton S. Hershey Medical Center campus that includes six new patient care, research, and education buildings including the new Penn State Hershey Cancer Institute and Penn State Hershey Children's Hospital. Prior to his appointment at Penn State, Paz served as dean of the Robert Wood Johnson Medical School and chief executive officer of Robert Wood Johnson University Medical Group for 11 years.

Board certified in internal medicine and pulmonary medicine, Paz remains clinically active with a special interest in patients with sarcoidosis, and his research focuses on the application of new technology in critical care medicine and the health-care delivery science. A recipient of numerous awards, Paz has served on corporate and scientific advisory boards in the biotechnology field. Paz currently serves on the Administrative Board of the Council of Deans of the Association of American Medical Colleges and the Board of Directors of the Association of Academic Health Centers.

Dr. Billie S. Willits

Billie S. Willits, PhD, is a graduate of the University of Iowa. She has served most recently as Chief Human Resource Officer and Associate Vice President for Strategic Planning at The Pennsylvania State University. Her most recent focus has been working to build a Regional Medical Campus at the University Park/State College location – including establishing clinic sites, hiring medical teams, and identifying and connecting research opportunities and projects for students and research faculty.

Willits has taught several courses in the areas of employee relations, human resource management, employment law, and public sector labor relations, and in the past has served in numerous human resource management capacities at various academic medical colleges and consults in private industry through WK Associates. She has been president of the Nittany Chapter of Labor and Employment Relations Association and serves on the board of directors for Skills of Central PA, Inc., a private, nonprofit human services organization, and on the board of directors for the M&T Bank Corporation.

Deirdre C. Weaver

Deirdre C. Weaver, MA, is a nonprofit professional with broad experience in planning, communications, development, corporate relations, and government relations. She is currently the Communications Specialist for the dean and chief executive officer at The Pennsylvania State University (Penn State) College of Medicine and Penn State Hershey Medical Center. She joined Penn State College of Medicine in 2007 after 7 years with the American Cancer Society, where her responsibilities included managing a wide range of health promotions, advocacy, and patient service programs.

Weaver is a graduate of Carleton College (Northfield, Minnesota) and holds a master's degree in history from the University of Wisconsin-Madison. She has taught world and European history at Truman State University (Kirksville, Missouri) and West Texas A&M University (Canyon, Texas).

Sean Young

Sean Young is the Chief Marketing Officer for The Pennsylvania State University (Penn State) Milton S. Hershey Medical Center and Penn State College of Medicine. His duties include managing the public relations and marketing functions for the organization. Prior to joining the Medical Center and College of Medicine in 2001, Young served as Broadcast Communications Coordinator for former Pennsylvania governor Tom Ridge. From 1997 to 2001, he managed media events, national and regional television and radio interviews involving the governor and Ridge administration officials, as well as statewide electronic communications functions for the governor's press office.

As a reporter, anchor, and program host for a local television station, Young earned two Associated Press Awards and four mid-Atlantic Emmy nominations for his on-air work. He has since earned a fifth Emmy nod for his work on a documentary about the origins of Penn State Hershey Medical Center: *Memories & Milestones*.

Chapter 8
•••••••••••••

Dr. Wilsie S. Bishop

Wilsie Bishop, DPA, MSN, is Vice President for Health Affairs and the Chief Operating Officer at East Tennessee State University (ETSU) with administrative responsibility for the Colleges of Clinical and Rehabilitative Health Sciences, Medicine, Nursing, Pharmacy, and Public Health. Prior to assuming that role in 2007, she served in various administrative positions at the university including Vice President for Administration and Chief Operating Officer, Dean of the College of Public and Allied Health, department chair in the College of Nursing, Assistant Vice President for Academic Affairs, and Associate Vice President for Health Affairs. Dr. Bishop has also taught in the nursing programs at ETSU, the ETSU Master of Public Management Program, and in the doctoral program in Public Health.

Dr. Bishop has been instrumental in developing and setting policies for faculty, staff, and students. She chaired university-wide task forces on the status of women at ETSU and on cultural diversity, both of which identified recommendations to enhance the diversity of the ETSU as well as identifying systemic changes to improve the campus climate as it relates to diversity and the role of women on campus. She is on the Board of Trustees for the Commission on Colleges, the recognized regional accrediting body in the 11 US southern states. She also serves on the Board of Directors of the Association of Academic Health Centers.

Dr. M. David Linville Jr.

M. David Linville Jr., MD, is the Assistant Dean and Director of Operations for the College of Medicine at East Tennessee State University (ETSU), serving as senior advisor to the dean of medicine. He also maintains his position as associate professor in medical education, serving as director of the second-year practice of medicine course. As Acting Associate Vice President and Executive Director at ETSU, Dr. Linville works with the Office of Rural and Community Health and Community Partnerships – working with faculty and communities and their organizations to interface, develop, and conduct community-based teaching and learning, service, and research.

Dr. Linville previously served as Interim Assistant Dean for Academic Affairs, overseeing and directing the 4-year medical student curriculum. His work at ETSU has focused on medical education, medical simulation, and curriculum development.

Chapter 9
• • • • • • • • • • • • • •

Dr. Stephen Smith

Stephen Smith, DSc, FRCOG, FMedSci, is Vice-President (Research) at the Nanyang Technological University and the Founding Dean of the Lee Kong Chian School of Medicine, Singapore. Dr. Smith led the formation of the United Kingdom's first Academic Health Science Centre, launched in October 2007 from the merger of Hammersmith Hospitals National Healthcare Service Trust and St. Mary's National Healthcare Service Trust and its integration with Imperial College London. He previously served as Principal of the Faculty of Medicine at Imperial College London and has been Chief Executive of Imperial College Healthcare National Health Service Trust since its inception, the largest such trust in the United Kingdom. Dr. Smith has also been at the forefront of the development of the United Kingdom's first Global Medical Excellence Cluster for London and South East England.

A gynecologist by training, Dr. Smith has published over 225 papers on reproductive medicine and cancer. He has served on and advised numerous committees for many organizations including the Medical Research Council, World Health Organization, the National Institutes of Health (USA), the National Health Service, the British Heart Foundation and the Wellcome Trust. He also sits on the Health Innovation Council of the National Health Service and is a Trustee of the Nuffield Trust.

Peter Davies

Peter Davies, BEng(Hons), MSc, CEng MIET, is a professional engineer who trained at the United Kingdom's Ministry of Defence (MOD), becoming a Chartered Engineer in 1997 with the Institute of Engineering and Technology. At the MOD he undertook a number of roles spanning project management and policy making before gaining a Master of Science in Management from the London Business School in 2001 as a Sloan Fellow. Upon his return to the MOD, he advised on reforming its planning processes, and was appointed to the Defence

Secretary's Private Office responsible for the personnel, acquisition, and military activity in the UK portfolios.

Using the insights he gained from his service as the Senior Civil Servant with policy responsibility for armed forces' pensions, compensation arrangements for injury and illness and wider veterans' affairs, he transitioned into the health sector, becoming Policy Adviser to the Imperial College Academic Health Sciences Centre in 2010. He is a trustee of a charity in Dublin, Ireland, that owns a hospital for the elderly, originally established for veterans, and in 2011 set up a consultancy firm advising organizations on engaging with Whitehall.

Chapter 10
• • • • • • • • • • • • • • •

Dr. William F. Owen Jr.

William F. Owen Jr., MD, served as the fourth president of the University of Medicine and Dentistry of New Jersey. Comprising eight health schools, including three medical schools, a nursing school, dental school, school of health-related professions, school of public health, and school of biomedical research, the University of Medicine and Dentistry of New Jersey has transformed under Dr. Owen's leadership to a top-tier university and the largest publicly funded health university in the United States.

Dr. Owen is the former chancellor of the University of Tennessee Health Science Center and Senior Vice President of Health Affairs for University of Tennessee, and was a tenured professor of medicine and a research institute director at Duke University. He also served as the Chief Scientist of Baxter Healthcare Corporation, a multibillion-dollar, global business. Since 1985, Dr. Owen has secured approximately $25 million in extramural funding for his research and published numerous journal articles, scientific reviews, and editorials, as well as book chapters and textbooks.

Dr. Owen serves on the governing boards for several major educational, business, and civic organizations like the New Jersey Presidents' Council, New Jersey Chamber of Commerce, New Jersey Council of Teaching Hospitals, New Jersey Hospital Association, Newark Alliance, Robert Wood Johnson University Hospital Health System, Tufts University Medical School, and the Association of Academic Health Centers.

Lee Miller

Lee E. Miller is the Managing Director of NegotiationPlus.com, with offices in the United States and Asia, and a career columnist with New Jersey's *Star-Ledger*. He works with individuals and organizations on how to become more effective in leading and influencing others, and his clients include universities, nonprofits, and Fortune 500 companies. An adjunct professor at Columbia University and at Seton Hall University where he teaches graduate courses in influencing and negotiating, decisionmaking, and human resources management, Lee has authored several books on negotiating and influencing power.

Mr. Miller has previously served as Senior Vice President of Human Resources at TV Guide Magazine, USA Networks, and Barneys New York, Inc., a Vice President of Labor and Employee Relations at R.H. Macy & Co. Inc., and a partner and cochair of the employment and labor group at one of the largest law firms in New Jersey. Lee is the former chair of the International Association of Corporate Professional Recruiters, Secretary to the Union County Motion Picture Advisory Board, and a Director of the American Repertory Ballet Company.

Chapter 11
••••••••••••••

Dr. Barbara Atkinson

Barbara F. Atkinson, MD, served as Executive Vice Chancellor of the University of Kansas (KU) Medical Center. She also concurrently served as the Executive Dean of the KU School of Medicine, and was the first woman in the country to hold both positions at a medical center. In her capacity, she oversaw KU's schools of medicine, nursing, and allied health, with more than 3100 students, as well as 2500 faculty and staff and a budget of $225 million. She focused on improving the region's health by bringing a National Cancer Institute-designated comprehensive cancer center to the Medical Center and advancing the Medical Center's prestigious research programs in cancer, neurology, liver, kidney, and reproductive biology.

Dr. Atkinson is a respected pathologist and is a Life Trustee and past president of the American Board of Pathology. In 2010 President Barack Obama appointed her to the Presidential Commission for the Study of Bioethical Issues. She has held editorial positions on various professional journals and has edited several books in cytopathology and gynecologic pathology. She was elected to membership in the prestigious Institute of Medicine of the National Academy of Sciences in 1997. She serves on the Board of Directors for Practical Bioethics and Audubon of Kansas.

C.J. Janovy

C.J. Janovy, MA, is Director of Communications at the University of Kansas Medical Center. Her previous positions include editor of the *Pitch*, an alternative weekly newspaper in the Kansas City metropolitan area, for which she has worked in various capacities for over two decades.

Dr. Marcia Nielsen

Marcia Nielsen, PhD, currently serves at the University of Kansas Medical Center as Associate Dean for Health Policy, Associate Professor within the Department of Health Policy and Management, and Associate Director of Public Policy at the Institute of Community and Public Health. Her prior positions include executive director of the Kansas Health Policy Authority – the state health-care agency in Kansas tasked with developing and maintaining a coordinated health policy agenda that combined the effective purchasing and administration of health care with promotion-oriented public health strategies.

Dr. Nielsen's experience includes serving as a Peace Corps volunteer working for the Ministry of Public Health in Thailand; during the debate over comprehensive health-care reform in the 1990s, she worked as a legislative assistant to then US senator Bob Kerrey (D-Nebraska). After completing her doctorate in health policy and management from Johns Hopkins School of Public Health, she worked as a health lobbyist and then assistant director of legislation for the American Federation of Labor and Congress of Industrial Organizations.

Chapter 12
••••••••••••••

Dr. D. Clay Ackerly

D. Clay Ackerly, MD, MSc, is a senior resident in internal medicine at Massachusetts General Hospital and a research fellow at the Duke Clinical Research Institute. Clay received his MD from Duke University as a Nanaline Duke Scholar, his master's in international health policy from the London School of Economics, and his bachelor's in health policy from Harvard College.

Prior to pursuing his medical training, he served as a special assistant to Dr. Mark McClellan at the Centers for Medicare and Medicaid Services (CMS), where he oversaw CMS's quality-improvement, pay-for-performance, and health information technology initiatives. Prior to CMS, Dr. Ackerly served as an industry economist at the US Food and Drug Administration and as a staff economist at The White House Council of Economic Advisers. Before his time in government, he also gained experience working in Bristol-Myers Squibb's Global Outcomes Research Group and Goldman Sachs' Healthcare Investment Banking group.

Dr. Krishna Udayakumar

Krishna Udayakumar, MD, MBA, is the Director of Duke Medicine Global and Interim Executive Director of the International Partnership for Innovative Healthcare Delivery at Duke University. He is responsible for global business development and coordination of international strategic initiatives for Duke Medicine in his role as Director of the Office of Duke Medicine Global. He works closely with entities such as the Duke Translational Medicine Institute, the Duke Global Health Institute, and the Duke Heart Center to expand Duke's international activities and develop global partnerships across translational and clinical research, global health, education and training, health-care management, and related areas.

Dr. Udayakumar also provides business strategy and business development support for the Duke Translational Medicine Institute, serves as Assistant Professor of Global Health and Medicine at Duke University Medical Center, and is Associate Program Director of the Duke Medicine Management and Leadership Pathway for Residents, an innovative graduate medical education program combining clinical and management training. As Interim Executive Director of the International Partnership for Innovative Healthcare Delivery, Dr. Udayakumar provides leadership for the recently launched nonprofit organization affiliated with Duke Medicine that seeks to support innovators to scale and replicate successful health-care delivery solutions globally.

Dr. Alex Cho

Alex Cho, MD, MBA, is an assistant professor of medicine who works with Chancellor for Health Affairs Victor Dzau, MD, on special projects related to health policy and new models of care, in particular innovative health-care delivery models as applied in developing countries. Working with the Center of Genomic Medicine at Duke University, he participated in key research focusing on the translation of genome sciences into clinical practice. He has helped lead and develop DukeEngage, a civic engagement program for undergraduates and Duke faculty encouraging service around the world.

In addition to authoring numerous peer-reviewed and non-peer-reviewed articles, he is a reviewer for the *Journal of Genomic Medicine*, *Genomic Medicine*, and the *Yonsei Medical Journal*, among other professional publications.

Dr. Victor J. Dzau

Victor J. Dzau, MD, is Chancellor for Health Affairs, Duke University, President and Chief Executive Officer, Duke University Health System, and the James B. Duke Professor of Medicine. Previously chairman of medicine at Harvard Medical School as well as chairman of the Department of Medicine at Stanford University, Dr. Dzau has significantly impacted health care through his seminal research on the renin-angiotensin system and his pioneering leadership in the discipline of vascular medicine and biology.

Dr. Dzau is internationally renowned as a leader in global health-care strategy and delivery and his vision is for academic health centers to lead the transformation of medicine through innovation, translation, and globalization. Leading this initiative at Duke, he with others developed the Duke Translational Medicine

Institute, the Duke Global Health Institute, the Duke-National University of Singapore Graduate Medical School, and strategic alliances with Peking University and others. The recipient of numerous national and international honors and recognitions, Dr. Dzau was honored with the prestigious Gustav Nylin Medal from the Swedish Royal College of Medicine as well as the Research Achievement Award of the American Heart Association. In addition to serving as the Board Chair of the Association of Academic Health Centers, Dr. Dzau has chaired and serves on many professional committees and boards, including the Institute of Medicine Council of the National Academy of Sciences, as well as board governor of Health Industry of the World Economic Forum.

Afterword

Dr. Richard I. Levin

Richard I. Levin, MD, FACP, FACC, FAHA, on decanal leave during the writing of this book, is Senior Scholar in Residence at the Association for Academic Health Centers. Prior to his Association of Academic Health Centers appointment, he served as Vice-Principal for Health Affairs and Dean of the Faculty of Medicine at McGill University in Montreal, Canada. He maintains positions of Professor of Medicine in the Division of Cardiology at McGill as well as Professor Emeritus of Medicine in the Leon H. Charney Division of Cardiology at New York University. Prior to becoming Dean at McGill, Dr. Levin was the Vice Dean for Education, Faculty and Academic Affairs, and Professor of Medicine at New York University School of Medicine. There, he was responsible for the entire spectrum of educational programs and he and his colleagues at the schools of New York University developed ALEX, a new ecology for learning and the platform for all medical education at New York University. Dr. Levin's scientific interests include endothelial cell biology, the prevention of atherothrombotic events, the role of the new information technologies in medical education, and the reformation of academic health centers for the support of implementation science and personalized medicine. He was awarded four patents for his work developing a device and system for coronary health intervention and for studies on the promotion of wound healing. He is a founder of a medical technology company, the author of numerous papers, has lectured throughout the world, served on numerous boards, and is the recipient of honors including a Clinical Investigator Award from the National Heart, Lung and Blood Institute of the National Institutes of Health in the United States, the Valentine Mott Medal, and the Esther Hoffman Beller Research Award. He was recently elected a Fellow of the Canadian Academy of Health Sciences.

Glossary

Academic Health Science Center
Also known as academic health center or academic medical center. As defined by the Association of Academic Health Centers, an academic health science center is an educational institution that includes a medical school and at least one additional health professions school (e.g., nursing, dentistry, pharmacy, allied health, public health, veterinary medicine, graduate school in biomedical sciences), and either owns or is affiliated with a hospital or health system. It engages in three essential activities: (1) educating the future health workforce through their health professions schools; (2) conducting cutting-edge biomedical and clinical research; and (3) providing comprehensive patient care.

Accreditation
A type of quality assurance process under which services and operations of institutions or programs are evaluated by an external body to determine if applicable standards are met. If standards are met, the appropriate governing body grants accredited status. The accreditation process can also ensure that certification practices are acceptable, typically meaning that they are competent to test and certify third parties, behave ethically, and apply suitable quality assurance. In the United States, private organizations or associations often offer accreditation services. In many other countries, accredited status is granted by government agencies.

Accreditation Council for Graduate Medical Education (ACGME)
A nonprofit private council responsible for the accreditation of post-MD medical training programs within the United States. Accreditation is accomplished through a peer-review process and is based upon established standards and guidelines.

Americans with Disabilities Act of 1990 (ADA)
US law originally enacted in 1990 to protect individuals with mental, physical, and cognitive disabilities from discrimination by all public entities in certain circumstances of daily life including employment, housing, transportation, and telecommunications. The intent of the law is to ensure that disabled individuals can participate in the mainstream.

Bayh-Dole Act of 1980

US law that gives US universities, small businesses, and nonprofits intellectual property control of their inventions and other intellectual property that result from government-funded research.

Case Mix Index (CMI)

A measurement of the severity of illness, used frequently in the United States, CMI is generally applied to a group of patients treated by a hospital or other health-care institution and helps determine the cost assigned to specific medical conditions. Fundamentally, CMI is a tool that helps explain the cost of treating a health-care institution's patient population.

Centers for Medicare and Medicaid Services (CMS)

US government agency that coordinates government financial assistance programs for health care. Generally, the Medicaid program is for certain people and families with low incomes and resources, and is jointly funded by the state and federal governments. The Medicare program is funded entirely by the federal government and focuses primarily on the older population.

Certification

A confirmation of competence or other characteristics as necessary for a specified status. For professionals, certification indicates an individual has met specific standards and is able to competently complete a job or task, usually confirmed by the passing of an examination and/or the study of required educational coursework.

Clinical Trials

Biomedical or health-related research studies that involve people as research subjects and follow predefined protocols. Investigators who observe and measure the outcomes of the study conduct clinical trials.

Collective Bargaining Agreement

An agreement reached as a result of negotiations between employers and all or a unit of its employees (usually represented by one or more trade unions in the negotiations process) regarding terms of employment such as wage scales, working hours, training, health, safety, and employment benefits.

Conflict of Interest/Commitment

A conflict of interest exists when an individual or an organization (in a relationship based on trust) engages in multiple activities, one or more of which may compromise the motivation for the activity and/or the basis of the trust. A conflict of commitment occurs when an individual or organization has a relationship that requires a commitment of time or effort to activities such that, either implicitly or directly, usual or expected obligations cannot be met or are compromised.

Continuing Medical Education (CME)
A form of education for those in the medical field to maintain competence and learn about new and developing areas within their field – often necessary to maintain current individual licenses to practice medicine. Courses are subject to certifying agencies for acceptability and may be in the form of live events, written publications, online programs, audio, video, or other electronic media.

Corporate Integrity Agreement
Legally binding detailed and restrictive arrangements that are imposed when serious misconduct (fraudulent or abusive action) is discovered through an audit or self-disclosure. The agreements usually remain in force for 4–5 years. For health-care providers they can result in compliance programs that are mandated as part of a legal settlement with the federal government.

False Claims Act
US federal law, also known as the "Lincoln Law" from its enactment during the American Civil War in the 1800s, that imposes liability on persons and companies (typically federal contractors) who defraud governmental programs. The law includes a *"qui tam"* provision that allows people who are not affiliated with the government to file legal actions on behalf of the government.

Family Educational Rights and Privacy Act of 1974 (FERPA)
A US federal law enacted to protect the privacy of student education records including grades or behavior. The law applies to all schools that receive funds under an applicable program of the US Department of Education. Generally, schools must have written permission from the parent or eligible student in order to release any information from a student's education record.

501(c) Organization
Refers to section 501c of the US tax code that determines eligibility for business income tax-exempt status of nonprofit corporations or associations.

Government Management Reform Act of 1994
In response to increasing public attention focused on improving the performance and accountability of US federal programs, the law mandates government management reform. Among the multiple means to improve government management, the law calls for better financial and performance information and

measurements for managers, and the adoption of integrated processes for planning, management, and assessment of results.

Graduate Medical Education (GME)

Post-MD medical training programs within the United States are referred to as graduate medical education. Students make residency, medical career, and specialty choices during this period of their medical education.

Head of Faculty

Also known as dean, chief executive officer, or vice president for health affairs, this individual usually oversees the management of the teaching faculty, staff, and students within the medical school and/or for the entire academic health center.

Health Information Technology for Economic and Clinical Health (HITECH) Act

Enacted as part of the American Recovery and Reinvestment Act of 2009. The American Recovery and Reinvestment Act contains incentives related to health-care information technology in general (e.g., creation of a national health-care infrastructure) and contains specific incentives designed to accelerate the adoption of electronic health record systems among providers. Because the act anticipates a massive expansion in the exchange of electronic protected health information, the act also widens the scope of privacy and security protections available under the Health Insurance Portability and Accountability Act of 1996.

Health Insurance Portability and Accountability Act of 1996 (HIPAA)

US law enacted in 1996, and amended since, regulates the availability and breadth of group health plans and certain individual health insurance policies. It also creates several programs to control fraud and abuse within the health-care system and requires the Department of Health and Human Services to draft rules that aim at increasing the efficiency of the health-care system by creating standards for the use and dissemination of health-care information. The Privacy Rule of the Health Insurance Portability and Accountability Act, enacted in 2003, regulates the use and disclosure of certain information held by "covered entities" (generally, health-care clearinghouses, employer-sponsored health plans, health insurers, and medical service providers that engage in certain transactions).

Human Resources (HR)

Refers to the function or division within an organization charged with the overall responsibility for implementing strategies and policies relating to the management of individuals and the organization's workforce. The term is also used to refer to the overall workforce itself as an organizational resource.

Informed Consent

A valid consent by patients or participants in human subject research indicating they have the cognitive abilities and adequate knowledge to participate and make fully informed decisions regarding their health care and/or clinical research participation. In order for the patient's consent to be considered valid, he or she must be considered competent to make the decision at hand and consent must be voluntary.

Institute of Medicine (IOM)

Established in 1970, the Institute of Medicine is the health arm of the US National Academy of Sciences. It is an independent, nonprofit organization that works to provide unbiased and authoritative advice and evidence to decision makers in government and the private sector to make informed policy to improve the nation's health. In addition to producing studies, the Institute of Medicine convenes forums, roundtables, and standing committees to address critical issues and facilitate discussion.

Institutional Review Board

A committee that has been formally designated to approve, monitor, and review biomedical and/or behavioral research (such as clinical trials) involving humans with the aim to protect the rights and welfare of research participants and subjects.

Joint Commission

An independent, nonprofit organization that develops standards for quality and safety in the delivery of health care and evaluates organization performance based on these standards. The Joint Commission is an accrediting organization that certifies health-care organizations and programs through on-site surveys at least once every 3 years (laboratories undergo surveys at least once every 2 years) to determine if safe and effective health care is being provided. Joint Commission certification is highly sought after.

Medical Students/Residents

Medical students receive a broad range of medical knowledge and basic clinical skills, and are provided limited experience in practicing medicine. Residency is a stage of graduate medical training beyond the medical degree that provides in-depth training within a special branch of medicine under the supervision of fully licensed physicians. Successful completion of residency training is a requirement to practice medicine in many jurisdictions.

Medicare/Medicaid

See Centers for Medicare and Medicaid Services (CMS).

National Cancer Institute Designation

The National Cancer Institute (NCI) is one of several Institutes that make up the US government's National Institutes of Health. NCI-designated cancer centers are recognized for their scientific excellence. They are a major source of discovery and development of more effective approaches to cancer prevention, diagnosis, and treatment. They also deliver medical advances to patients and their families, educate health-care professionals and the public, and reach out to underserved populations. An NCI-designated cancer center may be a freestanding organization, a center within an academic institution, or part of a consortium of institutions.

National Institutes of Health (NIH)

Established and funded by the US government, the National Institutes of Health conducts and supports biomedical research to expand the knowledge base in medicine and diseases and improve public health. Multiple institutes comprise the National Institutes of Health and are dedicated to conducting research and providing grants and other funding for scientists in specific research areas (e.g., the National Cancer Institute).

Payor (Private, Third-Party)

An organization other than the patient (first party) or health-care provider (second party) involved in the financing of personal health services. (Health insurance companies are an example of private payors; Medicare/Medicaid is an example of non-private/government payors).

Physician Payments Sunshine Act (Sunshine Act)

Part of the Patient Protection and Affordable Care Act (2009), the US Sunshine Act requires covered manufacturers (such as pharmaceutical and medical device companies) to track and report certain financial and ownership relationships with physicians and teaching hospitals (such as consulting fees, honoraria, travel, and entertainment). The Sunshine Act requires the Centers for Medicare and Medicaid Services to issue regulations that provide details on the process and requirements for reporting of physician payments and financial relationships as required by the Sunshine Act provisions. The act further calls for the information to be publicly disclosed on the Internet.

Physician Practice Plan/Physician Organization

Larger than traditional practices, these legal entities are established by groups of physicians allowing them to share overhead costs and services (e.g., billings, insurance, leasing). Many such practices were organized as a means for physician practitioners to leverage their economic and negotiating power with health insurance companies as well as compete with health maintenance organizations (health insurance companies that provide in-house medical services).

Recovery Audit Contractor (RAC)

The Recovery Audit Program was created by the Medicare Prescription Drug Improvement & Modernization Act of 2003 and was made permanent by the Tax Relief and Health Care Act of 2006. The program's mission is to reduce Medicare improper or overpayments. The United States is divided into four geographic jurisdictions under the program and contracts are awarded by the Centers for Medicare and Medicaid Services to firms (recovery audit contractors) to undertake the tasks of reviewing, auditing, identifying, and recouping improper Medicare payments made to providers for health-care services received by members of the Medicare program.

Residency Program (First-Year Resident)

Residency programs in the United States are post-MD graduate programs that provide more in-depth training for medical graduates within specific specialties under the supervision of licensed physicians. Most jurisdictions require a completion of a residency in order to be licensed to practice medicine. Duration of most medical residency programs can range from 3 years through to 7 years for a specialized field such as neurosurgery. A year in residency begins between late June to early July, depending on the individual program, and ends one calendar year later. In the past, a first-year resident was referred to as an "intern."

Resident Duty Hours

The US Accreditation Council for Graduate Medical Education defines duty hours as all clinical and academic activities related to the residency program; for example, patient care (both inpatient and outpatient), administrative duties relative to patient care, the provision for transfer of patient care, time spent in-house during call activities, and scheduled activities, such as conferences. Duty hours do *not* include reading and preparation time spent away from the duty site.

Safe Harbor Regulation

Generally included within a law's provisions or rules promulgated to enforce the law, "safe harbor" regulations describe various payment and business practices that, although they potentially implicate violation of a law, are not treated as criminal or civil offenses. For example, the regulations can limit or eliminate liability under a law provided the potentially criminal party acted in good faith or in compliance with defined standards.

Stark Laws

A series of US laws (named after the initial sponsor, Congressman Pete Stark of California) enacted to govern physician self-referral for Medicare and Medicaid patients. Physician self-referral is the practice of a physician referring a patient to a medical facility in which he has a financial interest, be it ownership, investment, or a structured compensation arrangement.

Technology Transfer

The process of transferring skills, knowledge, technologies, methods of manufacturing, samples of manufacturing, and facilities between governments or universities and other institutions to ensure that scientific and technological developments are accessible to a wider range of users who can then further develop and exploit the technology into new products, processes, applications, materials, or services.

Tenure

A job status or benefit of job security achieved by senior employees that guarantees the right not to have his or her position terminated without just cause. The status is generally received through a contractual arrangement with the employer and, in academia, is achieved after several years and by meeting specific institutional goals.

Translational Medicine

The process of applying the results of biological research discoveries into actual treatments or diagnostics for patients.

US Food and Drug Administration (FDA)

Federal government agency that regulates the use, sale, and marketing of food, medicine, and tobacco in the United States for purposes of protecting the public health. Food and Drug Administration regulations aim to assure the safety, efficacy, and security of human and veterinary drugs, biological products, medical devices, the nation's food supply, cosmetics, and products that emit radiation. The Food and Drug Administration also has responsibility for regulating the manufacturing, marketing, and distribution of tobacco products to protect the public health and to reduce tobacco use by minors.

Whistle-Blower

A person who discloses, or otherwise makes public, information about dishonest or illegal conduct in a government department, a public or private organization, or a company.

1

Introduction
The Hallmarks of Successful Academic Health Science Center Leadership

Steven A. Wartman and Stewart Gabel

From the Editor

Effective leadership is essential to the success of any organization. For academic health science centers, the usual hierarchical relationships are difficult to apply, since many of the faculty view themselves as highly accomplished individual professionals (and rightly so). This introductory chapter discusses the components of successful leadership that can be transformational for the institution.

—SAW

Academic health science centers are the part of universities that educate the next generation of health professionals, conduct leading biomedical and clinical research that leads to new treatments and diagnostic breakthroughs, and deliver comprehensive patient care from the basic to the most advanced. With budgets often in excess of a billion dollars and the constant need to continuously monitor and improve its education, research, and patient care functions, the job of academic health science center leaders is complex, requiring diverse skill sets and expertise. These leaders must master a staggering range of management and operational skills as they engage in all facets of the organization, ranging in scope from the scientific to the educational, legal to public relations, patient care to personnel management, and financial to philanthropy. Also, they must do so quickly, as too much on-the-job learning may limit the institution's ability to move forward. Yet, it is unrealistic to expect a new leader emerging from a specific area of academia to already have the necessary skill sets in place. Thus, this book is an effort to depict, in granular terms, those areas in which the leader should be knowledgeable, if not expert.

However, cognitive knowledge alone is not the hallmark of successful leadership of these complex entities. There are additional factors that must be considered, including institutional "fit," personality, and leadership style. This introductory chapter is intended to address these other dimensions. It is our contention that the best plans and strategies cannot be successfully implemented without the "right" leadership in place.

Searching for a New Leader

There is a traditional ethos in academic medicine that the best leaders often come from outside the institution that is seeking new leadership. These "outsiders" bring a fresh perspective and knowledge of how things can be done differently. Importantly, they have no internal "baggage" with them and are able to approach issues and relationships anew. The process that brings them to the institution usually involves a combination of professional search firms and faculty search committees, with the final decision usually made by the university president and/ or a board of trustees or their equivalent. On the other hand, an appropriately groomed internal candidate knows the institution well, has well-developed relationships, and has a much shorter learning curve than a person coming from the outside. Regardless of whether the institution chooses to go inside or outside for a new leader, the search process tends to be lengthy, at times cumbersome, and often flawed.

The process is flawed for a number of reasons. Search firms, while having some knowledge of the needs of the institution and a handy list of potential candidates, often do not understand the subtleties of the position for which leadership is sought. Faculty search committees tend to be dazzled by great academic curricula vitae and have inadequate understanding of the skills required to be a successful leader of a particular institution at a specific point in time, or whether a given candidate has those skills. As a result, candidates often rise to the top of the list based on a combination of past achievement in a narrow and perhaps less relevant field and charm or engaging confidence.

However, these attributes are not enough to ensure successful leadership of these enterprises. The candidate must have an eagerness to embrace (and learn about) a wide range of issues for which he or she may have limited knowledge. Most important, the candidate must be sufficiently self-aware to follow the principles of what has been described as *transformational leadership*.[1]

The Transformational Leader
••••••••••••••••••••••••••••••••••••

The study of leadership and its requirements has evolved over the course of recent decades, from a focus on the exceptional abilities, accomplishments, and singular efforts of one remarkable person, who often leads out of crisis, to a focus on the abilities and accomplishments of someone who engages and works collaboratively with others. The latter focus is a relationship-oriented manifestation of leadership epitomized by the concept of *transformational leadership*, an intuitively appealing, empirically supported form of leadership that emphasizes the "transformation" of subordinates and colleagues (and at times the leader and even the person to whom the leader reports) during the development by the new leader of principles-driven dedication to the larger organizational mission.[1] These various relationships, involving both subordinates and colleagues, are uniquely woven between professional schools, departments, institutes, and programs that often must be managed (and at times led) on a peer basis. The role of the leader in this environment is often complicated by the competitive nature of the relationships involved, including the gaining and/or use of resources, often in a zero-sum environment, and issues surrounding academic prestige. Further, the usual hierarchical relationships found, for example, in most business organizations are strained in academia where accomplished professors view themselves as independent professionals. Under these circumstances, the key challenge is to fulfill mission-driven objectives by building alliances and resolving conflicts.

The origins of the concept of transformational leadership are associated with J. M. Burns, who noted, "The transforming leader recognizes and exploits an existing need or demand of a potential follower … seeks to satisfy higher needs [of the follower], and engages the full person of the follower. The result of transforming leadership is a relationship of mutual stimulation and elevation that converts followers into leaders and may convert leaders into moral agents."[2] Transformational leadership, as described by Burns and others,[1,3,4] has four essential components: the four "I"s of *idealized influence* (which can be divided into idealized attributes and idealized behaviors), *inspirational motivation, intellectual stimulation,* and *individual consideration.*[1,3] Studies in health-care settings have demonstrated that staff members – followers – working with leaders who are rated higher on scales of transformational leadership have a greater sense of well-being and satisfaction with their work,[5-9] feel more empowered,[10] and have decreased burnout.[8,11] Leaders exhibiting higher levels of transformational leadership are also felt to be more effective.[5,6,12] Evaluations of patient care practices also suggest better outcomes with leaders considered transformational.[5]

Transformational versus Transactional Leadership
· ·

Transformational leadership is often contrasted with transactional leadership.[1,4] In the latter, the leader-subordinate relationship is characterized by strict performance and outcome criteria. Successful completion of tasks by the subordinate is associated with reward (e.g., promotion, pay raise), and lack of success at task completion is associated with lack of reward or punishment (e.g., failure to get a pay raise, demotion, or dismissal).

Transformational leadership, on the other hand, is based on principles-driven work and on the strength and quality of the leader-subordinate relationship. It is not based on reward and punishment (although the two types of leadership can and often are used together). Success in the workplace and "transformation" of the subordinate (and at times of the leader) seems to derive from the experience of leaders as role models, their abilities to motivate subordinates to join collective efforts based on values and principles, their abilities to challenge subordinates to question existing assumptions and create new solutions, and their deep support for subordinates in their work, growth, and development. Box 1.1 provides additional examples of competencies in the four core components of transformational leaders in any field.

Box 1.1 The Core Components of Transformational Leadership*

1. **Idealized influence**: leaders who exhibit idealized influence are perceived to be principles driven and values oriented in their pursuit of success. They are considered role models for others. They are persistent, dedicated and focused. Subordinates are proud to be associated with them and the values they espouse. For some, they are charismatic.

2. **Inspirational motivation**: leaders who exhibit inspirational motivation are perceived to be energetic, enthusiastic, confident, and forward-looking. Their views and behaviors inspire subordinates toward greater efforts in pursuit of principles-driven work.

3. **Intellectual stimulation**: leaders who exhibit intellectual stimulation challenge and expect subordinates to be problem solvers and to not accept the status quo. They recognize that creativity and imagination are important qualities that can further the work effort and achieve success in the mission.

4. **Individualized consideration**: leaders who exhibit individualized consideration show individual attention to subordinates. They mentor, coach, and support subordinates in their work, while recognizing the individuality of the subordinate and his or her own unique path toward further growth and development.

*Adapted from Bass[1,3] and Antonakis *et al.*[4]

The principles of transformational leadership and its relationship-oriented approaches can be applied to situations of either equal or unequal power/authority. These include peer-to-peer as well as supervisor-subordinate relationships. Transformational leadership constructs have been applied at individual, team, group, and organizational levels. Team members, for example, can be evaluated and trained to become more "transformational" to one another. Organizations can be described based on the degree of their adherence to transformational leadership principles.[13]

In the health-care arena, there are often relationships between leaders of equal authority (e.g., division heads of departments, department chairs of a medical or other professional school, deans of different professional schools). In these cases, the principles of transformational leadership must be modified to reflect different situations using the same four "I"s as depicted in Box 1.1. However, there are other competencies and skills that are not addressed in the usual transformational leadership format when leaders of comparable organizational levels interact. Some of these competencies are noted in Box 1.2 and a fifth principle, *interpersonal or intercollegial consideration*, is added. These modified characteristics and competencies focus mainly on the leader's abilities to model on a peer-level adherence and commitment to principles-driven approaches within the health-care organization, to understand organizational and interpersonal dynamics, to relate appropriately to these dynamics, to foster collaborative working relationships with other leaders, and to address successfully conflicted relationships, all while building allies and coalitions for future principles-driven work. In all of these cases, emphasis on mission-driven objectives, principles, and values, rather than personal desires or "ego-driven" objectives, should be foremost.

Box 1.2 The Basic Tenets of Transformational Leadership Expanded and Modified for Relationships with Other Organizational Leaders

1. **Idealized influence***: leaders demonstrating *idealized influence* are recognized as models within their organizations. They are individuals who uphold the principles and values of the organization and of their own particular organizational component. They espouse and pursue a vision that is consistent with the vision of the larger organizational system and of their own organizational component. They do this with energy, determination, and focus. They serve as reference points for other leaders who are proud of this collegial association. Core principles in medicine and health care such as beneficence, non-maleficence, respect for individual autonomy, and pursuit of lifelong learning are basic principles that help shape the vision of leaders holding *idealized influence*.[13,14]
2. **Inspirational motivation***: leaders demonstrating *inspirational motivation* communicate their vision, principles, and adherence to the organizational mission

and to the mission of their particular area of concern effectively, energetically, and with confidence. They do this in written and verbal forms, and their personal behavior and organizational activities follow them. They are able to engage other leaders around mission- and vision-driven objectives.

3. **Intellectual stimulation***: leaders demonstrating *intellectual stimulation* work with other leaders to evaluate and address mutual problems in the larger organizational context, question existing approaches, and formulate new ones. They challenge and stimulate themselves and other leaders to find new or innovative solutions to opportunities or problematic situations. They model and encourage other leaders to be resourceful and creative.

4. **Individualized consideration***: leaders demonstrating *individualized consideration* recognize the contributions of other leaders as they together pursue joint inter-programmatic or organizational efforts. They also recognize their colleagues' individuality and personal aspirations and goals for their own particular areas of concern. They are available to provide informal mentorship or coaching to other leaders around developmental or programmatic issues if this is sought. They are careful not to intrude on the domains of colleagues, but are forthcoming in support of other leaders if requested.

5. **Interpersonal (intercollegial) consideration**: leaders exhibiting *interpersonal or intercollegial consideration* recognize the complex nature of organizations, with their legitimate diversity of agendas among programs and entities that comprise the whole. This diversity of agendas extends to relationships outside of the organization, and includes other stakeholder groups. Leaders recognize the likelihood of conflicts among programs (or individuals representing these programs) based on the legitimate agendas and perceived needs of these programs.

*These four I's are modified and adapted from Bass[1,3] and Antonakis *et al.*[4]

Leaders of academic health science centers also recognize the likelihood of conflicts among individuals that are not based on the legitimate agendas of particular programs or the pros and cons of particular positions but, rather, on egocentricity, personality factors, rivalries, competition, and/or status concerns of individuals representing those programs. Leaders are mindful of potentially interfering factors in the pursuit of organizational objectives, especially when clear mission-driven agendas appear thwarted for little or no apparent reason. They are careful to evaluate the substance of arguments for and against particular proposals based on organizational and programmatic mission and vision-driven objectives. Leaders exhibiting *interpersonal or intercollegial consideration* take positions after evaluating principles based on the merits of a position, apart from the individual personalities, rivalries, or competition that may be involved. They nonetheless remain sensitive to "ego-driven," individual needs, concerns, and personalities that may fuel rivalries or competition among individuals. They communicate clearly the reasons for their positions and are able to justify to themselves and others that their positions stem from organizational and programmatic principles and values.

Leaders recognize that they too may be subject to personal factors and biases that inappropriately influence their own evaluations and judgments of others and particular positions. They are mindful of the need to be reflective about the reasons and implications of their own positions and the importance of continually returning to mission- and values-driven goals and objectives. Leaders are skilled at negotiating differences and conflicts based on mission- and values-driven principles rather than personal bias. Negotiations are based on recognized "win-win" solutions whenever possible.[15] Leaders are also mindful of the personal and position-related needs of others and recognize the importance to some organizational leaders of social status and prestige. They attempt to arrive at solutions that are viewed as positive from both sides, that "save face" whenever possible, and that do not establish "winners" and "losers." These leaders attempt to resolve conflicts and arrive at solutions that encourage collaboration with others, recognizing both the needs of the present and opportunities of the future. They attempt to set the stage for current adversaries to become future collaborators in principles-driven work.[15–17]

Finding the Right Leader

Regrettably, an individual's leadership style is rarely formally evaluated in the course of the search process for a new leader. Indeed, it is not uncommon that a new leader is selected on the basis of a strong personality (and ego), while relatively little effort is made to more deeply assess that individual's personality characteristics and behavioral traits in the context of a clear set of leadership skills. The answer to a simple question is a good start: can this individual put the institution's interests ahead of his or her own and "bask in the reflected glow of others"? Therefore, it is incumbent upon institutions, search committees, search firms, and university presidents to commit to taking a much more in-depth look at the personality traits of candidates that suggest a good fit for the institution. In particular, an emphasis on transformational leadership is essential if institutions want to thrive in a highly competitive and challenging era.

A competent leader is usually proficient, at least initially, at "managing down" in the organization – that is, overseeing the work of assistants, faculty, chairs, center directors, and so forth who work *for* him or her. However, equally important – and frequently absent – are skill sets to "manage parallel" and "manage up": to work efficiently and productively with peers at the same level in the organization and with those to whom the leader reports. Indeed, failure to successfully manage "parallel and up" is a leading cause of institutions falling short of their potential; it is also a cause of leaders losing their jobs.

Another critically important concern in the search for leaders of academic health science centers is the quality and quantity of potential candidates. Unfortunately, creating a substantial interest in pursuing careers in academic administration can be problematic. The path to leadership is highly variable and often is not viewed by potential candidates as attractive. Faculty too often belittles academic administration with slurs such as "suits" or "crossing over to the dark side." The result is that individuals from within these ranks who desire to advance to positions of administrative leadership often have a poor idea of what this leadership actually entails, and may even be discouraged from pursuing it. There is a strong need for academic administration to be "demystified" by more transparently displaying its value for all to see and by encouraging those with potential talent in this area to pursue it. Efforts to create "leadership programs" are needed along with comprehensive institutional succession planning, whether it be through grooming internal candidates or determining that a leader of a certain type is needed from the outside. Ultimately, the message must be clearly sent that effective leadership is the single most important parameter for institutional success.

Because academic health science centers are such critically important institutions, it is incumbent upon these institutions, their search committees, search firms, and university presidents to commit to taking a much more in-depth look at the personality traits of candidates who suggest a good fit for the institution. Also, talented individuals need more preparation in assuming the leadership of these critically important institutions. This book provides an overview of many of the skills that are required with the hope that it proves useful to current and future leaders.

Author's Personal Reflections

I've visited more than 80 academic health centers in the United States and around the world, where I've been privileged to encounter some of the most principled, most intelligent, and hardest-working people I've ever known. Leaders of academic health centers are fighting for the noble missions of education, research, and patient care, and often with great obstacles in front of them. These leaders are constantly dealing with unexpected crises – environmental, political, scientific, financial, or otherwise – but, somehow, they are able to articulate a set of principles for which they stand, and evolve strategies for managing those crises without wavering from their principles.

The truly transformational leaders I've met engage others around them. They have the capacity to take their ego out of the job, and bask in the reflected glow of the professionals under their leadership. They truly appreciate, admire, and give credit to other people. They listen to others, and, perhaps most important, they have the intelligence to change their minds when presented with compelling arguments. In this way, they are able to move their institutions forward and advance their essential work.

Leaders have so many demands thrust upon them that I believe it's important for them to have some kind of personal project that will speak to the leader but also be a game changer for the institution. This is not about being engaged with the institution in the traditional ways – giving lectures, seeing patients, mentoring students – all those are a given. When I served as an academic health center leader, I founded a center for medical humanities and ethics. I felt that this was an important project for my institution. This was not essential for accreditation, but it filled a need, it added value to the institution, it was a good thing to do, and it inspired me personally.

It's difficult to fully prepare someone for the challenges of leading an institution as complex as an academic health center, but this book is a good start. The best advice I can give to someone preparing to take on a leadership role is the classic Greek adage: know thyself. The most successful leaders I've met understand themselves very well. They understand their strengths, and they understand their weaknesses. They do everything they can to enhance their strengths and compensate for their weaknesses.

I believe there is nothing more stimulating or challenging than being a leader in health care today. No other field gives you such intimate access to individuals as health care, whether you're treating patients, mentoring students, working with researchers, collaborating with communities, or intersecting with the business, political, and philanthropic spheres. All of it is exciting, and it's all geared toward one goal: improving health and well-being.

—SAW

References

1. Bass BM. *The Bass Handbook of Leadership: theory, research and managerial applications*. 4th ed. New York, NY: Free Press; 2008.
2. Burns JM. *Leadership*. New York, NY: Harper & Row; 1978.
3. Bass BM. Two decades of research and development in transformational leadership. *Eur J Work Org Psychol*. 1999; **8**(1): 9–32.

4. Antonakis J, Avolio BJ, Sivasubramaniam N. Context and leadership: an examination of the nine-factor full-range leadership theory using the Multifactor Leadership Questionnaire. *Leadership Quart*. 2003; **14**(3): 261–95.

5. Xirasagar S, Samuels ME, Stoskopf CH. Physician leadership styles and effectiveness: an empirical study. *Med Care Res Rev*. 2005; **62**(6): 720–40.

6. Spinelli RJ. The applicability of Bass's model of transformational, transactional, and laissez-faire leadership in the hospital administrative environment. *Hospital Topics: Research and Perspectives on Healthcare*. 2006; **84**(2): 11–18.

7. Failla KR, Stichler JF. Manager and staff perceptions of the manager's leadership style. *J Nurs Adm*. 2008; **38**(11): 480–7.

8. Cummings GC, MacGregor T, Davey M, *et al*. Leadership styles and outcome patterns for the nursing workforce and work environment: a systematic review. *Int J Nurs Stud*. 2010; **47**(3): 363–85.

9. Weberg D. Transformational leadership and staff retention: an evidence review with implications for healthcare systems. *Nurs Adm Q*. 2010; **34**(3): 246–58.

10. Larrabee JH, Janney MA, Ostrow CL, *et al*. Predicting registered nurse job satisfaction and intent to leave. *J Nurs Adm*. 2003; **33**(5): 271–83.

11. Corrigan PW, Diwan S, Campion J, Rashid F. Transformational leadership and the mental health team. *Adm Policy Ment Health*. 2002; **30**(2): 97–108.

12. Menaker R, Bahn RS. How perceived physician leadership behavior affects physician satisfaction. *Mayo Clin Proc*. 2008; **83**(9): 983–8.

13. Orr RD, Pang N, Pellegrino ED, *et al*. Use of the Hippocratic Oath: a review of twentieth century practice and a content analysis of oaths administered in medical schools in the U.S. and Canada in 1993. *J Clin Ethics*. 1997; **8**(4): 377–88.

14. Rancich AM, Pérez ML, Morales C, *et al*. Beneficence, justice and lifelong learning expressed in medical oaths. *J Contin Educ Health Prof*. 2005; **25**(3): 211–20.

15. Fisher R, Ury W, Patton B. *Getting to Yes: negotiating agreements without giving in*. 2nd ed. New York, NY: Penguin Books; 1991.

16. Moore CW. *The Mediation Process: practical strategies for resolving conflict*. 3rd ed. San Francisco, CA: Jossey-Bass; 2003.

17. Bush RAB, Folger JP. *The Promise of Mediation: the transformative approach to conflict*. Rev. ed. San Francisco, CA: Jossey-Bass; 2005.

Academic Health Science Centers in the New World Order

Optimizing Structure and Governance for High Performance

Jean E. Robillard

From the Editor

Academic health science centers – despite historical, cultural, and economic differences – have the common goal of aligning their academic functions of education and research with their clinical role of the delivery of patient care. This chapter presents a framework for structure and governance of these entities that seeks to maximize institutional effectiveness in a challenging health-care environment.

—SAW

The mission of academic health science centers (AHSCs) is to develop the next generation of health-care professionals, including physicians, nurses, physician assistants, physical therapists, and other health-care providers; to create knowledge by conducting both basic and clinical research; and to provide both primary and specialty medical care to the population, including the underserved.[1] These three missions are interdependent and need to be managed together, especially during challenging times. Most AHSCs are part of either a public or a private university and comprise a medical school, one or multiple-owned or separate/affiliated teaching hospitals, and a faculty practice plan that may have different organizational structures depending on the history and culture of the institution.

In some cases, the AHSC may also oversee other health professional schools (e.g., pharmacy, dentistry, nursing, public health).

By their very nature, AHSCs are extremely complex entities that must respond to the demands and needs of multiple constituents often with different and diverging agendas. Although they are known to set high-quality standards, they are also viewed as more expensive and less efficient than their non-teaching counterparts.[2] At the same time, AHSCs have to be entrepreneurial, assuming measured risks while maintaining their mission-related activities and, simultaneously, being cognizant that these actions and decisions may have dramatic repercussions on the stability of their own universities.[3,4] Moreover, AHSCs today face rapid and potentially unparalleled changes in health care, including dramatic changes in the basic relationships between physicians, hospitals, and patients – all set against a backdrop of increasing public expectations for access and high-quality care.

The Changing Health-Care Landscape

The transition to a new "post-reform" business model will likely bring new competitors and encourage consolidation of hospitals and physician practices,[5,6] similar to what was experienced in the mid-1990s.[7] Consolidation, which is already occurring in many other industries, will become a necessity for health-care organizations – including AHSCs – to insure their survival by negotiating better contracts with commercial payors and allowing fixed costs to be spread over a much larger patient base. In addition, with pressure from patients and payors to take cost out of the system ("bending the cost curve"), we should experience major market shifts. In all likelihood, these will include new forms of reimbursement based on value and quality rather than just physician productivity, increased demand for evidence-based care, and the establishment of integrated health-care organizations that take risks and share rewards.

In response to the changing landscape, AHSCs must recognize the interdependent and complementary nature of their different components (medical school, research enterprise, hospital, and practice plan), demonstrate levels of financial discipline and transparency at all levels and across their entire organization, bring discovery not just from the bench to the bedside but also to the community, and play a larger role across all health sciences. AHSCs will be well positioned to respond effectively to these challenges if they are able to create structures that integrate physicians and the hospital in ways that lower costs, improve quality and safety, and provide better and more convenient service to patients.

The urgency of eliminating the traditional silos and redundancy of efforts in AHSCs has become even more acute in the context of health-care reform and ongoing concerns over access to care, quality, and safety of clinical services, and the imperative to reduce costs. The underlying premise is that enhanced integrative relationships across the academic enterprise (medical school, research enterprise, practice plan, clinical delivery system, and other health sciences schools and colleges) are key for the success of future innovation in medical education, research (basic, clinical, population, and health services research), and medical care. To achieve these goals, AHSCs need an internal governance structure and a management system that emphasize discipline and teamwork, allowing the institution to react rapidly and take advantage of this "new world order" in health care.

Challenges Facing Academic Health Science Centers

Without a doubt, AHSCs today face significant challenges. At a macroeconomic level, a number of factors are adding a great deal of instability to an already complex industry. These include the uncertainty and the unknown in implementation of health-care reform, the unpredictability of traditional funding streams and the uncertainty of third-party reimbursement associated with the unknown impact of changes in reimbursement models, pressure from both state and federal lawmakers to control the costs of health care, changes in demographics, and the impact of globalization on the transmission of diseases. In addition, the rapid increase in new knowledge concurrent with expanding and transformative changes in technology and increased patient expectations for better outcomes place additional demands on AHSCs to offer patients more personal – and personalized – care, while at the same time improving quality and safety. Decisions about how best to satisfy these demands, train the next generation of health-care professionals, advance biomedical discovery, and fulfill the AHSC mission to take care of vulnerable populations are among the many challenges AHSCs must address.[2,3]

For example, in the area of education, AHSCs are expected to lead innovation and develop health professionals who will be prepared to respond to the demographic, social, economic, and technological changes of the future. In addition to providing graduate medical education and training to the next generation of medical specialists, AHSCs need to take the lead in transforming medical education and developing new educational models to train all health-care professionals in the delivery of integrated care with a patient-centered approach. To achieve these goals, and as proposed by the Institute of Medicine in 2004,[8] AHSCs need to develop interprofessional curricula that start in the classroom and expand to clinical rotation sites. Teaching team-based care and developing a health-care workforce capable of delivering integrated care are essential to meeting the needs of patients who are expecting affordable, accessible, and patient-centered care.

AHSCs have a mandate to redesign and restructure care processes and to take a larger role in improving the health of the population.

At the same time, the public also expects AHSCs to develop new diagnostic tools, to test new therapeutic approaches, and to improve clinical outcomes and the health of the population. Let's not forget that AHSCs are the recipient of large amounts of public support for their research and educational missions, as well as a disproportionate share of funds to care for low-income and uninsured patients. AHSCs need to create an environment where there is increased collaboration at all levels – from the basic scientists to the clinicians – to focus on the health of patients and populations. This will only be achieved if AHSCs foster innovation and coordinate care in a cohesive fashion. Addressing these questions appropriately is essential to maintaining the financial integrity of these centers, and the survival of their parent universities, as well as to create and deliver the kind of health care the nation expects.[8,9]

Academic Health Science Centers in the New World Order

Over the last 20 years, universities, medical schools, hospitals, and practice plans have created and developed AHSCs using different models of integration, ownership, and affiliation.[10–12] However, irrespective of their heterogeneity, all play a crucial and essential role by creating new knowledge for the benefit of the populations they serve, training the next generation of physicians and health-care providers, providing the most advanced care and specialized services often not available in community hospitals, serving an essential societal role in taking care of the poor and the underserved, and by providing leadership in making health care more efficient while improving accessibility, quality, and safety in our health-care system.[1]

Faced with changing social, political, and economic contexts, the changing nature of public health issues (including the obesity epidemic), the increased incidence of diabetes, and problems associated with the natural aging of the population, AHSCs need to become more agile and nimble to respond to these challenges. Thinking creatively about what AHSCs will be like 10–20 years from now is almost impossible when there is so much uncertainty surrounding the anticipated changes in the health-care covenant over the next few years. However, scientific progress in biomedical research[13] and technological innovations in diagnosis, treatment, and clinical information systems will continue to evolve and should influence and accelerate the need to reshape how we deliver care.

At the same time, we must remain mindful that our resources are limited[14] and that investing in prevention,[15,16] and providing better access to those who cannot presently afford care,[17] will improve the general health of Americans and decrease the overall costs of health care. Furthermore, as treatments advance, we should continue to see a further increase in outpatient care while inpatient care will focus more and more on highly specialized and complex cases. Hospitals will become more complex technically, will have more intensive-care beds, and will be smaller overall. In other words, one may envision that AHSCs will become the critical-care hub of a network of smaller clinical facilities and remote-care sites linked by elaborate electronic information systems and advanced critical care transportation.

Community clinical care will be provided by groups of providers (e.g., physicians, physician assistants, nurse practitioners, physical therapists, pharmacists, and so forth) and coordinated based on the needs of the patient.[18] New technologies, while increasing prevention and improving care, will create competitive disruption in the market place.[19] New technology is already in use to rapidly distribute information to patients and to increase efficiency in processes. Because of newly available electronic access to health-care providers, patients will become more involved and more accountable for managing their own care. This new technology, which could integrate with social networking, such as Facebook and Twitter, could be used to target information to patients and their families, coordinate interaction between patients, family, and care team, and to notify patients of out-of-range values. This, along with the new media available for use by patients, should lead eventually to decreased health-care utilization and possibly decreased needs for costly emergency department visits.

While patients are becoming empowered, the fee-for-service model that currently incentivizes the number of provider encounters and rewards overuse and often duplicative services, rather than encouraging effective and efficient care, will be phased out or modified. We are already seeing both private and government payors moving toward a system that rewards coordination and efficiency of care, emphasizes prevention and control of chronic conditions, maximizes quality outcomes, and reduces costs. Most health-care stakeholders and policy makers have concluded that effectively reducing medical cost trends to the level of economic indicators that guide businesses requires reform of both payment and delivery systems, as well as a focus on maintaining or improving the overall health of a population such that the incidence of chronic diseases declines.[15,16]

The ability of AHSCs to assume responsibility for effectively coordinating and managing all the health and medical services provided to a population will require establishing a proactive and comprehensive approach to population health management.[18] Since core processes for the population will not all be provided "directly" by AHSCs, services provided by other medical providers, community agencies, and regional hospitals will need to be coordinated.[18] To effectively participate in this transformation in health-care delivery, AHSCs will have to carefully review the way they are training the health-care workforce,[20] and how they are structuring themselves to assume responsibility for the total care of patients.[21-23] Data sharing of outcomes, quality, and costs with the goal of determining best practices may become a way of life for AHSCs. The future offers great potential for those who have the courage and readiness to recognize the implications of changing market dynamics, and who are positioned to face anticipated challenges, including hospital-physician integration.

Variations in Academic Health Science Center Structure and Governance

The structural organization of AHSCs and the range of relationships between medical schools, teaching hospitals, and physician organizations vary widely across the country. According to a September 2010 survey by the Council on Teaching Hospitals, of the nation's 133 medical schools (79 public and 54 private), 107 were part of an "integrated" AHSC (62 public and 45 private); defined[24] as either under common ownership with a college of medicine or as free-standing hospitals that are part of an AHSC in which the majority of the clinical chiefs of service are department chairmen in the affiliated medical school. Of the 107 medical schools that were part of an integrated AHSC, common ownership of the hospital and the medical school was observed among 42 (28 public and 14 private), while ownership of the hospital and the medical school was separate in 65 (34 public and 31 private).

Over the years, AHSCs have periodically reassessed their organizational structure, leading to various models and levels of integration between medical schools, hospitals, practice plan/physician organizations, and in some cases, insurance entities.[10,12,25] In the context of today's rapidly changing health-care environment, one wonders if the prevailing organizational and governance structures in AHSCs meet their present needs and prepare them to face the challenges ahead. A recent review of their many organizational variants suggests two general AHSC models.[12,26,27] The first is the "single fiduciary, one executive leader model," as defined by Wietecha.[26] In this model, the medical school dean, chief executive officer of the teaching hospital, and often the chair/executive director of the practice plan report to a single executive leader (vice president or vice chancellor) who reports to the president of the university and its respective board. The second model is the "multiple fiduciary, multiple executive leader model."[26] In this model, the dean of the medical school, the chief executive officer of the hospital, and, often, the practice plan leader report to different entities and separate fiduciary boards. A review of the different forms this model takes can be found in a paper published by Barrett.[12] More often than not, the second model has led to confrontations and conflicts over clinical and academic priorities and the allocation of resources across the AHSC's different missions.

However, the single fiduciary approach does not necessarily guarantee success; some institutional failures have also occurred under the single executive leader model.[26] One of the main reasons for these failures has been the inability to blend corporate and academic cultures and to successfully integrate workers within a corporate hierarchy.

Overall, the single fiduciary model has been successful in reducing conflicting interests while supporting the clinical, educational, and research missions of the institution. It has been quite effective in many AHSCs around the country, including the University of Michigan, the University of Pennsylvania, the University of California, Wake Forest University, and, more recently, at the University of Iowa, to name a few. All things considered, the single fiduciary model appears to hold greater promise for AHSCs to achieve optimal performance in the modern health-care environment.

It is important to note that the success or failure of a model is predominantly a function of who holds leadership positions. The "right people" can make most any system work (although poor structures make it harder and may discourage the best people), but the right structure will never make the "wrong people" successful.

Ten Principles Leading to High-Performing Academic Health Science Centers

Whatever the model, the future success of AHSCs will depend on a clear set of basic principles on which a strong governance structure can be built. First and foremost, the AHSC exists to support the academic mission. The university hospital provides an important public service and serves the public good, but only as a by-product of the academic mission. No university, especially in today's climate, would operate a health-care delivery system if it did not have the academic intent.

Second, the AHSC should function as a transparent organization so that its component entities (medical school, research enterprise, practice plan, and hospital) work together in an atmosphere of trust and mutual respect. Transparency fosters openness of thought, free exchange of ideas, and increased participation in decision making. An environment of transparency will assist the leader(s) of the enterprise to seek a proper balance between competing priorities and demands.

Third, the mission, vision, and values of the different enterprises comprising the AHSC need to be aligned. The AHSC should have one single strategic plan with all entities sharing the same goals. In addition, tying financial performance incentives for each member of the leadership team to the performance of others, as well as of the enterprise overall, should theoretically encourage further alignment and constructive leadership and operations performance.

Fourth, the different entities within an AHSC should be aligned under a single organizational structure (i.e., a single point of accountability). Efficient AHSCs have been able to consolidate their financial, human resources, legal, government relations, information technology, communication and marketing, and strategic planning offices under a single reporting structure to serve the medical school, research enterprise, hospital, and practice plan. This alignment under a single corporate structure decreases divergence between the different units, aligns the interests of clinical and academic elements with the overall goals of the organization, and enhances operational effectiveness. This coordinated approach should improve the ability of the organization to compete in a new health-care landscape while continuing to excel academically.

Fifth, the stability of the organization should be built on collaboration and accountability while eliminating barriers between the different entities. It is the role of the vice president/vice chancellor for health affairs to make sure that both the dean of the medical school and the hospital chief executive officer understand and respect the needs of one another's organization in order for the enterprise to thrive.

Sixth, AHSCs need to be self-critical and more open, with a commitment to continual self-assessment and benchmarking, to promote ongoing improvement. AHSCs will provide better value and outcomes for their patients if the leadership is able to set specific goals and measure performance against a clear set of metrics designed to drive improvements. There should be a serious commitment to organizational performance measurement and transparency in presenting the results both internally and externally. Performance measures, when used in positive and constructive ways, can become critical tools for organizational improvement overall and attracting new patients.[28] The mission, vision, values, and goals need to be well articulated and understood by all, and the entire organization should measure itself against metrics established to gauge progress.

Seventh, the administrative structure of AHSCs should be flexible and adaptive with an appropriate balance of centralization and decentralization. This is especially true since AHSCs exist on the boundary between the market-based economy driven by health care and the university's commitment to research and academic demands, which often contradict the health-care organization's needs for flexibility and nimbleness.

Eighth, AHSCs should have clear succession planning and should invest in the development of new leaders with the ability to listen, communicate, make difficult decisions, and take appropriate risks. Good leaders should to be able to "prudently" risk the assets of the organization in order to ensure a better future. Failure to take measured risks and being content with the status quo are "major diseases of success" and often lead to the failure of the organization.[29]

Ninth, leadership should recognize the diverse requirements of the AHSC and balance investments accordingly. AHSC leaders are responsible for fulfilling the tripartite mission of delivering patient care, educating the future workforce, and creating new knowledge. Yet the expectation that each component of the overarching mission should be self-supporting is unrealistic and poses a threat to the overall organization. Cross-subsidization of the missions is often necessary. When needed, cross-subsidization should be done with clear goals and objectives, and the outcome of these investments should be monitored and measured using unambiguous metrics and comparable benchmarks. Leadership must also be ready to shift or end support when outcomes are not achieved or priorities change. This will ensure that valuable resources can be redirected as needed in order to continually advance collective goals.

Tenth, trustees need to embrace their responsibilities rather than delegate them to the appointed executive leader(s) of the AHSC. To achieve this goal, the board of trustees needs the time and expertise to understand the clinical and academic issues and dilemmas facing the AHSC, and to question the strategy and decision-making process of its leadership team. There is growing evidence that suggests the quality of governance impacts the operating performance and success of health-care organizations.[23] In particular, active and engaged governance boards play a vital role by putting appropriate leadership in place to ensure the best patient care possible while functioning efficiently, effectively, and economically. Specifically, trustees should demand that AHSC executives are fully transparent with respect to the funds flow between different components of the organization. A strong governance structure with trustees who have a good understanding and knowledge of modern health-care systems, understand the relationship between the AHSC and its host university, and are versed on many of the complex financial issues that could affect the capital resources of the AHSC and university is essential to the success of the AHSC.

Conclusion

The dynamics affecting AHSCs shape the education of our students and residents; impact the relationship between nurses, physicians, and staff; and, sooner or later, influence the quality of patient care and patient outcomes. In today's new world order of health care, a frustrated public demands increased accountability and greater efficiencies in the health-care delivery system. The government and payors want better care at lower cost. To respond to these challenges, AHSCs must go beyond the traditional model of education, research, and patient care toward developing integrated systems of care involving team-based approaches that reach patients in their own community and improve population health. In addition, AHSCs need to develop strategies to improve patient satisfaction, educational outcomes, and research excellence. An organizational structure that allows for seamless integration of the AHSC's different missions is a key first step to achieving this vision for high performance and, ultimately, better health.

Author's Personal Reflections

The most rewarding part of overhauling our governance at the University of Iowa was to bring the whole health system under the new structure, and to see the various parts of our organization enrolled in a single vision, and moving toward a single future. We created one corporate structure for the whole university health-care system. We established one legal office, one single human resources office, one communications department, and one strategic plan. We eliminated redundancy, and by doing so, we developed one voice to speak for the institution. So when a decision is made, the whole institution is able to move in the same direction. We've had success in both the clinical and the academic areas. We've built a large academic research building. We're starting a new children's hospital, and we're building a subspecialty clinic off campus. None of these projects would have been possible without the streamlining of our governance and working collectively.

Competitiveness is part of human nature. Every good organization knows that it's important that people come to the table with different skills and ideas, and that everyone should have a chance to express their opinions. However, in the end we have to make one unified decision. The governance structure allows you to do this, but it's really about the people you choose to work with. A healthy governance structure forces you to get the right people. One example is our decision to move off campus. We sought to bring many clinics off campus and develop a $70 million building where they could all reside. It involved the hospital and the practice plans, and it was a real change of culture. We were asking faculty to practice medicine as if they were engaged in a private practice, with the goal of increasing the quality of service. The hospital paid for the building, but the practice plan operated the facility and was ultimately responsible for the bottom line. This would not have been possible to achieve without imposing that larger governance structure. We came with a template, and gave them autonomy to work inside the template, but we set very clear boundaries. We will open the clinic in less than 12 months, and so far it has been going very smoothly.

We are achieving our goals by working with one strategic plan for the entire organization. The strategic plan is a living document that we all use to make decisions. We review the plan together every quarter, and we present it to the Board of Regents twice a year. This has really changed the way people think. We can always add to it, but the plan helps us to order our priorities, and to reassess the organization on an ongoing basis. It's a lot easier to go where you're going if you know where you're going. It's rewarding to enable people to work together toward achieving a set of shared goals. As a leader of an academic health center, you need to surround yourself with a team of great people to make the organization a success. It's not just about making big decisions; it's also about the process of making the decision. How do we establish the best decisions and get people working together?

There is always pressure to cut back, but you can't shrink to greatness. Yes, there are financial challenges, but academic health centers must invest. They have to continue to take measured risks, and be bold, and look at growth. Growth is not about taking business from a neighbor, it's about being creative, and generating new products and new treatments. Academic health centers have to be entrepreneurial, and if we do that, we will do well, and the country will do well.

Health care is changing, and those changes are exciting, because they make us rethink what we do. I believe the delivery of care will be better, and the application of research to clinical care will also improve. The issues we're facing are serious, but there were issues in the past that were also serious. It's up to us to use those challenges as an incentive to do better. In the end, we may have a delivery-of-care system that is better than we have presently, and probably at lower cost. There are ways to do this, but we have to be creative and be willing to change the system. We have to change the education system, the way we deliver health care, and the way we train and use our entire workforce. Also, we have to make sure there is more interface between basic science discovery and clinical application in the community. For example, electronic medical records will supply us with a wealth of data that we never had before. Eventually, patients should be able to schedule their own visits, and see their results an hour after they come to the clinic. These things are happening. The times are changing, but they are changing for the best.

—JER

References

1. Task Force on Academic Health Centers. *Envisioning the Future of Academic Health Centers.* The Commonwealth Fund; 2003.
2. Fisher ES, Wennberg DE, Stukel TA, *et al.* Variations in the longitudinal efficiency of academic medical centers. *Health Aff (Millwood).* 2004; Suppl. Variation: Var19–32.

3. Rodin J. A revisionist view of the integrated academic health center. *Acad Med*. 2004; **79**(2): 171–8.

4. Kastor JA. *Governance of Teaching Hospitals: turmoil at Penn and Hopkins*. Baltimore, MD: Johns Hopkins University Press; 2004.

5. Krauskopf L. Humana to buy Concentra for $790 million to diversify. New York, NY: Reuters; 2010.

6. Ascension Health, Oak Hill Capital Partners team on hospital acquisitions. *St. Louis Business Journal*. February 21, 2011.

7. Blumenthal D, Edwards N. A tale of two systems: the changing academic health center. *Health Aff (Millwood)*. 2000; **19**(3): 86–101.

8. Committee on the Roles of Academic Health Centers in the 21st Century. *Academic Health Centers: leading change in the 21st century*. Kohn LT, editor. Washington, DC: National Academies Press; 2004.

9. Kirch DG. *A Future that Inspires: AAMC President's Address; 2010 Annual Meeting*. Washington, DC: Association of American Medical Colleges; 2010.

10. Culbertson RA, Goode LD, Dickler RM. Organizational models of medical school relationships to the clinical enterprise. *Acad Med*. 1996; **71**(11): 1258–74.

11. Weiner BJ, Culbertson R, Jones RF, *et al*. Organizational models for medical school-clinical enterprise relationships. *Acad Med*. 2001; **76**(2): 113–24.

12. Barrett DJ. The evolving organizational structure of academic health centers: the case study of the University of Florida. *Acad Med*. 2008; **83**(9): 804–8.

13. Lifton RP. Individual genomes on the horizon. *N Engl J Med*. 2010. **362**(13): 1235–6.

14. Chernew ME, Baicker K, Hsu J. The specter of financial Armageddon: health care and federal debt in the United States. *N Engl J Med*. 2010; **362**(13): 1166–8.

15. Simonson B, Lahiri S; for Lewin Group; for Pharmaceutical Research and Manufacturers of America (PhRMA). *The Prevalence and Cost of Select Chronic Diseases*. Washington, DC: PhRMA; 2007.

16. DeVol R, Bedroussian A. *An Unhealthy America: the economic burden of chronic disease*. Santa Monica, CA: Milken Institute; 2007.

17. Institute of Medicine, Committee on Health Insurance Status and Its Consequences. *America's Uninsured Crisis: consequences for health and health care*. Washington, DC: National Academies Press; 2009.

18. Berwick DM. Launching accountable care organizations: the proposed rule for the Medicare Shared Savings Program. *N Engl J Med*. 2011; **364**(16): e32.

19. Kaufman, Hall & Associates. The transformation of America's hospitals [lecture]. Presented at University HealthSystem Consortium CFO Council Meeting, Chicago, IL; 2011.

20. Association of Academic Health Centers. *Out of Order, Out of Time: the state of the nation's health workforce*. Washington, DC: Association of Academic Health Centers; 2008.

21. Goldstein L, Martin L, Nelson JC; for Moody's Investors Service. *Special Comment: transforming not-for-profit healthcare in the era of reform*. Report No. 124883. New York, NY: Moody's Investors Service; 2010.

22. Lee TH. Putting the value framework to work. *N Engl J Med*. 2010; **363**(26): 2481–3.

23. Goldsmith J. Analyzing shifts in economic risks to providers in proposed payment and delivery system reforms. *Health Aff (Millwood)*. 2010; **29**(7): 1299–304.

24. Association of American Medical Colleges. *Council of Teaching Hospitals and Health Systems: survey of hospital operations and financial performance*. Washington, DC: Association of American Medical Colleges; 2010.

25. Task Force on Academic Health Centers. *Managing Academic Health Centers: meeting the challenges of the new health care world*. The Commonwealth Fund; 2000.

26. Wietecha M, Lipstein SH, Rabkin MT. Governance of the academic health center: striking the balance between service and scholarship. *Acad Med*. 2009; **84**(2): 170–6.

27. Wartman SA. *The Academic Health Center: evolving organizational models.* Washington DC: Association of Academic Health Centers; 2008.
28. Lee TH. Turning doctors into leaders. *Harvard Business Review.* April 2010: 50–8.
29. Keough DR. *The Ten Commandments for Business Failure.* New York, NY: Penguin Group; 2008.

Organizational Structure, Data, and Academic Health Science Center Transformation

Robert I. Grossman and Robert Berne

From the Editor

Management of complex entities like academic health science centers requires access to reliable information that can effectively guide operational decision making. In this chapter, a case study is presented that demonstrates how good data can lead to a successful transformation of the enterprise.

—SAW

Organizational structure as a determinant of organizational culture and perform-ance is central to the function of academic health science centers (AHSCs). Data is a driving force to facilitate management and the transformation of an AHSC into an integrated hospital and school with effective board oversight and university relations, as well as the creation of a culture of transparency and accountability. This chapter examines AHSC transformation from both the internal management and the medical center board/university perspectives – two different but related points of view. The case study presented here highlights the importance of deep, real-time, simply presented data to the transforma-tion. Applying a *clinical* focus on internal management processes and a *finance* focus for board/university assessments to an institution's reorganization strategy, thereby highlighting the differences in decision making and perspectives, is use-ful to illustrate the importance of such data utilization in achieving a successful AHSC transformation.

New York University Langone Medical Center: A Case Study in Academic Health Science Center Transformation

Background

Over the past 4 years, New York University Langone Medical Center (NYULMC) has been engaged in a transformation from an ad hoc management and decision-making organization to a centralized, data-focused enterprise driven by its vision to be a world-class patient-centered integrated academic medical center. This was necessitated as much by the economic and imminent value-based purchasing realities of twenty-first-century medical care as it was from a deep desire to be part of an endeavor that held excellence as a core value. Both the internal medical center management and the governance structure, in this case the boards of both New York University (NYU) (the university) and NYULMC, needed to be highly aligned in terms of the medical center's vision.

It is relevant that NYU (as a university) has undergone its own transformation from a regional commuter university to a national and international research university over the past 30 years. The almost 170-year history of NYULMC is that of a medical school-centric mission focused on education and research, distinct from institutions that begin as hospitals caring for patients and later add a medical school. Indeed, one of the reasons why a 1998–2001 merger with such an institution failed was because of significant operational differences between "hospital" and "school" cultures.[1]

The legal de-merger took over 5 years and provided NYU an opportunity to structure its governance and management of the medical center in a way that balances the needs and risks of both the university and NYULMC. In terms of revenues, the medical center (hospital and school of medicine) contributes roughly half for the entire university. Before the failed merger, both the school and hospital were constituents of the university, reporting to the president and board. During the merger period (1998–2006), the school remained a part of the university and NYU was one of two corporate members of the merged Mount Sinai–NYU Hospital.

Post merger, it became clear that one of the most important steps for the hospital and school of medicine was to begin operating as an integrated AHSC, while remaining connected to the university; also post merger, for academic reasons, it was important for the school of medicine to remain a part of the university. To address issues of risk, the university became the sole member of the hospital, a separate 501(c) organization with its own board, with its debt in an obligated group separate from the university (including school of medicine) debt.

The remaining major structural question was how to operate the medical center as an integrated AHSC consistent with this governance system. A hospital board was created with legal responsibilities for governance of the hospital. The board is appointed by the university and also serves as the advisory board for the school of medicine. Thus the one board acts as a medical center board. Further connection to the university is ensured, as eight members of the university board are also appointed as NYULMC board members. When the university board and its committees review medical center matters, it is with the knowledge that, at the medical center, both independent and overlapping board members have been involved in the process, ensuring alignment.

In terms of post-merger medical center leadership, when the dean/chief executive officer (CEO) stepped down in 2007 it was clear that the hospital needed a leader with strong business skills while the school required a strong academician. There were arguments that it would be unlikely to find both strengths in a single person. The counterargument was that true integration could not take place without one person, a physician with combined "business" and "academic" skills in the position. Moreover, beginning with a search for one person would allow the opportunity to change course; a search for two would be conducted if a person with the combined strengths did not emerge. Fortunately, the search resulted in a single leader, the dean CEO, who reports to both the university president through the executive vice president for health and to the medical center board. This governance system can lead to a successful transformation if the medical center and the university have a high level of alignment between them.

For the leadership team, the consequences of the de-merger also required rebuilding the organizational structure of NYU Medical Center.* Prior to 2007, the reconstituted organization was directed by the position of dean/CEO. However, in reality it was two separate organizations with a hospital president, reporting to the dean/CEO, responsible for all hospital activities and a dean and vice dean for education accountable for the education and research missions. The faculty practice was in the school of medicine and accountable to the vice dean for clinical affairs. Additionally, there were separate chief financial officers, chief information officers, and so forth for the hospital and school (*see* Figures 3.1 and 3.2). Variations of this organizational scheme exist at many AHSCs and can be viewed as a system of checks and balances with considerable discussions and negotiations taking place between the hospital and the school. In these scenarios the hospital is the revenue generator and the academic missions, requiring subsidies, are funded through agreed-upon mission payments (from the hospital to the school).

New Organization

In 2007, a new organization table was developed (*see* Figure 3.3). The position of hospital president was eliminated and hospital functions were divided between

---

* In 2008, NYU Medical Center was renamed the NYU Elaine A. and Kenneth G. Langone Medical Center.

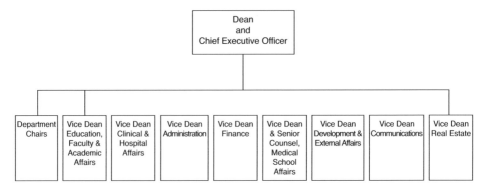

FIGURE 3.1 New York University School of Medicine table of organization, 2006

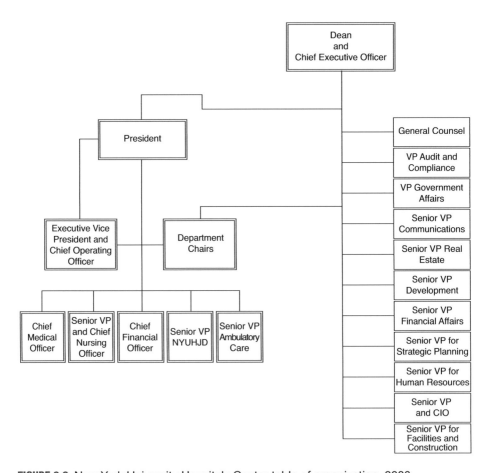

FIGURE 3.2 New York University Hospitals Center table of organization, 2006

those that involved operations ("throughput") and those that involved generation of patient volume. In addition, single medical center leadership positions were created for chief financial officer, chief information officer, human resources, and so forth. The institution evolved from one with separate hospital and school silos to one with a medical center focus, enabling alignment of all aspects in the organization. The alignment diminished friction between hospital and school organizations and facilitated efficient resource management.

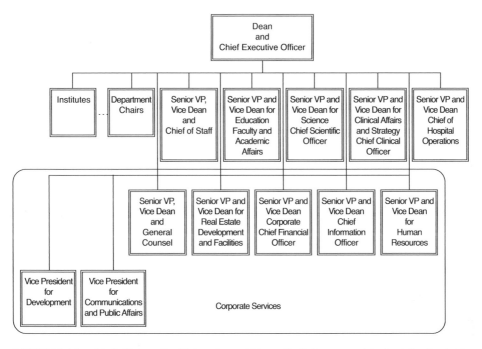

FIGURE 3.3 New York University Elaine A. and Kenneth G. Langone Medical Center table of organization, 2011

The ability to manage as a single entity dramatically improved the effectiveness of the decision-making processes. Recruitments did not involve separate hospital and school negotiations. Mission payments for research and education became straightforward, and all members of the enterprise viewed themselves as employees of the medical center instead of working for the school or hospital.

The structure of an organization is directly related to its function. In a mission-based configuration, emphasis is placed on agility and performance rather than whether a service is rooted in the hospital or school. Under the new paradigm, a strategy could be developed that exploits strengths, creating five strategic areas (Neuroscience, Cancer, Musculoskeletal, Children's Services, and Cardiovascular) and positioning the institution to respond favorably to the rapidly shifting landscape of health-care reform. Foundations of excellence were established in the three missions (research, clinical care, and education), with a cascading effect of embellishing reputation, improving the ability to recruit and retain students and faculty, and positioning the medical center for a metrically driven reimbursement environment that was clearly on the horizon, while at the same time addressing significant financial challenges.

Dashboard

Having data is a key element of strategy, and where there are multiple users of such information differences in perspective and interpretation often occur. In AHSCs, endless arguments from entrenched positions concerning data "quality" are, unfortunately, the norm. These conflicts are often predicated on established interests attempting to maintain the status quo. Good data can be an important initiator of behavioral change. The first step in data-driven management is to produce high-quality data and to make certain that discussions are concentrated on interpretation of data rather than its quality. The onus is on the individuals whose data is being analyzed to be certain that the facts are correct. From the data a fundamental understanding can be derived of how the health-care enterprise and its components are functioning as well as where it must improve.

One aspect of this approach has been the design and implementation of an *enterprise data dashboard*. The dashboard contains up-to-date information about the clinical, research, financial, education, and quality aspects of the AHSC. All the departmental chairs are provided their own dashboard focusing on their particular components of the missions (*see* Figure 3.4a–e: screen shots of dashboard and components).

The dashboard data can be divided into three broad categories: (1) leading indicators; (2) lagging indicators; and (3) coincident indicators. An example of a leading indicator (predictive but not necessarily accurate) might include the number and value of grant applications, as a certain percentage of them will translate into funded research. A lagging indicator (momentum defining) might be the number of hospital readmissions. Tracking trends in this data provides a view of the quality of the medical care being rendered. A coincident indicator (contemporaneous state) is the daily cash, or number of full-time employees per adjusted occupied bed, which provides liquidity or efficiency measures.

Many hospitals and health systems are highly inefficient, opaque businesses larded with legacy systems that fail to yield quality information in real time. Superimposed on this structure is the reluctance of hospital leaders to change their approach to management. To state that "good data" are an essential ingredient for quality and financial stability is to proclaim the obvious, yet it is clear that many institutions have neither "good data" nor the desire to fundamentally use data to change processes or operations.

Once there is consensus among users that the data are of high quality, the

FIGURE 3.4A Dashboard snapshot: data on research-related activities

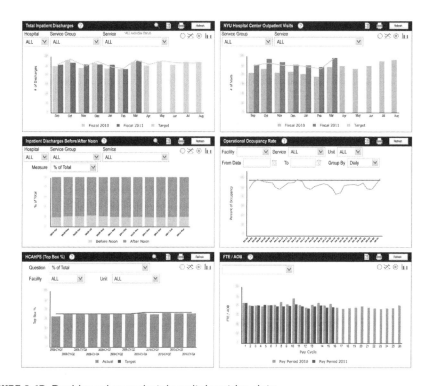

FIGURE 3.4B Dashboard snapshot: hospital metrics data

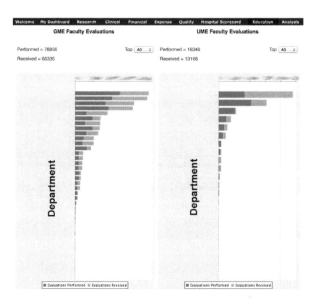

FIGURE 3.4C Dashboard snapshot: graduate and undergraduate medical education evaluations data

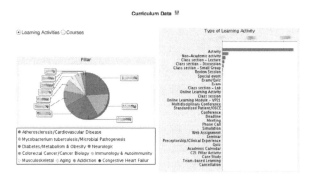

FIGURE 3.4D Dashboard snapshot: medical student learning activity data

next appropriate step is organizational alignment and behavior modification. By approaching data with a medical center perspective, where all the missions are coequal and responsibility is obvious, "finger pointing" and opacity are minimized. The medical-centric approach can vastly improve agility in decision making across the enterprise and can result in an improved bottom line.

Exemplar

The strongest correlation with hospital margin is 1/average length of stay (ALOS). ALOS is a common metric that is used to evaluate hospital quality, efficiency, and costs. It is a critical factor in hospital cost structure and quality care. Embedded in ALOS measures are a plethora of issues and processes, including hospital

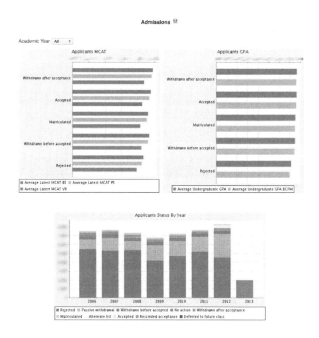

FIGURE 3.4E Dashboard snapshot: medical school admission data

complications and efficiencies. In many circumstances, hospitals receive a fixed fee for a particular diagnosis-related group. The best-case scenario for the hospital is to admit and discharge the patient in the shortest possible time using the least number of tests, treating the patient appropriately, and obtaining the best outcome. Anything interfering with the "ideal" scenario adds expenses, erodes margin, and affects outcome. Neither physicians nor nurses have much incentive to rapidly move patients along. By not paying on a per diem basis the "risk" is transferred to the hospital.

ALOS can be separated into four basic components: (1) Physician, (2) Hospital, (3) Nursing, and (4) Family/Social situation; to approach ALOS issues requires examining all of these components.

Physicians

Physicians should prescribe the very best in medical/surgical therapy, including eliminating artistic impressionism, and implementing evidence-based medicine (when available). They should pay appropriate attention to all of the conditions that impact quality care, not just the primary patient complaint, including correct testing and correct interpretation of tests performed in a timely fashion. The ALOS for all of our physicians is available on the dashboard (*see* Figure 3.5).

The ability to compare ALOS among those who perform the same tasks is a powerful force in driving ALOS down and in understanding differences in

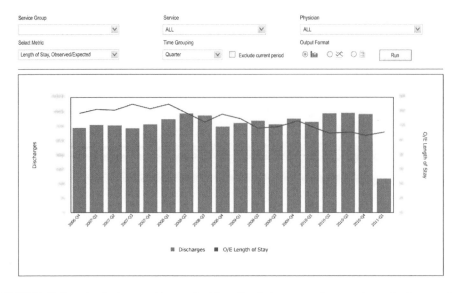

FIGURE 3.5 Graph of observed/expected length of stay superimposed on discharges for quarterly time periods

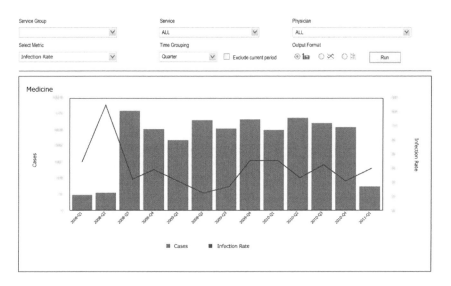

FIGURE 3.6 Example of review of variations of average length of stay: comparison of infection rates

particular practice patterns – for example, where there are x number of surgeons who perform similar surgical procedures and a variation is observed in ALOS. To explain the variation in ALOS, infection rates are reviewed (*see* Figure 3.6), showing significant differences. Equipped with the appropriate data, surgeons with the higher ALOS can be approached with a focus on practice issues.

Hospitals

The hospital must ensure that all of the components of service are supplied in an efficient manner. That includes social work, discharge planning, imaging studies, blood drawing, medications, and so forth. Cleaning and preparation of the room must be expeditious. This efficiency can be measured in early discharges (*see* Figure 3.7).

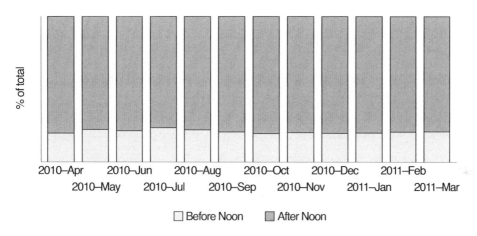

FIGURE 3.7 Example of efficiency measurement: comparison of early and late hospital discharges (Langone Medical Center)

Nursing

Nursing assistance is essential. Continuous improvement in workflow and prioritization is central to enabling early discharge. Ensuring that testing, instructions, prescriptions, and logistics are completed is the responsibility of nursing. The dashboard can also be drilled down to the nursing component level with respect to ALOS.

Family

The family has to be ready to receive the patient. This requires physician, nursing, and social service performing their given tasks.

By continuously monitoring the data, identifying hurdles, working as a team, and celebrating progress, improvement of ALOS without affecting quality of care becomes a reality (*see* Figure 3.8). That translates to the bottom line and to better patient care – less time in the hospital, less chance of a complication.

The dashboard enables a comparison of physicians with similar types of practices (breast surgeons, hip surgeons, cardiologists, and so forth). Evaluation of their data highlights differences in methods within analogous procedures or practices when normalized for case mix. Refining this information generates an

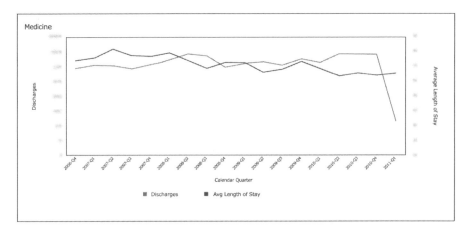

FIGURE 3.8 Graph of average length of stay superimposed on discharges for quarterly time periods

approach to improvement in quality. The overall effect, in a particular area of practice, with access to one another's data cannot be understated. This immediately leads to more attention to quality and performance improvement. In our setting, initial areas of concentration were readmission rates, ALOS, infection rates, and observed-to-expected mortality (*see* Figure 3.9). The effect of data can be tracked over time on an enterprise-wide basis, departmentally, or for the individual physician (*see* Figure 3.10).

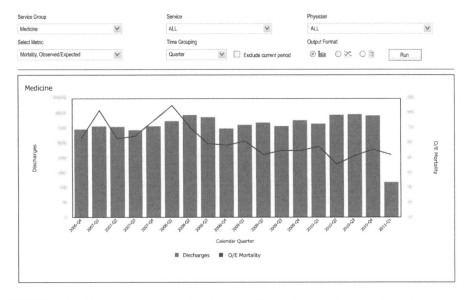

FIGURE 3.9 Quality and performance tracking: mortality observed/expected, by department

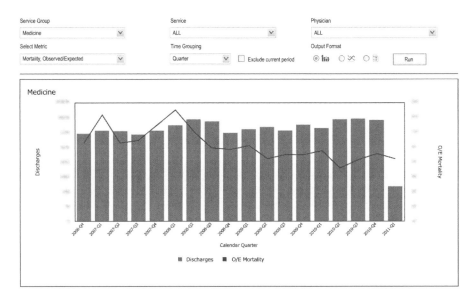

FIGURE 3.10 Quality and performance tracking: mortality observed/expected, by physician

Departmental Snapshot

A second part of the management process is dialog created by the "departmental snapshot." This process includes a yearly intensive departmental review by the dean/CEO and vice deans. Dashboard data are embedded into a two-page summary of each department (*see* Addendum at end of this chapter, Figure 3.11a and b). The snapshot contains the following: (a) the year's key accomplishments, strategic plan including short and long priorities, and the challenges that the department foresees as impediments to achieving its goals; (b) data on the department's research, educational, and clinical endeavors; (c) foundational information regarding finances and faculty productivity; and (d) graphic information on clinical or research longitudinal data.

After preliminary discussions with the department chair's office are concluded and all the objective issues are harmonized, a meeting between the chair and the dean/CEO is followed immediately by the budget meeting between the vice deans, finance, the department chair, and the department administrator. Here, final budgetary issues are agreed upon.

Governance and Financial Goals

The medical center-university structure and governance must be aligned to strongly support the transformation of the medical center. The school of medicine is part of the university's legal entity and obligated group for debt, while the hospital is a separate entity with its own debt (not guaranteed by the university).

The goal is to manage both as an integrated AHSC that is, itself, related to the university. At NYULMC, shortly after the de-merger and before the leadership change in 2007, the school of medicine had a large structural operating deficit that was unsustainable. Moreover, the hospital was roughly break-even, and thought at the time to be underperforming. Going forward, from both medical center and university perspectives, the goal was for above break-even financial performance for the medical center as a whole, which translated to drastically reducing the structural deficit of the school and improving the financial results of the hospital, while simultaneously achieving ambitious clinical, research, and education goals. In addition, the financial performance needed to be sufficiently positive such that, with philanthropy and sustainable borrowing, support for previously neglected capital would be forthcoming.

A challenge in a potentially transformational period is finding the "right" level of overall financial oversight by the university and medical center boards when potentially too much or too little could impede the transformation. In this case, a key was to drive efficiencies in operations while being willing to make strategic investments in programs, infrastructure, and systems that would meet clinical, research, and educational goals. It was unlikely that the full set of goals could be met by "cutting" alone, as the three mission goals would not improve and the vision would not be achieved.

Meeting these financial goals in the midst of a transformation required active and committed board-level finance committees for both the medical center and the university, with key roles played by independent and overlapping board members. The university finance committee met four times per year while the medical center finance committee met nine times per year and delved deeper into the medical center's financial performance than the university committee could, as the medical center was a key agenda item in two to three of the four finance committee meetings.

A key tool to enable this appropriate level of board involvement was a sophisticated, and understandable, long-range forecast that included operating and capital flows over a 10-year period. The medical center and university finance committees were the first to recognize that uncertainties of such a plan increase in the out-years, but these committees also knew its value in terms of instilling a level of financial discipline illustrating the ramifications of various decisions and trends, and allowing the modeling of what-ifs in terms of alternative investments in relation to financial targets. The long-range forecast was built from the bottom up with substantial detail at every level – numbers of faculty and staff; clinical activity divided by subspecialty; funded research by department; changes in volume, rates, and prices; and so on. With the least amount of uncertainty in year one of the plan, it can become, with greater level of detail, the operating and capital budget for the coming year, with the cycle repeated annually. Further, by using a consistent approach and format over time for the plan and the budget, both board committees develop increased understanding of and confidence in these as tools to assess short- and long-term performance.

With the medical center as its sole focus and more meetings, the medical center finance committee can delve into considerable details surrounding NYULMC's finances. Financial statements are produced monthly, within 5–6 days after each month's end. In addition to examining operating trends in revenues, expenses, margins, cash, and receivables and payables, the committee discusses clinical trends in measures such as inpatient discharges, ALOS and case mix index, and outpatient visits. The committee also delves into periodic capital financing and addresses issues such as debt structure, pension investments, fixed versus variable rate instruments, and debt issue timing. The focus varies between the medical center as a whole and the school of medicine and hospital. For the school, issues such as trends in research funding and performance of the faculty group practice are commonly on the agenda. For the hospital, changes in payor mix, pending state and federal budget actions, cash management, quality measures, and rating agency reports are examples of the matters that the committee discusses regularly. On occasion, the committee assesses the performance of a subunit such as the cancer center or department of surgery. Items such as fringe benefits are examined regularly.

Building on the work of the medical center finance committee, the university finance committee focuses on the "bigger picture" of the medical center and its relationship to the university. With pent-up capital demands creating the need for substantial investment at the medical center to accomplish the transformation, the university finance committee scrutinizes the overall capital and borrowing plans of the medical center, distinguishing between the necessary capital spending and debt that is part of the school of medicine (and thus the university) and that which is part of the hospital. Even though the medical center debt is part of a separate obligated group, the rating of the hospital and the school are examined together by the ratings agencies – thus the need for coordinated management of the medical center and university debt levels and capital plans.

Evaluating the Transformation

Over the past 4 years we have experienced a fundamental transformation at NYULMC. The culture has shifted from "I" to "we" – from school- and hospital-centered to enterprise-centric with a healthy relationship to the larger university. Appropriate investing performed for the benefit of the medical center has enabled agile recruitment, swift acquisition of space, improvement in facilities, and opportunistic investments in education and research.

Some tangible results from the transformation include: (1) continuous improvement in the operating margin and cash positions of the medical center and hospitals; (2) continuous improvement in bond ratings; (3) a net addition of over 2 million square feet of space (as of 2017); (4) improvements in quality ranking surveys, including being in the top 10% of hospitals in the United States for overall recommended care based on Centers for Medicare & Medicaid Services (CMS) data; (5) successful clinical and research faculty recruitment; (6) growth in sponsored research; and (7) an intangible feeling that the medical center is moving in the right direction. This direction has been validated by the remarkable philanthropic support that has been received. Over the past 4 years our institution has raised over $1 billion.

Conclusion

Predominant elements that can facilitate the transformation of an AHSC are an integration of the hospital and school, a focus on objective data, effective board oversight and university relations, and the creation of a culture of transparency and accountability. By managing our enterprise as a medical center rather than a school and hospital, we dramatically improved our decision-making ability and eliminated traditional school versus hospital squabbling. This reorganization resulted in a cultural transformation underscoring the importance of organizational structure as a determinant of function. Driving management by data is a continuous process that must be reinforced. The quality results have followed: We are recognized by *US News & World Report* as among the best in the country in 14 specialties and second in the New York metro area overall. In addition, we are ranked in the top 10 nationwide for overall performance by the University HealthSystem Consortium and, according to WhyNotTheBest.org (an online aggregator of government measures of health-care quality), in the top 10% of hospitals nationwide for "Overall Recommended Care" our 30-day mortality rates place us number one in the nation for heart attack and heart failure, and fifth in the nation for pneumonia.

In summary, organizational structure, data focus, and transparency have been prime movers in our transformation.

Author's Personal Reflections

Let me give you an example of how the proper use of data can make a difference. We sought to improve our before-noon discharges, so we could refill our beds and serve people more efficiently. But we couldn't seem to do it. We had all this information about before-noon discharges and how hard

---

it was to improve the number of before-noon discharges. We examined all the aspects of why it was so hard to change. It turned out that there were a whole series of issues. First off, the patients needed to make arrangements for someone to be there to take them home. But there was a host of issues involving our own processes: a combination of nursing, pharmacy, attending physician, family, and social work factors. By looking at this single metric and deconstructing it, we understood why we couldn't just say we wanted the patient discharged before noon and make it happen overnight. There were so many components to address first.

For example, many times, patients wait for their lab results before they can get discharged, so they stay in the hospital so they can get blood drawn and get the results back. It turns out that the blood drawing teams started their shifts at 8 a.m., and so they couldn't possibly get the results back before 11 a.m. That doesn't leave a lot of time for the attending physicians to review the results and talk to the patient. So we retaught the nurses to draw blood at 6 a.m., so patients would have lab results ready when the attending physicians began their rounds. By taking the issue apart, and dealing with the constituent problems, we were able to refill our beds more quickly, but it also changed our whole focus. Everybody now understood it was a multifactorial problem.

But you also can't get too bogged down in the detail. You have to enroll people in a larger vision. We developed a vision statement, and we stayed very focused on it, and I think it generated a lot of passion in people who worked here, but also in those who were associated with NYU, and in the philanthropic community. Our vision is to be "a world-class, patient-centered, integrated medical center." And I believe that this vision led us to raise more than a billion dollars over 3 years.

Leading an academic health center is about understanding the culture of a particular institution and being a steward of the best part of that culture. When you get to the role of CEO, it isn't about you anymore, even though you've done things, and you may have your own individual accomplishments. It's about making the organization better. That's where the fun is: in enabling the transformation of an institution. I'm starting my fifth year and I think the institution is a different place from when I started. Seeing that transformation has been an enormously satisfying experience.

You have to have confidence in yourself and in your vision, and you should think big. This job is a marathon, not a sprint. There will be ups and downs, and you can't worry about those things. You have to be focused on the vision and its fulfillment. Integration is key to that. Sometimes it's difficult to get people working together in a unified way. In academic health centers, the school of medicine and the hospital sometimes have entirely separate organizational structures. We have integration of our academic, research, and clinical care enterprise. There's no hospital president. There's a chief operating officer of the hospital, and there's an individual who is head of our faculty practice. The chief operating officer is responsible for hospital throughput, and the faculty practice is in charge of volume. So we have to work together in a much more functional way. After all, you can't have throughput without volume, and vice versa. So you have to be integrated.

Health care is an incredibly exciting and important field, and it is begging for innovation all the time – not just innovation in research and clinical care but also in organization, and in the way we do things. People in health care are passionate about what they do because they're doing something very important, and they know it: they're improving people's lives in meaningful ways.

—RIG

Addendum

Figures 3.11A and 3.11B provide a snapshot that serves as a basis of discussion between the dean and department chair regarding the progress during the year as well as setting future goals. They contain data from research, education, and clinical care. They also contain the department's key accomplishments and future goals.

Reference

1. Grossman RI, Berne R. Commentary: less is better; lessons from the New York University-Mount Sinai merger. *Acad Med.* 2010; **85**(12): 1817–18.

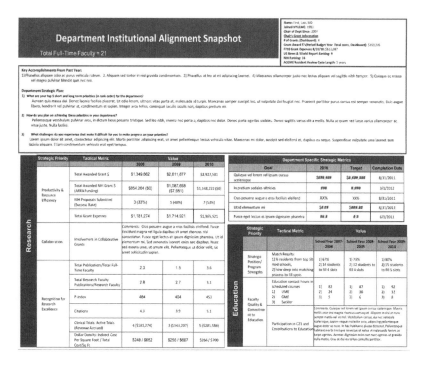

FIGURE 3.11A Example of evaluation tool used to determine a given department's productivity

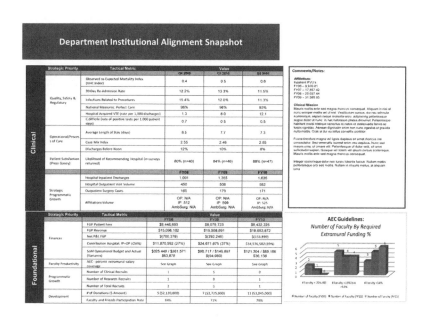

FIGURE 3.11B Example of evaluation tool used to determine a given department's productivity

Contemporary Challenges in Academic Health Science Center Financial Management

Jeffrey R. Balser, Edward R. Marx, and John F. Manning

From the Editor

Because of its multiple functions (education, research, and patient care), an academic health science center must effectively channel fund flows to areas of need and promise, while reducing expenditures in other areas. This chapter presents a discussion of and a plan for managing the finances of these complex entities.

—SAW

As emphasized repeatedly in this volume, academic health science centers (AHSCs) are among the largest and most complex organizations, largely because of the formidable diversity in their three traditional, core missions. It is this tripartite mission (patient care, education, and research) that makes not only the operational but also the financial management of AHSCs complex and challenging.

The various governance models and organizational structures co-mingled among the medical school, physician practices, hospitals, and clinics further add to the complexity of AHSC financial management. Strategies to manage finances must balance the interests of stakeholders with independent fiduciary interests, while also attempting to support the broader goals of the AHSC that, by definition, must cut across these separately managed operating entities.

AHSCs are now under unprecedented pressure to function more cost-effectively. These pressures stem from two related sources: (1) the massive federal budget deficit, which is constraining health care and research revenues on which most AHSCs depend (Medicare, Medicaid, and National Institutes of Health [NIH]); and (2) the large year-over-year increase in US health-care costs borne by employers. There is general agreement that these rising costs are no longer sustainable, and employers and insurers are taking aggressive steps to drive down rates of reimbursement to all health-care providers, including AHSCs.

In this chapter, we will focus on broad themes that impact the financial management of an AHSC, in the context of the contemporary budgetary challenges all AHSCs are actively managing in the United States, and in many cases outside the United States. We will also use our experience to illustrate strategies that can be helpful in adapting to the changing landscape. There is little doubt that as the AHSC has become, and must remain, a vital national resource, its fiduciary oversight and management deserves as much attention as its core programmatic objectives in health care, research, and education.

Cross Subsidy: The Conundrum of Academic Health Science Center Financial Management

In almost all AHSCs, patient care activity, both inpatient and outpatient, has provided the greatest potential to generate a positive margin (revenue exceeding expense).[1] At the same time, education and research typically require large subsidies to meet not only student and faculty needs but also accreditation standards. Hence, the architecture of cross-subsidization is fundamental to the financial management of AHSCs and poses a distinctive challenge in the academic health-care setting.

Adding to the complexity of cross-subsidization, the clinical departments in medical schools typically collect professional revenue for patient care services (physician fees), while the hospitals and clinics separately collect revenue related to patient hospitalization, testing, procedures, and other ancillaries associated with the provision of health care. For most AHSCs, hospital and clinic activity are a greater source of positive margin than physician reimbursement.[1] Hospital subsidies supporting physician compensation and their academic professional activities have grown, while medical schools have been increasingly challenged to provide both market-competitive compensation and academic resources supported by professional fees alone.[1]

An illustration is helpful in shedding light on the importance and magnitude of cross-subsidies in the modern AHSC. Vanderbilt University is home to Vanderbilt University Hospital, The Monroe Carell Jr. Children's Hospital at Vanderbilt, the Psychiatric Hospital at Vanderbilt, and a number of clinic and outpatient surgery facilities. These facilities and programs, entirely owned and operated by the university, experienced more than 55 000 inpatient admissions and nearly 2 million outpatient visits during fiscal year 2011. At the same time, the schools of medicine and nursing are providing education for nearly 3000 graduate and professional students and residents. The medical school's biomedical research programs are among the nation's 10 largest in NIH research funding. Collectively, the revenues and expenses of the medical center, including all patient care, education, and research-related costs, approach $3 billion annually and have grown by 11.3% annually over the past 10 years.

Because Vanderbilt entirely owns and operates these entities (the "simplest" of the many AHSC governance models, as discussed later in this chapter), it can transfer funds between the various academic and health-service entities at the discretion of its own management team. Nonetheless, the decisions and processes governing cross-subsidy, even in a single-ownership model, are far from simple. Roughly speaking, there are three general categories of cost that require cross-subsidies in AHSCs (see Figure 4.1).

1. *Costs for staff and faculty compensation related to research not funded by outside sponsors.* Even when research projects are supported by outside sponsors, components of salary may not be recognized by the funding agency. For example, legislation at the end of calendar 2011 lowered the "salary cap," the maximum salary amount that NIH will recognize in reimbursing faculty research efforts at medical schools, to Executive Level II, $179 700, a $20 000 reduction from Executive Level I. Many faculty physician scientists performing both research and patient care at medical schools are paid market-based salaries that exceed this government-imposed limit. Medical schools are competing not only with each other internationally for these highly talented individuals, but also with a private sector that has no "salary cap." In these cases, a medical school will "cost share" the gap in support. For example, if a physician scientist is paid $229 000 per year ($50 000 above the "NIH cap"), and is devoting 50% of his or her effort to directing an NIH-supported project, the medical school must provide $25 000 in subsidy or "cost share" for time devoted to the NIH-funded project.

2. *Faculty support for time spent in educational activities.* Unlike undergraduate education and professional training in many other disciplines, medical school tuition charges do not cover the actual cost of educating medical students. The minimum requirements for quality medical education include costly, oversight-intensive activities, including sophisticated laboratory and simulation training environments. Moreover, medical education requires time devoted to teaching in the classroom, as well as clinical care at the bedside. For many years in the last century, the attending staff voluntarily contributed much of these costs. However, voluntarism has slowly disappeared in a cost-accounting era. These critical educational activities displace or slow

compensated patient care and research activities by faculty, and therefore are a source of unreimbursed cost for the medical school. The cost of training interns and residents is only partly covered by the support received from Graduate Medical Education funds provided through the nation's Medicaid and Medicare programs. Hospitals spend approximately $13 billion each year on residency training costs, and recover only 23% of their direct expense for these costs.[2]

3. *Startup packages for new investigators and research infrastructure costs, "the indirect costs."* While the NIH spends approximately $30 billion each year supporting research at the nation's medical schools, the medical schools themselves also spend billions of dollars supporting the research programs of young faculty members as they mature to a level where they can compete successfully for NIH funds. Generally speaking, this "start-up" period requires up to 5 years, and medical schools routinely invest $500 000–$1 000 000 of internal funds supporting a single new investigator over this maturation period.[3] Further, the nation's medical schools are not fully reimbursed by sponsors for their infrastructure costs associated with sponsored research. Examples include human subject protection, animal care, chemical safety, compliance and regulatory costs, and plant maintenance and energy costs. Nationwide, the "gap" in overhead cost supported by university medical centers is exacerbated by the NIH indirect cost reimbursement model that limits administrative costs to 26% (the "administrative cap").

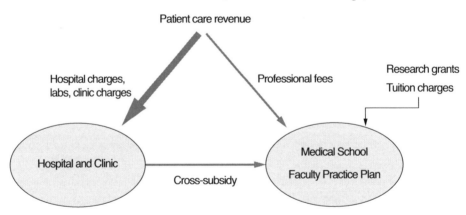

Note: Arrow width is indicative of disparate size in revenue streams; cross-subsidy amount steers revenue from the hospital to the school.

FIGURE 4.1 Overview of Academic Health Science Center revenue streams and cross-subsidies

At Vanderbilt, our costs associated with these three categories exceed $200 million per year, and are not atypical across the industry. Clearly, sources of revenue must be applied to these funding gaps for an AHSC to maintain financial integrity. For both public and private institutions, few medical schools have endowments and/or technology transfer royalties that are capable of offsetting more than a fraction of these costs. Public institutions face the additional challenges of state funding subjected to the discretion of political and budgetary climates. As such, nearly all AHSCs subsidize these costs with margins generated by providing health care. Moreover, given that professional fee margins coming directly to medical schools have diminished over the last decade and will continue to diminish over the next, this gap in funding is largely supported at many AHSCs by margins generated at their associated hospital and clinic entities.

While AHSCs depend on the hospital and clinic margin to provide gap funding, the hospitals and clinics face their own margin challenges. Perhaps foremost among these is the payor mix of AHSCs, which typically includes a large portion of Medicaid and charity care. Across the United States, AHSCs provide more than 40% of the nation's charity care in 6% of the nation's hospital beds.[4] As the major tertiary resource in many communities, AHSCs provide care for patients suffering from trauma, burns, or other complex injuries, regardless of the ability to pay. In fulfilling its mission of service to the region, Vanderbilt provided $370 million in uncompensated care during fiscal year 2011. As with many AHSCs, Vanderbilt provides nearly half of the uninsured care in its region.

These illustrations clarify why AHSCs often have a higher cost structure when compared with community hospitals: they are often the sole provider of highly specialized (and expensive) tertiary acute care services to all patients in a large region, including the uninsured; AHSCs manage a significant infrastructure and faculty development investment in discovery science that is not recoverable from third-party research sponsors; and finally, AHSCs subsidize a substantial percentage of the cost of education for the nation's health-care workforce.

Governance as a Key to Financial Success

Health-care reimbursement pressures, within and outside of AHSCs, are unprecedented, and are certain to greatly impact AHSCs disproportionately given the historic reliance on these revenues to support not only clinical care (for the insured and uninsured), but the research and educational missions. In managing through an era of scarce health-care financial margins, AHSCs recognize the need to engage in a number of efforts to become more economically efficient. These efforts range from the more traditional cost-cutting efforts to more cutting-edge projects aimed at making health-care delivery more cost-effective through innovation. Clearly, nationwide adoption of health IT, spurred by the federal Health Information Technology for Economic and Clinical Health Act of 2010, could facilitate a move toward greater cost efficiency industry-wide, but only if health IT is utilized in a manner that improves and standardizes the process of care, and does not simply serve as a documentation resource.

In an era of scarcity where cost-cutting, resource sharing, and ever-more challenging negotiations over cross-subsidization are required, the AHSC governance model and related cultural norms will become increasingly important. Governance models in place at AHSCs are tremendously varied. For instance, the term "medical dean" implies budgetary responsibilities ranging from oversight of the research and educational areas in a medical school, typically less than $500 million per year, to oversight of a comprehensive health system with multiple hospitals, clinics, and schools training a host of professionals, with staff exceeding 20 000 and budgets as large as $5 billion.

In many cases, medical deans are partnered with one or more hospital chief executive officers, who may or may not report to the same organization or even share identical goals, particularly in cases where the hospitals that generate the majority of the AHSC health-care margin are separately owned and managed. In such cases, negotiations around cost-subsidies for academic activities, key to the success of both the hospital and the medical school, depend not only upon personal style and alignment of the leaders (usually the dean and the hospital chief executive officer) but also often upon the historic and cultural alignment of the two organizations. For example, financial support by a hospital partner in supporting the cost shortfall for residency training that occurs within the hospital walls may be a simpler matter to resolve than support for funding gaps the medical school experiences in its research mission. Conversely, even when these missions are entirely owned by the university, and report to a single "dean," "executive vice president," or "vice chancellor," resolving the internal negotiations around the amount for subsidization for the education and research mission remains challenging and complicated. For example, will scarce capital resources be invested in replacing outdated imaging equipment or supporting a laboratory renovation for a new investigator?

The process of balancing these competing priorities is not only the challenge but also the real substance of AHSC financial management. For an AHSC to be successful, particularly in the future, the approach to these negotiations would ideally reflect a cohesive strategic vision that is shared by key leaders responsible for managing all three (clinical, research, and education) mission areas.

Empowering Mission Leaders for Strategic Alignment

Historically, the degree to which chairs of clinical departments, and even deans of medical schools, engaged directly in the "business" side of clinical care has varied.

Given the governance of medical school faculty practice is typically distinct and separate from the organizational oversight of the staff and resources in the clinic and hospital, there are considerable opportunities for failure to align operational and strategic goals in key domains that involve resource utilization (staff time, equipment needs, and so forth). These misalignments affect not only finances but also the quality of patient care.

Robert Heyssel, MD, examined this financial and strategic alignment issue in an AHSC.[5] He implemented a model at Johns Hopkins University where the medical school clinical chairs were given true budgetary responsibility not only for clinical faculty but also for areas of the hospital business such as nursing units. While elements of this model persist at Johns Hopkins University to some degree even today, across the United States the more typical approach has been the creation of patient care centers. These structures "anneal" leaders from the medical school departments, hospital nursing, and hospital administration in a coalesced oversight structure. Patient care center models have met with both successes and failures, and are largely dependent upon the personalities and voluntary engagement of the participating leaders.

As described throughout this text and emphasized in the previous chapter, alignment of the goals and accountability of medical school and hospital leaders can be accomplished in any number of ways, but two ingredients are essential for success: (1) shared operating performance data and (2) aligned incentives focused on this data. Monthly or quarterly reports have been traditionally utilized for this purpose, and can be helpful management tools, but are often outdated by the time they are issued. Online systems or "dashboards," capable of reporting real-time operating performance that both clinical and administrative leaders can effectively use to jointly manage the financial performance of clinical programs, typically require a significant financial investment by the AHSC. These dashboards also require agreements relating to data access and security, particularly in cases where the faculty physicians, nursing management, and hospital administrators report to separate fiduciary organizations. While "off the shelf" tools can be useful, they often require custom tailoring to meet the specific operating setting and goals of the individual AHSC.

At Vanderbilt, we have implemented an Executive Summary Dashboard that is available to hospital, clinic, and medical school leaders and managers. The tool provides, in real time, patient care revenue, inpatient and outpatient clinic visit and discharge volumes, inpatient bed utilization, inpatient length of stay, and other variables. All values are reported relative to the current budget. The dashboard is updated daily so the management team can develop a routine of examining the results each morning. A benefit of using an electronic dashboard instead of a report is its interactive nature, allowing one to "drill down" into specific details and quickly analyze the root cause of a budget variance. For example, if inpatient discharges are falling behind budget in an operational area, one can examine discharges by Major Diagnostic Category and can see the estimated margin, length of stay, and case mix index for this general area of clinical activity. The analysis can be broken down further into individual Diagnosis Related Groups, to determine whether admissions related to particular medical conditions are involved. Alternatively, if the dashboard reveals a variance in outpatient visits, the utility provides a detailed view of clinic visits by individual clinic location, with volumes relative to budget and prior year. This level of detail allows all members of the management team to quickly identify issues of concern, and to work together to put plans in place to address operational challenges impacting financial performance.

Complementing the availability of real-time information driving financial performance is an effort to align incentives. Again, medical school leaders have long been provided incentives, but these have traditionally been related financial parameters limited to funds collected by the school, such as research funds or drivers of professional fees such as "relative value units." At Vanderbilt, we have developed a set of department chair incentive goals that focus on the performance of the hospitals and clinics, and across multiple domains of functionality – financial performance, quality, and service – in areas their departments directly affect, individually or collectively. On a periodic basis, chairs come together with health system administration for an update where all share progress in a mutually supportive atmosphere on each of the goals. The discussion is structured to promote robust discussion around metrics, ideas for improvement, and ways to collaborate to more fully understand the drivers of performance. Through this approach, medical school leaders can develop greater accountability, sense of control, and psychological ownership over the key operating performance metrics that drive hospital and clinic financial performance. Success in achieving metrics improves the hospital margins, and in doing so creates greater financial flexibility to support cross-subsidies aimed at improving the academic (research and educational) missions of the health science enterprise.

Summary

The complexity of AHSCs extends through their operations into the intricate management of their finances. Their tripartite mission of patient care, education, and research results in a complex financial matrix, as funds must be diverted to subsidize the mission-critical arenas of education and research. Success in managing these subsidies requires recognition and acceptance of their importance, a clear strategy for working within the many distinctive AHSC governance structures to align incentives between hospitals, clinics, and faculty, and a means to provide real-time information across domains that can be used to improve health-care metrics driving quality of care and financial performance.

At Vanderbilt we have seized upon many of these opportunities, improving our operating margin from 0.8% in fiscal year 2001 to 3.7% in fiscal year 2011. Through the use of information technology and health-care innovation, alignment of medical school and hospital incentives, provision of real-time financial information, and frequent discussion of shared strategic goals and accompanying funds flow throughout the medical center, we have been able to improve our financial performance while advancing in our missions of patient care, education, and research. Nonetheless, with the formidable challenges posed by the federal budget deficit, health-care payment restructuring, and likely reductions in support to the NIH, many AHSCs will be called to undergo difficult systemic changes to deliver the unprecedented degree of operating efficiency required for financial viability in the new health-care economy.

Author's Personal Reflections

One of the big challenges for academic health centers is the division of control between hospital and clinic ("health system") finance, and the budgets controlled by department chairs, which are typically limited to professional fees for the physician faculty. The hospital and clinical budget is by far the largest financial entity, and its revenues largely subsidize the research and educational activities of the school. Even though the department chairs don't manage the hospital budget, they heavily influence it, since it is their physicians who determine clinical volume and resource utilization. When the hospital budget is running behind, it's sometimes necessary to "rally the troops" in the school of medicine to improve the hospital and clinic performance.

There was a period of time at Vanderbilt when the hospital and clinic budgets were running behind because of a combination of factors related to clinical volume and severe weather, which temporarily closed down much of our elective business activity. I gathered together the clinical enterprise leaders from the school of medicine and the hospital and clinics, and for the first time, I made the case that we all needed to be working as a consolidated team to improve the financials of the hospital.

We implemented a number of measures to achieve that goal, and those efforts were successful, but the psychology of the clinical departments "owning" the hospital and clinic performance was the real breakthrough. My chairs now have incentives in their compensation tied to volume and other major factors of hospital and clinic performance, not just the performance of their individual departments. What we've found is that those measures that improve quality also improve financial performance. So rather than emphasizing some line in the budget, what we do is emphasize those functional measures that we know will not only improve the financials, but which will also improve patient care.

The truth is, managing finance in a large institution is linked to managing culture. For me, it's fulfilling to improve culture, or to recognize positive aspects of our culture here at Vanderbilt. Each quarter, we assemble 1000 leaders from throughout the clinical and academic enterprise, and we recognize colleagues who have performed in exceptional ways. A culture that is mutually supportive and has strong values around important things is far easier to manage financially than a culture with sharp elbows.

When you examine academic health centers from 50000 feet, you see that they have evolved into large, multibillion-dollar businesses. What separates us from other large entities is that we sit atop gigantic research engines, and so we are constantly innovating. As a leader of one of these institutions, the amount of change one faces on a daily or weekly basis is extraordinary. You learn to view the unexpected problem as an opportunity, and not just something that trashed your schedule.

—JRB

References

1. Wietecha M, Lipstein SH, Rabkin MT. Governance of the academic health center: striking the balance between service and scholarship. *Acad Med.* 2009; **84**(2): 170–6.
2. Perlberg H. *Doctor Shortage Looms Amid Hospital Funding Gap.* Bloomberg.com. October 4, 2011.
3. Dorsey ER, Van Wuyckhuyse BC, Beck CA, *et al.* The economics of new faculty hires in basic science. *Acad Med.* 2009; **84**(1): 26–31.
4. Association of American Medical Colleges. *How Do Teaching Hospitals Serve America's Communities?* Available at: www.aamc.org/linkableblob/70256-3/data/teachhosp facts2-data.pdf (accessed February 1, 2012).
5. Heyssel RM, Seidel HM. The Johns Hopkins experience in Columbia, Maryland. *N Engl J Med.* 1976; **295**(22): 1225–31.

Conflicts of Interest and Commitment

Policy Making in the Academic Health Science Center

Raymond J. Hutchinson, Sanjay Saint, and James O. Woolliscroft

---

From the Editor

Because academic health science centers and their faculty, students, and staff serve the public good, maintaining integrity and trust is essential. In this chapter, the authors discuss conflicts that may arise when the interests of faculty are in potential conflict (real or perceived) with the institution or the scientific and educational communities.

—SAW

In an ever more complex society and regulated environment, the academic health science center (AHSC) in the twenty-first century must continue to strive to fulfill its multifaceted missions. In the United States, as has been true in the past, the AHSC remains accountable to those who underwrite its missions – the American public, the US Congress, various federal agencies, private donors, and students. Equally, AHSCs are accountable to the clientele they serve – the public, patients, and students and trainees. This task has become more complex – if not more difficult – by virtue of interactions with the biomedical industry.

Staying True to Mission
• •

AHSCs share common goals with the biomedical industry, such as developing new diagnostics and treatments for patients afflicted with a wide range of illnesses and advancing information about innovations to both caregivers and patients while ensuring proper use of new products. As the AHSC research enterprise expands from traditional basic science research to include translational medicine and clinical trials,[1] and with the decline in the relative dollar value of the National Institutes of Health (NIH) budget,[2] AHSCs have increasingly turned to industry partnerships to fulfill their research mission. Further, researchers and scientists at AHSCs have been encouraged to expand their entrepreneurial horizons, both by their home institutions and by the US government through the Bayh-Dole Act of 1980.[3]

Often, these entrepreneurial efforts result in the creation of new biomedical companies with the express purpose of developing novel diagnostics and therapies. Typically, the founding investigators and associated university own equity in the company and retain royalty rights deriving from the intellectual property developed in the course of the research, with prospects for considerable financial remuneration upon the licensing of the intellectual property and approval for use in humans of a drug, device, or diagnostic test by the US Food and Drug Administration.

As significant financial rewards become potentially associated with research findings, it is perhaps no surprise that public concern has arisen regarding the validity of research results and the possibility that personal biases and conflicts of interest (COI) may influence research practices and the interpretation of research results.[4,5] Furthermore, the association of the AHSC with biomedical industries has extended beyond the research realm, specifically into patient care, educational, and philanthropic domains.

Recognition that huge financial rewards can accrue to biomedical companies when a product is successful has raised concern regarding the fashion in which these companies engage physicians – both within and outside of the AHSC – to endorse their products, to teach peers about those products, and to prescribe these products in their patient care activities. Recently, Congressional investigations have revealed outsized payments by biomedical companies to physicians who use or prescribe company products.[6] While some of these payments are justifiable and based on seminal intellectual contributions toward a product's development, it appears that some payments are disproportionately large given the physician's actual contribution. The US Congress has conducted investigations into these practices, given concerns about the degree to which physician practices may be driven by ties to biomedical companies.[6]

The need for the AHSC to remain true to its diverse missions – fostering ethical scientific inquiry, delivering sound patient care, and ascribing to unbiased educational practices – as well as the increased external oversight, has led to a tightening of regulations of financial interest disclosures of professional activities occurring outside of the AHSC. AHSCs are evaluating these disclosures closely, searching for inappropriate influence on an individual's research and, more recently, on their patient care and educational practices. Moreover, AHSCs have developed and are still developing management strategies to reduce and eliminate COI in these three areas.

While engaging in positive steps as they strive to reduce unwanted influences, AHSCs must maintain a fine balance between achieving tight regulation of what is allowed in the AHSC-biomedical industry interface and unduly thwarting scientific advances that have the potential to reduce human suffering. Another potential downside to using regulations alone to control human behavior is that those being regulated may come to depend upon regulations for determining the course of their professional lives, rather than developing solid principles of professional ethical behavior. After all, there is no substitute for internalized sound ethical principles to guide the behavior of individuals who on a daily basis are called upon to make decisions that significantly affect the lives of their patients.

AHSCs must continue to promote appropriate principles of behavior across their cultures, for without those, regulations will not achieve the desired goals. This chapter will discuss the balance that exists between maintaining and advancing the missions of the AHSC and the powerful, but unavoidable, influences that can threaten to derail those missions.

Federal Regulations Affecting the Academic Health Science Center

Federal laws encourage AHSCs to work with the biomedical industry while simultaneously proscribing various activities that are deemed inappropriate. On the one hand, the federal government has taken a proactive stance in fostering relationships between universities and their AHSCs and the biomedical industry through passage of the Bayh-Dole Act of 1980, transformative legislation in promoting such synergy.[3] On the other hand, because of concerns with rising health-care costs and recognition that misbehavior occurs, federal legislation has been enacted to ensure that federal expenditures in health-care programs are ethical and legal. Anti-kickback legislation, Stark laws, and the False Claims Act are examples. Recently proposed laws, including the Physician Payments Sunshine Act,[7] will require biomedical industries to publicly disclose all payments to physicians above a minimal threshold; the provisions of these laws are likely to be enacted over the next 3–4 years.

In response, some companies and some AHSCs have already begun to create public websites for faculty-physician disclosures. Comparisons of industry and AHSC websites are inevitable; the public will be interested in the similarities and differences in the remuneration reports for a given outside interest. In addition to these notable regulations, the Internal Revenue Service and many state governments have regulations in place that affect prescriptive and purchasing practices within the AHSC.

During the last decade, public concern and media scrutiny have increasingly focused on the impact of individual physician-industry relationships on all three core missions of the AHSC: biomedical research, education, and clinical care. Each of these realms will be discussed in the following sections.

Managing Conflict of Interest in Biomedical Research

In large part because of federal requirements for identifying and managing COI in sponsored research, policies and implementation of the same are more advanced than in the educational and clinical arenas. The NIH has required disclosure of significant financial interests related to public health service-funded research since 1995.[8] As a consequence, all universities receiving such funding from the NIH and other federal agencies have had policies in place establishing financial thresholds for disclosure of outside interests, for defining review procedures of outside interests, for assigning relationship to funded research, and for reporting such related significant financial interests to the funding agencies.

Typically, AHSCs have COI offices and faculty committees with assigned responsibility to review and assess outside financial relationships, and create management plans to reduce or eliminate the conflict. A public health service advance notice of proposed rule-making in 2009,[9] once established as a rule, will likely lower the reporting threshold from $10 000 to $5000, will lay the responsibility for determining relatedness of a significant financial interest at the feet of the institution receiving the funds rather than at those of the investigator, will increase reporting requirements to the NIH, and will require ongoing monitoring of management strategies. It is likely that other federal funding agencies will follow suit in their requirements.

Currently, most AHSCs and universities have committees to address potential COI in funded research activities. The principles at stake in research include the scientific integrity of research findings, the health and well-being of patients who enter clinical trials as human subjects, the public trust as the primary recipient of advances made in biomedical science, and the federal agencies and other sponsors, including biomedical companies, which provide funding for biomedical research. These committees review many factors in determining whether an investigator's extra-institutional interests should be considered in evaluating their research projects. These factors include whether the outside interest is related to their professional activities, particularly their specific research; whether the outside interest is a compensated activity and, if so, the amount of compensation accruing to the investigator; and the potential direction that influence from financial remuneration may have on research outcomes and human subjects protection. Considerations that come into play include financial ties to a biomedical company, such as equity interest in a company; the opportunity to earn royalty payments; and service in a leadership capacity at the company, as an officer of the company, as a consultant to the company, or as an advisory board member for science, research direction, or administrative direction for the company.

If the COI manager or the committee identifies a COI, a management plan is developed to reduce the risk of undue influence of company-related interests upon the research. The management plan often includes the expectation that the investigator either step away from his/her financial interest with the company or not serve as principal investigator for the related research. Additional proscriptions may include prohibiting the investigator from recruiting potential research subjects or from obtaining informed consent from subjects and creating auxiliary reporting relationships for junior faculty or trainees working on the research to assure that a conflicted supervisor does not compromise their career and educational goals. Further, all relevant ties to biomedical industries, financial or otherwise, are expected to be disclosed in all research presentations and publications.

Despite well-established principles for managing COI in research, new opportunities, such as Small Business Innovation Research (SBIR) and Small Business Technology Transfer (STTR) funding, continue to provide challenging scenarios for proper management. Because of the intended close working relationship between the AHSC and the biomedical company, there are less distinct boundaries between work done at the AHSC and that done at the company. On occasion, company personnel may travel to the AHSC to perform specialized tasks in completing the research; this may raise regulatory and security concerns at the AHSC. Oversight to assure that the academic goals of doctoral and postdoctoral students and other trainees engaged in SBIR or STTR projects are met becomes particularly important in the context of this academic-business relationship. Further, the primary investigator at the AHSC is likely to have a fiduciary relationship with the company while performing AHSC-based research that may benefit the mission of the company. The challenges posed by SBIR and STTR funding are a contemporary topic at many national meetings of those engaged in managing COI at AHSCs.

Managing Conflict of Interest in Education
• •

Over the last decade, medical schools have become increasingly concerned with the impact that financial ties to biomedical industries may have on the quality of teaching delivered by their faculty. This concern relates to the possibility that payment by a biomedical company to a faculty member may bias that faculty member's educational effort. Clearly, students and the public expect that professors will present evidence-based medical information free from bias. It is noteworthy that students in many institutions have played an important role in encouraging their institutions to adopt strong policies that control external influence. To that end, several medical associations have published guidelines on the acceptance of funding from biomedical companies for educational activities. These organizations include the American Association of Medical Colleges (AAMC),[10] the Institute of Medicine,[11] and the American Association of Universities.[12]

Recently, increased attention has focused on the receipt of funds from biomedical companies to support continuing medical education (CME). There have been concerns that funding directed toward support of an educational activity in which a faculty member has a particular interest will curry favor with that faculty member and result in a feeling of reciprocity toward the company sponsoring the education. The Accreditation Council for Continuing Medical Education (ACCME) has established standards for conditions under which funding may be accepted from biomedical companies.[13] Similarly, the AAMC issued its report *Industry Funding of Medical Education: Report of an AAMC Task Force* in 2008.[10] The report included recommendations that: (1) AHSCs develop audit mechanisms to assure compliance with the standards of the ACCME; (2) AHSCs should establish a central CME office for reviewing and coordinating all requests for support and receipt of funds supporting biomedical CME; and (3) programs with biomedical industry support should be offered only by ACCME-accredited providers according to ACCME standards.

Medical schools across the country have taken various approaches to address concerns about biomedical support for CME-related activities. The University of Michigan Medical School has been among the leaders in reducing undue biomedical industry influence on patient care and medical education, with a strong vendor policy and a recently enacted prohibition of acceptance of biomedical industry support for continuing medical education for which CME credit is awarded.[14] Applying these varied approaches to this complex issue, US medical schools share the common goal of preserving the integrity of medical education in an environment in which ever-changing educational tools will make the preservation of evidence-based, unbiased teaching an increasing challenge.

Another important element of ensuring transparency in the delivery of medical education is ensuring that students and trainees are made aware of any relevant financial interests of the faculty or staff teaching them. Such relevant financial interests include equity interests in companies supplying medication or other patient supplies; receipt of royalties for use of a drug, biologic agent, device, information technology application or medical supply used in treating patients or in medical education; and consultancy or service on a board of advisors for a company. Some AHSCs have chosen to post physician ties to biomedical industries on institutional websites which detail faculty profiles and are accessible to students and trainees. Other institutions require faculty and staff to disclose outside financial interests of relevance to students and trainees at the beginning of a class or clinical rotation.

Managing Conflict of Interest in Clinical Care

In clinical care, the physician's primary interest must be the welfare of the patient. The clinical care delivered must be guided by best practices and must be evidence based. However, there are a multitude of influences that compete with the altruism expected of physicians. Financial considerations are inescapable in the modern practice of medicine; among these are the expectations of third-party payers, the financial stability of physician practices, the impact of different physician compensation plans on practice patterns, and the influence of physician-owned medical services on utilization of various technologies and health-care services.[15]

Physician interactions with drug, device, and biotechnology industries raise additional concerns in assuring that patients receive optimal care. For more than a century, US medicine has depended upon professionalism to ensure that patient needs remain foremost. However, the increased complexity and frequency of physician ties to biomedical industries over the past two decades have raised many questions which have the potential to erode patient and public confidence in medical care.

In the eyes of many, conflicts in clinical care activities are dealt with less formally than those in research and education.[15] While most institutions have well-established policies for reviewing and managing conflicts in research, and many have developed or are developing policies for managing educational bias created by financial ties to biomedical industries, fewer have clear policies on oversight and management of industry influences on patient care. Yet, it is these latter conflicts that pose the greatest direct risk to the public in the form of misuse or overuse of diagnostic tests, surgical devices, or pharmaceutical agents.

A major concern is that physicians who participate in the development of drugs or devices, and as a consequence earn royalties for their use, could over-prescribe the drug or device in order to increase earnings. A commonly employed strategy to manage the use of drugs and devices in a setting in which a physician and/or a hospital derives financial benefit is to require that the company selling the product not pay royalties either for their product's use in patients of the physician-inventor or to the hospital or AHSC where the patient is being seen. In practice, this may be hard to accomplish, although several device companies do have systems in place to assure that royalties do not accrue to physicians or medical centers when a device is implanted at the relevant site.

Beside royalties, other forms of industry payment to physicians that raise concerns include: provision of gifts; payment of travel expenses to meeting venues where a deliverable is not expected of the physician traveler; provision of expensive meals to physician and nursing groups; payment for participation on speakers' bureaus where the physician or nurse serves largely as a promotional agent for the company; and service on advisory boards or boards of directors with little or no defined deliverable provided by the physician or other care-provider. Many AHSCs have already taken measures to preclude these activities.

In addition, physician ownership of laboratory or radiology facilities or of rehabilitation or medical supply companies poses a significant conflict management issue, as well as tricky legal issues. A number of AHSCs have now established clinical COI committees to implement policies eliminating the most egregious practices and subsequent guidelines and guidance to physicians and hospital units on some of the more complex, less clear-cut issues.

In 2010 the AAMC published a position paper on interactions between health-care providers and the biomedical industry, with emphasis on the impact of physician financial relationships on clinical decision making.[15] The paper emphasized the essential roles of professionalism and self-regulation, highlighted by independent and objective judgments in clinical decision making. Further, the importance of highly principled physician behavior during mentorship for medical students and residents was underscored. Recommendations in the AAMC report include:

- alignment of physician compensation mechanisms with patient interests
- creation of standards for interactions with the biomedical industry by medical professional societies
- institutional identification of physician-industry financial relationships, with evaluation for potential COI and appropriate management
- establishment of thresholds for reporting financial relationships to the institution, for requiring management of significant financial interests, and for reporting on relevant financial interests to patients
- evaluation and management of institutional financial relationships with biomedical industries in the context of clinical care delivery

- establishment of methods, style, and context for public disclosure of physician and institutional financial interests.

As for public disclosure, it is important to recognize that patient needs for elements of disclosure may not coincide with the institutional need for oversight, that providing information on financial relationships without a faculty or institutional context may not serve patient welfare sufficiently, and that balancing dollar amounts in faculty disclosures between the institution and industry websites will require much attention to definition of the types of activities disclosed and the timeframe for disclosure. Even with detailed attention, it's likely that innocent discrepancies will occur, with the possibility for public misinterpretation of such differences as constituting misbehavior.

As is true in the educational realm, transparency in the delivery of patient care is essential. Various approaches to patient notification have been undertaken. These include patient-accessible websites, including physician profiles with their industry-related financial interests,[16] printed material delivered to patients at their initial encounter with the AHSC that provides contact telephone numbers and/or e-mail addresses to learn about their physicians and their industry ties, and physician-specific printed material defining relevant industry ties and delivered by the physician or his or her office staff to patients.

Assessing and Managing Individual Conflicts of Commitment
• • • • • • • • • • • • • • • • •

While properly managing COI for faculty and staff within the AHSC is a concern for both internal and external parties, conflict of commitment is a matter of primary interest to the leaders and administrators of the AHSC. This directly relates to dedication of an adequate amount of time to the tasks that an individual must commit in performing a job well, despite the distractions of outside interests.

Oftentimes, decisions regarding potential conflicts of commitment are left to the discretion of a chairperson or a supervisor; in such circumstances, there is considerable variability in the level of comfort that the supervising person experiences in making decisions regarding the acceptability and sustainability of outside interests for an employee. The discomfort can be due to uncertainty regarding the institutional stance on outside activities, inadequate information on the activity and the time commitment involved, or the management characteristics of the supervisor or the unit. In addition, standards at the AHSC may vary depending upon whether the employee in question is faculty or staff; the expectations regarding time commitment are often different for faculty than for staff, resulting in varying standards. For example, the University of Michigan covers conflict of commitment in its standard practice guide on COI and conflicts of commitment by indicating that faculty and staff with appointments of 50% or more owe their primary professional commitment to the University of Michigan.[17] Despite this expectation, the university does recognize the value of having faculty and staff engage in outside activities. Furthermore, there is variability in application across job categories and also across colleges and units as to how they evaluate time commitments for faculty and staff. This occasionally creates contentious situations for administrators trying to strike the necessary balance.

Ideally, an AHSC will have a well-defined policy on conflict of commitment, denoting expectations for both faculty and staff in disclosure of outside interests, the circumstances under which time may be committed to those activities, particularly during AHSC work hours, the degree to which AHSC resources may be used by those undertaking outside activities, and the measures which should be taken to assess and avoid conflicts with key activities of the AHSC. An important component in making such a policy work is a robust system for disclosing outside activities; this system should collect information in detail sufficient that a reviewer can easily determine the relationship of the outside interest to the discloser's job within the AHSC and the total amount of time to be devoted to the activity for a given period, usually annual.

Finally, should adjudication of faculty and staff be required regarding the continuance of their outside activities, there is a possibility for strong differences of opinion. Chairs and administrators will benefit from an established appeal process – for example, a dedicated institutional committee constituted by faculty and representatives from key areas of the AHSC, such as medical staff affairs, administration, nursing, pharmacy, and purchasing. Such a committee, with formal institutional endorsement, carries with it the weight of broad representation and institutional authority, with less risk of allegations of capricious decision making to resolve contentious situations.

Policies and Strategies to Manage Institutional Conflict of Interest

Recognition that institutional COI can impact the missions of the AHSC has resulted in recent public and federal interest, given the disclosure of ties between AHSCs and biomedical industries. Many AHSCs have developed, or begun to develop, institutional policies to identify areas of potential institutional COI. Somewhat slower to develop have been the management strategies required to mitigate the potential influence of such relationships on patient care, research, and education conducted at AHSCs. This is due to several factors, each of which will be discussed further:

- the concept that institutional financial interests are far enough removed from patient care, research, and education as to not influence those endeavors (firewalls)
- difficulties in recognizing all of the institutional financial areas in which the AHSC interfaces with a specific biomedical company
- balancing institutional benefits in senior leadership participation on biomedical company advisory boards versus the risk to AHSC missions because of undue influence on institutional decision making.

Firewalls

In some academic institutions, investment patterns are not apparent to the workforce, reducing the potential that institutional employees would conduct patient care or research in such a manner as to benefit institutional financial interests. While this is often true for investments in publicly traded companies, it is not likely true for start-up companies originating from the AHSC; in these situations, the faculty and/or employees whose work sparked the development of the start-up are typically well aware of the institution's financial interest in that company, thus creating the potential for undue influence in negotiations with the company and for the introduction of bias in evaluating research results and progress reports generated by the company. These latter situations clearly require institutional policy, including rules as to when sign-off is required by institutional boards of regents or directors, guidance and a mechanism for assessing whether clinical trials sponsored by an AHSC spin-off can be conducted at the AHSC, rules for determining who may sign off on financial matters for the AHSC in AHSC-company dealings, guidance on dual employment by the AHSC and the start-up and for appropriate mentoring of trainees and graduate students whose academic goals may be intertwined with research activities of the start-up, and an expectation that an institutional COI committee will engage in ongoing oversight of all of these areas.

Recognition of Institutional Patterns of Interaction with the Biomedical Industry

At complex institutions like most AHSCs, it is very difficult to discern all of the AHSC's interactions with a specific biomedical company, particularly those that are designated as "Big Pharma." Most financial/purchasing interactions occur well out of the sight of practicing physicians, as well as biomedical researchers and educators. As noted earlier, the potential for undue influence is relatively small. However, some AHSCs have chosen to set a threshold for institutional investment in a large biomedical company, which then triggers institutional review processes for product selection and purchasing practices from that company. For start-up companies, product selection and purchasing issues are far less complex;

however, the institution may benefit greatly and directly if a novel piece of intellectual property makes its way to production and use in medical practice. For this reason, it is important to have a formal policy governing relationships between AHSCs and start-up companies.

Balancing the Benefits of Participation by Academic Health Science Center Institutional Leaders on Biomedical Industry Boards with Potential Conflicts of Interest

Given the unique institutional vantage point of leaders within the AHSC, it is certainly reasonable to argue the advantage of having such individuals interact with biomedical industries, thereby learning about corporate strategies and priorities. The AHSC may benefit in its research initiatives through awareness of biomedical industry focus and trends; indeed, when institutional research priorities overlap with those of a biomedical company, synergy in research collaboration may result. Further, biomedical industries have an interest in working with academic leaders who may be able to provide insight into relevant lines of scientific inquiry and the directions of health-care delivery. A problem can arise when AHSC leaders are in a position to make or appear to make a financial or policy decision favorable to the biomedical industry with which they are engaged. Various strategies can be utilized to avoid real or perceived COI.

Creating obvious firewalls in decision making, particularly with reference to policies governing purchases from biomedical industries with which an institutional relationship exists, will go a long way to reducing anxieties and limiting claims of improper influence in research, educational, and patient care missions. An additional strategy for consideration is to limit compensation related to board participation by AHSC leaders to fair market value, as defined by an average faculty salary standard rather than by what could be viewed as fair market value for a chief executive officer. Indeed, an argument can be made that such board work, *performed for the institution's good*, should be considered as an institutional role with institutional compensation already provided and sufficient for the AHSC officer. In any case, all such outside board work must be disclosed within the AHSC, reviewed by the appropriate institutional official, and subject to review for approval or denial by the institutional COI committee or by the governing board of the AHSC.

Should Academic Health Science Centers Accept Biomedical Industry Funding for Capital Expenses?

With the intense focus on individual COI, faculty and staff often raise questions about their institution's willingness to accept large amounts of money from biomedical companies to support institutional facilities, capital development expenses, and the creation of endowed professorships. There is, as yet, no well-articulated philosophy regarding the wisdom of accepting such funding. Clearly there is a risk that the public may view acceptance of industry funds as posing a risk to the missions of unbiased purchasing and evidence-based prescriptive practices. Of course, the degree to which decisions to accept funding at a high administrative level affect the performance of individuals charged with making purchasing decisions or caregivers selecting a drug to prescribe is uncertain at best and likely not a major factor in day-to-day operations.

Research into the sociology of major gift giving and the resultant reciprocity can be instructive in answering these questions. For the present, institutional leaders tasked with making decisions regarding acceptance of major gifts should be guided by the ethic of ensuring that the AHSC remains true to its multiple missions, and leaders should make efforts to assure independence from undue influence for those making purchases and those delivering care for patients.

Implementing Conflict of Interest Policy in the Academic Health Science Center

Many factors challenge the successful implementation of proper COI policy at AHSCs. Some occur with any policy implementation, regardless of venue, and some are related to the specific nature of policy creation – for example, in areas that touch on personal behaviors and professional ethics. Most health-care administrators, providers, educators, and researchers take their professional responsibilities very seriously, striving to reduce undesirable biases in their work. In fact, many do not think that influences from their interactions with representatives, scientists, and leaders from biomedical industries impact their work negatively. Indeed, while it is known that reciprocity develops as a natural occurrence in the course of interpersonal collaborations, not much is known about how such reciprocity extends to the conduct of professional duties affecting third parties – for example, patients, students, trainees, the public. Therefore, it is often hard to convince professionals within the AHSC that their actions must be guided by a set of principles that they may feel they already adhere to without the need for third-party oversight.

Aside from personal convictions that COI policy is not needed, there are several challenges that should be discussed further: (1) the importance of carefully conceived definitions for the activities of interest; (2) achieving consensus among the faculty and staff of the AHSC; (3) creating systems that can effectively monitor the activities to be regulated; (4) limiting policy to activities within the control of the AHSC; and (5) assuring that information about faculty, staff, and institutional financial interests reach the committees and entities responsible for making and monitoring purchasing decisions, for validating proper patient care, and for assuring the quality of student education.

Definitions

The importance of tight definitions cannot be overemphasized, given the ambiguity surrounding certain activities, such as speakers' bureaus, and the fact that the same activity can be denoted by very different names, either by chance or by intention to circumvent regulatory standards. It is essential to define the precise activity that the policy is intended to regulate. In the case of speakers' bureaus, the concern primarily relates to situations in which faculty serve as advertising agents for biomedical products and receive compensation for so doing. Clearly, the elements of promotional speaking and of compensation provided for such activities need to be woven into the definition. Careful attention to definitions will also reduce the possibility that activities adding value to AHSC missions will not be dealt an inadvertent and fatal blow. Finally, crisp definitions will reduce ambiguity for faculty and staff and will enhance the culture within the AHSC for compliance.

Achieving Consensus

A primary requirement for ensuring compliance is to engage the faculty and staff early in the process of policy development; engagement of faculty should be broad-ranging across academic departments, academic ranks, and appointment and promotional tracks. While complete consensus is unlikely, soliciting input from faculty and staff and incorporating their suggestions in the policy as it develops will result in heightened awareness of the issues and in a more consistent culture across the institution. At the University of Michigan Medical School, the leadership held a series of symposia on topics related to engagement with biomedical industries; the symposia included discussions by faculty with existent ties to biomedical industries and by a representative of a biomedical device company. These symposia raised the level of interest in and knowledge regarding the impact of faculty and staff working with the biomedical industry as they conduct clinical care, education, and research. As recommendations were being developed, sessions for engaging faculty input were held; at these sessions, individual faculty members were given the opportunity to express their thoughts and concerns regarding various aspects of potential policy considerations – for example, industry support for CME activities and speakers bureau participation. Interest in these sessions was high, and available scheduled time slots were readily taken.

Effective Monitoring of Policies

In general, policy creation should be accompanied by a method for monitoring compliance with the policy mandates. AHSCs should not be creating policies that merely serve as window dressing. Recently, the public, Congress, and the press have taken leading AHSCs to task for failing to adhere to the policies that they created and advertised. A corollary to this approach is that the creation of policies that either cannot be tracked or effectively enforced represents more of a shell game than an effort at sound policy implementation.

Limiting Policies to Issues within the Control of the Academic Health Science Center

Following on the discussion in the preceding section, it makes little sense for the institution to ban activities occurring beyond its doors. First, there are not enough institutional resources to track the activities of faculty beyond the confines of the institution. Second, attempts to regulate activities beyond the institution will undoubtedly lead to random, and perhaps capricious, whistle-blowing by faculty distressed that they are limited in their activities by policies which others ignore. Third, and most important, in policy adherence, as in other key activities within the AHSC, institutional leaders and regulatory officials must always depend upon the personal professional integrity of care providers and other staff.

Policies and rules serve to regulate and prevent egregious misadventures by faculty and staff; nevertheless, dependence on a culture of personal integrity is essential for all of the vital day-to-day interpersonal encounters occurring throughout the center: physician-patient interactions in general, maintaining patient trust during the performance of surgery and procedures on anesthetized and sedated patients, collecting personal private information for medical uses and for financial reimbursement while preserving confidentiality, and meeting the expectation that accurate personal health information will be delivered to patients, however difficult the content and whatever the time commitment to deliver. Most often, a healthy culture based upon sound principles of ethical behavior will be much more important in achieving the missions of the AHSC than simply enforcing adherence to rules and regulations.

Coordination of Relevant Entities within the Academic Health Science Center to Achieve the Goals of Conflict of Interest Policies

In order to track relevant activities and financial interests and to enforce policies regarding COI, there must be robust coordination among the various entities within the AHSC responsible for compiling information on faculty and staff disclosures of outside interests, for reporting to patients on the relevant physician and caregiver relationships with biomedical companies producing drugs and devices for patient use, for overseeing student and trainee education with appropriate disclosure of the financial interests of the instructors, for tracking institutional purchasing decisions, and for monitoring relevant external financial interests of the institution, institutional leaders, and the board of directors.

Summary: Key Issues in Conflict of Interest Policy Development
••••••••••••••••

As in all areas of regulatory oversight, attempts to achieve perfection should not become the enemy of producing good guidance and policy development. Efforts to achieve compliance solely with rigid regulations will fail. As stated earlier, no matter how sophisticated our information technology systems and no matter how tightly wound the regulations, AHSCs will still depend upon personal professional integrity to guide the vast majority of personal and financial interactions. A principled culture within the AHSC, coupled with balanced regulations aimed at meeting federal, state, and institutional standards while emphasizing the values held most dearly by the AHSC, will go a long way toward reassuring the public, the press, and federal regulators that the public's interests and public funding are being protected.

While establishing and promulgating institutional culture, it is important to engage faculty, administration, and staff in discussions relating to policy, in order to assure that policies meet desired goals and that important aspects of patient care, medical education, and biomedical research are not wedged into impossible corners by virtue of well-meaning, but poorly conceived regulations that look good on the surface but which do not enhance the public good. Several of the controversial activities resulting from the engagement of biomedical industries with the AHSC are not absolutely good or bad; the AHSC must sort through the many shades of gray and arrive at practical solutions, guided by mission-critical principles, that allow it to promote the primacy of patient well-being, the centrality of evidence-based medical education, and the integrity of basic, translational, and clinical research.

Author's Personal Reflections

COI is of paramount concern to all academic health centers. We are particularly sensitive in our research. In order to develop the next generation of treatments, academic health centers conduct basic research. But in order to take those basic science discoveries and make them useful to patients, we need to partner with private industry in effective and transparent ways. There are legitimate questions about the degree of interaction between

---

biomedical industry and education. The biomedical industry would like a close relationship with academic health centers. They would like to engage with us to educate patients, students, and trainees, and of course, they'd prefer if we prescribed their products and treatments. So in those areas, we have to be cautious about our interactions, and prevent any undue influence. But the biomedical industry does have an important role to play in the development of new treatments and procedures, so the question is: how do we manage that relationship?

First, we have to recognize that the vast majority on both sides are honest, hard-working people who seek to improve the lives of others. The biomedical industry itself has changed their behaviors, and they're sensitive to the issue as well. Then we have to make sure we're doing everything we can ourselves to live up to the highest ethical standards. At the University of Michigan, we've enacted several measures and policies to prevent even the appearance of COI. First, we created a firewall between industry and students. We have a fairly strong vendor policy that has been in place for several years, which provides guidance around vendor interactions with physicians, students, and other trainees. Vendors have to sign in, and they must make appointments to meet with people. In addition, there are constraints placed upon vendor behaviors inside the institution. For example, we don't allow them to bring food or drink anymore. We also enacted a new policy on lectures. Anyone giving a lecture to trainees, students, or physicians must disclose their ties to the biomedical industry at the outset. The same is true for physicians who make rounds on inpatient service. These policies increase transparency and reduce the possibility that someone may promote drugs or treatments in which they have a vested interest.

We have taken a stance that the medical school will not accept biomedical industry funds for any activity sponsored by the medical school, whether on campus or elsewhere. This is probably one of the most restrictive policies of its kind in the country. Other places have put limits or restrictions on funds; we've taken an absolute stance on it. The point of this policy is to ensure that our educational processes are not influenced in any way by our ties to biomedical industry. This new policy was met with a lot of concern here at the University of Michigan. CME activities achieve a lot of good. So the dean established a separate fund to help subsidize the loss of funds created by the restrictions on biomedical industry. As a result, the concern at our institution subsided.

We've tried to elevate the culture in a positive way. Also, there's a real desire for people to do the right thing. For example, we have a pulmonologist who has extensive ties to the biomedical industry. This is a nationally renowned expert, so it makes sense that he would have such relationships.

This individual reaches out to me on a regular basis to make sure that he's in compliance with the letter and spirit of our policies. We also established an institutional COI committee to review our role in conducting clinical trials that are sponsored by biomedical companies that have spun off from the University of Michigan. These were companies that were developed around a particular drug or device with the involvement of one or more of our faculty members, who may now have a financial interest in the outcome of the trials. This committee makes sure that those influences don't affect patient safety or data integrity emerging from those trials. We have a community member on that committee, and at least one member from another university who's on that committee. They provide an outside, impartial perspective.

Of course we want the trials to occur. Part of our mission is to develop novel treatments that have positive impacts on patient health. If our faculty develop something through the preclinical stage but aren't allowed to take it to patients, that doesn't make sense. So what we do is to try to create firewalls for financially invested parties, but work to allow the trial to take place within our academic health center, provided that the process retains the highest integrity. We have independent data-monitoring committees whose two main goals are to protect human subjects and to ensure validity and integrity of data that emerge from trials, so that we can make honest assessments and results.

Being compliant is important, but I don't want to make it a religious experience. Our goal is to protect our faculty in the health system from outside circumspection that could be viewed as negative or problematic, and also to foster the research activities of our faculty. The burden of regulation has become increasingly great, for faculty and others. It's important to maintain regulatory compliance, but not to be excessively restrictive or burdensome. You have to have a balanced perspective. There are things we do to preserve our mission and integrity, and there are other things we do so that our efforts are properly understood by the public and press. The relationships we have are integral to the development of new treatments and scientific advances, and we have to be careful to preserve those, while balancing them against our service mission and explaining them to the public. But we can't become too subservient to external pressures when the values of the university are at risk.

—*RJH*

References

1. Dougherty D, Conway P. The '3T's' road map to transform US health care: the 'how' of high-quality care. *JAMA*. 2008; **299**(2008): 2319–21.

2. Loscalzo J. The NIH budget and the future of biomedical research. *N Engl J Med*. 2006; **354**(2006): 1665–7.

3. Assistant Secretary for Technology Policy, US Department of Commerce. *Rights to Inventions Made by Nonprofit Organizations and Small Business Firms under Government Grants, Contracts, and Cooperative Agreements*. 37 CFR, Pt. 401. 2002. US Government Printing Office via GPO Access. Available at: www.access.gpo.gov/nara/cfr/waisidx_02/37cfr401_02.html (accessed March 10, 2011).

4. Kassirer JP. *On the Take: how medicine's complicity with big business can endanger your health*. New York, NY: Oxford University Press; 2005.

5. Weber T, Ornstein C. Dollars for docs: who's on Pharma's top-paid list? *ProPublica*. November 1, 2010. Available at: www.propublica.org/article/profiles-of-the-top-earners-in-dollar-for-docs (accessed March 2, 2011).

6. Harris G. Drug maker told studies would aid it, papers say. *New York Times*. March 19, 2009.

7. United States. *Transparency Reports and Reporting of Physician Ownership or Investment Interests*. Patient Protection and Affordable Care Act of 2010, Pub. L. no. 689–696, § 6002. Congressional Record, 2010. Available at: www.gpo.gov/fdsys/pkg/PLAW-111publ148/pdf/PLAW-111publ148.pdf (accessed March 10, 2011).

8. US Department of Health and Human Services. *Responsibility of Applicants for Promoting Objectivity in Research for Which PHS Funding is Sought*. 42 CFR, pt. 50, subpart F. US Government Printing Office via GPO Access, 1995. Available at: http://grants.nih.gov/grants/compliance/42_cfr_50_subpart_f.htm (accessed March 2, 2011).

9. US Department of Health and Human Services. *Responsibility of Applicants for Promoting Objectivity in Research for which Public Health Service Funding is Sought and Responsible Prospective Contractors, etc. Advance Notice of Proposed Rulemaking*. FR Doc 2010-11885, 21 May 2010. Available at: www.thefederalregister.com/d.p/2010-05-21-2010-11885 (accessed March 10, 2011).

10. Association of American Medical Colleges. *Industry Funding of Medical Education: report of an AAMC task force*. Washington, DC; June 2008.

11. Institute of Medicine of the National Academies. *Conflict of Interest in Medical Research, Education, and Practice*. Consensus Report. April 21, 2009.

12. Association of American Universities. *AAMC, AAU Issue New Guidelines on Managing Conflicts of Interest*. February 28, 2008.

13. Accreditation Council for Continuing Medical Education. *ACCME Standards for Commercial Support: standards to ensure the independence of CME Activities*. 2007.

14. Singer N, Wilson D. Debate over industry role in educating doctors. *New York Times*. June 23, 2010.

15. Association of American Medical Colleges. *In the Interest of Patients: recommendations for physician financial relationships and clinical decision making; report of the Task Force on Financial Conflicts of Interest in Clinical Care*. Washington, DC; June 2010.

16. Stanford School of Medicine. *Community Academic Profiles: profiles that include disclosures*. Available at: http://med.stanford.edu/profiles//frdActionServlet?searchterms=disclosures&submit=+&choiceId=searchFRD&search=all (accessed March 5, 2011).

17. University of Michigan. *Standard Practice Guide: conflicts of interest and conflicts of commitment*. No. 201.65-1. Reviewed July 15, 2009. Available at: http://spg.umich.edu/pdf/201.65-1.pdf (accessed March 10, 2011).

Regulation, Accreditation, and the Compliance Function

Cynthia E. Boyd and Larry J. Goodman

From the Editor

Academic health science centers are among the most highly regulated of institutions. This chapter puts the regulatory environment in perspective and offers concrete approaches to effectively meeting these requirements.

—*SAW*

In an era of health reform and increasing internal and external examination and scrutiny, academic health science centers (AHSCs) are facing new trends and a host of unanticipated challenges. These challenges include areas in which AHSCs have already developed particular expertise, such as regulation, accreditation, and compliance. This chapter reviews several examples of important shifts in these processes.

The Era of Expanding Accreditation and Regulatory Requirements

Hospital accreditation has shifted away from onsite visits, interviews, standard adherence check-ups, and reviews of sentinel event root cause analysis summaries to the use of core measures including: risk adjusted outcomes, failure mode effect analyses, and other approaches to measuring processes and outcomes.

The Liaison Committee on Medical Education for medical students and the Residency Review Committees and Accreditation Council for Graduate Medical

Education for residents have also significantly changed the way programs must perform to earn continued accreditation. Medical schools must include meaningful self-directed learning experiences and provide evidence that their educational methods have been effective. Once again, measurable outcomes are required. Residency programs, too, must demonstrate more specifics about a resident's or a fellow's training. The training must meet certain experiential requirements and must include evidence that it was effective. Learning objectives and measurements against these objectives are more important than ever before. Additional expectations of training programs include cross-disciplinary experiences and a community impact assessment.

Research requirements and expectations have also changed, with much of the change driven by Congress and the public. Regulatory requirements of institutional review boards, appropriate informed consent, contract review, and data integrity remain critical components of any research enterprise. Additionally, a much more transparent process of exposing any potential conflict of interest is now expected. The research mission of most AHSCs is now expected to provide an obvious link to improvements in patient care or community health in a much more direct way than ever before. Finally, funding pressures because of impaired endowment funds, limited start-up funds for new investigators, and reductions in National Institutes of Health and industry awards place additional stress on this important mission component.

The last decade has also been marked by an enhanced requirement to document the medical record work done to meet a given billing level. Medicare has recognized significant savings by closely monitoring this requirement and has now outsourced this process through the use of recovery audit contractors. Training physicians and other health-care workers in billing requirements, as well as appropriate transfers to the electronic medical record, is now a significant undertaking. In some settings, this limits patient throughput or changes the typical doctor-patient interaction because doctors are typing while they are interviewing the patient. Similarly, "never events" (those events Medicare will not pay for because they should "never" occur in a hospital) and various pay-for-performance plans each share a new emphasis on data collection, sample review, and outcome analysis with statistical review.

Underlying each of these changes is the most significant point that each accreditation, regulatory, or compliance monitoring body has put forth – the AHSC institution itself is responsible for its practitioners, educators, researchers, and programs. To ensure that the responsibilities are carried out thoroughly and effectively, a robust central process of education, monitoring, self-reporting, and evidence-based best practices must be in place.

Health-care reform has further stimulated AHSCs to plan for a different future that includes forming new partnerships with physicians, aligning with accountable care organizations, developing electronic connectivity, and improving transparency in quality and cost. If the last decade was a time of data collection, the future is one of data sharing. More than ever before, programs must be cohesively managed, and AHSCs must recognize that they themselves are part of a team. Coordinating health-care delivery utilizing best practices and appropriate research, and incorporating these practices into our educational models, is required. Similarly, electronic connectivity and extensive training for all health-care practitioners in these new models and requirements is essential. Finally, in order to address all of the aforementioned changes, new leadership-training methods will be required.

An Approach to Accreditation and Regulatory Processes

There is no singular recipe that assures accreditation success. Like patient care, some things cannot be anticipated, and if anticipated, they may not be remediable. Nevertheless, attention to requirements and program performance can greatly improve the chances of a positive outcome.

The key components of a successful accreditation or regulatory program include: (1) content expertise, (2) data collection, (3) training of individuals involved in the program, and (4) a clear line of authority that includes the department, the program, a senior manager, the chief executive officer (CEO), and the board.

It is vital for an institution to have staff with in-depth understanding of its program requirements. For medical school accreditation, it is also helpful to have leaders who have participated as site visitors in the accreditation process of other schools. First-hand experience of the difficulties in sorting through the data provided and putting it in the context of the requirements, then comparing the school's written submission (self-study) with the onsite interviews and other findings, is invaluable. Regularly attending update presentations by Liaison Committee on Medical Education and Accreditation Council for Graduate Medical Education leadership, Residency Review Committee updates, or Joint Commission updates and incorporating these into the program training and data collection process is critical. But this is not enough. A successful program should include regular reports that measure performance against requirements and goals.

For example, a change in the call schedule for first-year residents must meet new duty hour limitations, but must also meet the overall educational requirements of the program. Even if clearly specified by a policy and a call schedule, the compliance program must collect information to assure reviewers that trainees are adhering to the schedule. Successful programs train everyone involved from the director to the trainee. A teaching physician may not realize the risk involved in keeping a trainee after hours – even if it is "just" for teaching purposes.

Most important, and despite its difficulty, a line of authority and accountability must be established – all the way to the Board. A senior administrator outside the program should have oversight responsibility and regularly update the dean or president, the CEO, and the board on program status. If trainees are provided some of their training at partner institutions, an institutional agreement that clearly specifies this relationship and an individual who tracks the performance of the relationship must be in place. The board should be regularly updated on accreditation, regulatory, and compliance issues, and itself, receive training.

Academic Health Science Centers and Corporate Compliance

Eradication of health-care fraud and abuse became the federal government's mantra of the 1990s. In fact, in 1994, then United States Attorney General Janet Reno declared fraud and abuse her agency's number-two priority behind violent crime.[1] A series of well-publicized compliance investigations, the most notorious involving the hospital giant Columbia/HCA, resulted in criminal indictments and staggering fines for alleged failures to comply with health-care laws and regulations.

One impetus for the federal government's increased focus on health-care compliance is the political dilemma faced by America's elected officials – how to ensure the availability of modern and often costly health-care services to an aging population without raising taxes. Federal officials have seized on an industry that has many processes and decisions with poor documentation, providing estimates on the extent of health-care fraud. There have also been some examples of egregious behavior that contributed to the suspicion that such behavior might be widespread. In 1992, the US General Accounting Office estimated that health-care fraud amounted to approximately 10% of total national health-care expenditures, or up to $100 billion annually.[2] Politicians suddenly blamed "fraudulent" health-care providers for the nation's health-care crisis. The US government characterized health-care fraud as the "crime of the nineties."[3] During this time there was a significant increase in the number of criminal and civil cases filed against health-care providers and the government was very successful in its attempts to prosecute cases of what they considered to be health-care fraud. In 1997, the Department of Justice announced that health-care fraud convictions had increased 270% during the Clinton administration.[4] The impression given the general public and the Congress by the Office of the Inspector General (OIG) for many years was that the runaway inflation in federally financed health-care costs was partially attributable to rampant fraud and abuse at all levels of providers and suppliers to the Medicare and Medicaid programs.

In an open letter to all health-care providers published in early 1997, the OIG declared a zero tolerance for fraud asking health-care providers to adopt and maintain compliance programs to assist the US government in eliminating health-care fraud.[5] The enforcement efforts of the OIG have tended to use the term "fraud" rather than "abuse," although there is a common law distinction between abuse with criminal intent and abuse that is clearly negligent. This has led to supplemental legislation permitting severe "civil" sanctions that can be imposed under the less difficult to prove "preponderance of the evidence marshaled" rather than the "guilty beyond a reasonable doubt" criminal standard. The use of extremely narrow "safe harbor" regulations promulgated in 1991 effectively and materially increased the scope of conduct that could be determined as unlawful.[6]

The OIG released its Model Compliance Program for Clinical Laboratories in 1997 and its detailed Compliance Program Guidance for Hospitals in February 1998. Since 1997, the creation of compliance program guidelines has been a major initiative of the OIG of the Department of Health and Human Services in its efforts to engage the health-care community in fighting fraud and abuse risk areas, to identify and limit the submission of erroneous claims, and to provide the industry with general guidelines for establishing effective programs for compliance with federal health-care program rules and regulations. As a result, a new industry of health-care consultants, information systems experts, accountants, attorneys, and ethicists has emerged to assist health-care providers in their compliance efforts.[7]

In the 1990s, virtually every health-care provider began to implement corporate compliance programs in an effort to prevent being caught up in government health-care antifraud oversight and prosecutions. The government actively encouraged health-care organizations to voluntarily adopt compliance programs; in an open letter, the OIG of the Department of Health and Human Services invited the nation's health-care providers to join the OIG in fighting fraud and abuse by adopting compliance programs that "promote a high level of ethical and lawful corporate conduct."[8] The OIG published a series of compliance program guidance documents through Federal Register notices directed at various segments of the health-care industry including clinical laboratories; hospitals; physicians; home health agencies; nursing facilities; third-party billing companies; pharmaceutical manufacturers; and durable medical equipment, prosthetics and orthotics supply industries. Among the first of these compliance documents was a notice encompassing principles applicable to hospitals and a wide variety of organizations that provide health-care service to beneficiaries of Medicare, Medicaid, and other federal health-care programs.

While there are many segments within the health-care industry that are highly regulated, hospitals face some of the more challenging and complex governmental regulations that have been imposed in the context of preventing and curtailing fraud and abuse, particularly hospitals affiliated with AHSCs. It is imperative that health-care institutions establish Compliance Programs, and that these programs are functional, effective, and tailored to the particular mission and structure of that organization.

The Importance and Fundamentals of a Compliance Program

The increased level of scrutiny in health-care compliance is a fact of business. Providers must devote significant resources to comply with the requirements of the Medicare/Medicaid reimbursement system, health-care insurers, and other private payors. Competitive pressures within the health-care industry and limited government funding of health care add to the challenges in consistently identifying additional resources that must be allocated for compliance.[9]

A corporate compliance program is a coordinated group of activities designed to prevent, detect, and remedy both intentional and inadvertent violations of law or corporate policy. Establishing a compliance program process is an important step an organization takes in assuring the internal organization, the community at large, and the government that it intends to comply and adhere to all federal government standards, recommendations, and other regulatory requirements applicable to the health-care community. A compliance program is integral to an organization's accreditation process, its compliance with regulatory requirements, and its overall business ethics within the community. Fundamentally, compliance efforts are designed to establish a culture within a hospital that promotes prevention, detection, and resolution of conduct that does not conform to federal and state law; federal, state, and private payor health-care program requirements; and the hospital's ethical and business policies.[10]

A compliance program demonstrates an organization's commitment to an ethical and proper way to do business. It encourages problems and errors to be reported, reduces the threat of whistle-blower lawsuits, minimizes the risk of wrongful behavior, helps to deter or avoid a Corporate Integrity Agreement, and reduces the risk of government fines, sanctions, or exclusion from the Medicare program.

An effective organizational infrastructure sets the tone for a successful compliance program with a chain of authority that runs from the board of directors or governance to the CEO to the corporate compliance officer. This infrastructure sends the message that management places significant importance on the compliance program. An effective compliance program begins with a formal commitment by the hospital's governing body to include all of the applicable elements based on the seven steps of the Federal Sentencing Guidelines.[11] At a minimum, comprehensive compliance programs should include elements as set out by the OIG:

1. The development and distribution of written standards of conduct, as well as written policies and procedures that promote the hospital's commitment

to compliance (e.g., by including adherence to compliance as an element in evaluating managers and employees), and address specific areas of potential fraud, such as claims development and submission processes, coding, and financial relationships with physicians and other health-care professionals.

2. The designation of a chief compliance officer and other appropriate bodies – for example, a corporate compliance committee, charged with the responsibility of operating and monitoring the compliance program, who report directly to the CEO and the governing body. The OIG recommends that a compliance committee be established to advise the compliance officer and assist in the implementation of the compliance program. The committee's functions should include:
   - analyzing the organization's industry environment, legal requirements with which it must comply, and specific risk areas
   - assessing existing policies and procedures to promote compliance with the institution's program
   - recommending and monitoring, in conjunction with the relevant depart- ments, the development of internal systems and controls to carry out the organization's standards, policies, and procedures as part of its daily operations
   - determining the appropriate strategy/approach to promote compliance with the program and detection of any potential violations, using tools such as hotlines and other fraud-reporting mechanisms
   - developing a system to solicit, evaluate, and respond to complaints and problems; the committee may also address other functions as the compliance concept becomes part of the hospital operating structure and daily routine.

3. The development and implementation of regular, effective education and training programs for all affected employees. Education and training is discussed in more detail later in this chapter.

4. The maintenance of a mechanism, such as a hotline, to receive complaints, and the adoption of procedures to protect the anonymity of complainants and to protect whistle-blowers from retaliation. The hotline as a reporting mechanism is discussed in more detail later in this chapter.

5. The development of a system to respond to allegations of improper/illegal activities and the enforcement of appropriate disciplinary action against employees who have violated internal compliance policies, applicable statutes, regulations, or federal health-care program requirements.

6. The use of audits and/or other evaluation techniques to monitor compliance and assist in the reduction of the identified problem areas. (The audit or review process is discussed in more detail later in this chapter.)

7. The investigation and remediation of identified systemic problems and the

development of policies addressing nonemployment or retention of sanctioned individuals.[12]

Compliance programs benefit an organization in many ways, but the most important reasons to establish one are to: prevent noncompliant events from occurring; detect events or errors early and correct them before they may become systemic in nature and are reviewed by external intervention; and reduce or mitigate the negative consequences that can result from external investigations in the event that noncompliant issues may arise.

Ensuring Program Effectiveness and Continual Improvement

While a comprehensive compliance program should include the seven elements described above, there are *three critical components* of a compliance program that are integral to program effectiveness and continual program improvement: (1) education and training, (2) auditing and monitoring, and (3) an internal communication and reporting process. Once an organization sets the tone regarding ethical business conduct with policies and procedures, it is the ongoing efforts and activities of these three critical elements that will determine and define how well that program is able to prevent, detect, and correct any potential errors, risks, or noncompliant activity that may occur.

Education and Training

The education and training of an institution's workforce is the first and most important line of protection and the key preventive aspect of a compliance program. It is critical that employees at all levels understand their roles and how to recognize and internally report compliance issues. In order to achieve an institution-wide culture change, the education process must provide the same information to all employees. The institution should educate different groups of employees and contractors in those areas of relevance to their specific duties. Targeted or role-specific training (e.g., regarding billing and coding, patient care documentation, potential anti-kickback violations, relationships with physicians) should be presented to specific groups or individuals within the organization for whom noncompliance may pose a greater risk. The education and training process should be based on the results of a risk assessment that includes both internal and external threats to noncompliance, with a well-planned education program to address each of the identified high-risk areas.

One study showed that effective training programs are delivered in person, interactive, more than one contact hour in length, and periodically repeated.[13] By contrast, training programs delivered primarily by means of video, interactive technology, or in game format were ineffective or harmful to a company's compliance environment. The OIG has expressed its preference for training programs delivered in person over other methods. Eileen Boyd, a former deputy inspector general stated:

> I'm a big believer in hands-on training, where people have a chance to ask questions and get tested on what they were supposed to learn. Putting a manual on a shelf – or herding people into an auditorium to watch a video – doesn't do it for me. If the health-care industry is foolish enough to put in compliance programs that aren't viable, they're making a serious mistake.[14]

Given the fact that billing compliance remains at the core of the OIG's focus in AHSCs, it is imperative to have focused in-person education on documentation and coding matters for those individuals who bear these responsibilities. Other specialty areas for focused education include Stark, anti-kickback, and physician relationships. Most institutions require mandatory compliance as a condition of continued employment; failure to complete required training can result in disciplinary action, including possible termination. Important in the training process is emphasizing and communicating to employees, and the institution as a whole, the positive goals of preventing noncompliant conduct from occurring. Finally, the education/training process should be dynamic and flexible to allow for improvements based on an analysis of workforce feedback and evaluations.

Auditing and Monitoring

Audits or reviews are vital for the success and effectiveness of any compliance program. Careful periodic reviews of a provider's activities and practices is critical in determining the organization's level of compliance and risk with some very complex and often confusing rules and standards that are applicable to health care. The audit or review process helps to tailor the compliance program activities to meet the specific needs of the organization. The Federal Sentencing Guidelines provide:

> The organization must have taken reasonable steps to achieve compliance with the standards, by utilizing monitoring and auditing systems reasonably designed to detect criminal conduct by its employees and other agents and by having in place and publicizing a reporting system whereby employees and other agents could report criminal conduct by others within the organization without fear of retribution.[15]

Similarly, OIG guidance states:

> An ongoing evaluation process is critical to a successful compliance program. The OIG believes that an effective program should incorporate thorough

monitoring of its implementation ... Although many monitoring techniques are available, one effective tool to promote and ensure compliance is the performance of regular, periodic compliance audits by internal and external auditors.[16]

The organization's annual auditing and monitoring plan is partially based on those activities that have been included in the OIG's Annual Work Plan. During the fall of each year, the OIG publishes its Work Plan for the coming calendar year and most compliance programs utilize this information to assess and plan their own internal compliance audit activities. The OIG Work Plan sets forth various projects to be addressed during the fiscal year by the Office of Audit Services, Office of Evaluation and Inspections, Office of Investigations, and Office of Counsel to the Inspector General. The Work Plan includes projects planned in each of the department's major entities: the Centers for Medicare and Medicaid Services; the public health agencies; and the Administrations for Children and Families, and Aging. Information is also provided on projects related to issues that cut across departmental programs, including state and local government use of federal funds, as well as the functional areas of the Office of the Secretary. Some of the projects described in the Work Plan are statutorily required, such as the audit of the department's financial statements, which is mandated by the Government Management Reform Act of 1994.[17]

Compliance programs that conduct regular and periodic audits or reviews should make certain that the internal community understands and is aware of the type of reviews that are being conducted. It is not unusual for employees, physicians, and others who constitute the workforce at an AHSC to express concern and anxiety when compliance reviews are conducted in their particular area of activity or practice. This anxiety is partially based on the language that is sometimes conveyed or used either before or during the course of a routine audit/review. Indeed, employees have noted and expressed feelings of anxiety or fear similar to what may be experienced with the announcement of an Internal Revenue Service tax audit. As a consequence, compliance programs should adopt language and an approach that is friendly, non-threatening, and that explains the purpose of their activities. Employees should be made aware that compliance reviews are typically conducted on a "not for cause" or routine basis as part of the organization's routine compliance audit plan.

An audit or review may be conducted for a variety of reasons. Some are conducted to provide the compliance officer and the organization with a baseline to measure the organization's current level of performance and compliance with a particular rule or statute. This provides a risk assessment that can later be used to prioritize compliance audit activities. An audit or review may also be conducted as a teaching opportunity to help employees and others become aware of their current compliance with coding, billing, Health Insurance Portability and

Accountability Act privacy and security, or an array of other governmental rules and regulations.

It is important that the results of audits or reviews are shared and communicated using clear language in a non-threatening and transparent fashion. This type of practice helps promote the compliance program and obtain the trust and respect of the employees just as a "not for cause" audit or review is conducted as a routine activity to assess the current status of compliance in a particular area. A for-cause audit is just the opposite and may result when a specific complaint, suspicion, or allegation (e.g., via a "hotline" call) has been made regarding areas identified by the government as potentially problematic or at high risk for fraud and abuse. Another type of for-cause audit may be imposed on an individual provider by the government under the mandate of a Corporate Integrity Agreement (compliance programs that are mandated as part of a legal settlement with the federal government). Clearly, this type of audit will have specific parameters and requirements that have been negotiated between the provider and government and the provider has no choice but to comply or face significant fines and penalties.

Notwithstanding the reason for the audit or review, the primary purpose of conducting such reviews is to measure the organization's level of compliance with specified health-care rule(s). The scope, duration, and the periodicity of an audit or review will be dictated by the circumstance under which it is being conducted and the type and/or extent of the findings once the review has been completed.

Hotlines and Other Forms of Communication

The third critical element that serves to ensure compliance program effectiveness is an internal communication process that provides employees with a mechanism for communicating questions, complaints, and concerns to the chief compliance officer. In each of the OIG compliance guidances released to date, the OIG comments on the significance of open communication between employees and the compliance officer. The OIG encourages establishing procedures so that hospital personnel may seek clarification from the compliance officer or members of the compliance committee in the event of any confusion or question about hospital policy or procedure. The OIG encourages the use of hotlines (including anonymous hotlines), e-mails, written memoranda, newsletters, and other forms of information exchange to maintain open lines of communication.[18]

The overwhelming choice of reporting mechanism for health-care providers is the "hotline," typically a telephone line dedicated to receiving calls from employees who wish to report a compliance issue in the workplace.[19] However, an organization's reporting mechanism choice will ultimately depend on the culture of the organization. Regardless of which mechanism an organization chooses to implement for communication and reporting purposes, several important policies must be enacted and communicated to employees to ensure the mechanism's effectiveness. These policies address:

1. ensuring the confidentiality of information in the report and the individual making the report
2. guaranteeing that no retaliatory disciplinary actions will be taken against any individual making a "good-faith" report
3. listing the steps of the investigatory process to ensure consistency and thoroughness.

The organization must also publicize the reporting mechanism to its employees, explaining the purpose of the mechanism and how it will operate. Employee awareness is crucial if the reporting mechanism is to be effective. Finally, it should be noted that most Corporate Integrity Agreements require outsourced hotlines.[20]

Hotlines operated by commercial vendors are typically staffed 24 hours a day, 7 days a week, with personnel available to answer the phone "live" and transcribe the caller's information into a written report. Outsourced hotlines typically do not have caller ID-type capabilities nor do they make information regarding the origin of calls available to the organization except in emergencies. Commercial vendors typically employ persons specially trained in responding to employees reporting concerns. These specialists are trained to ask questions and cull information from a caller that might otherwise be missed. Getting as much information as possible is vital since the more efficient and complete the initial report is, the more efficient and effective the compliance investigation can be.[21]

In order for a hotline to be effective an organization must undertake concerted efforts to make employees and other agents aware and informed of its existence and purpose. Posters, newsletters, tabletops, and making certain to inform new employees during the organization's employee orientation process are all appropriate means to publicize a hotline. Organizations should publicize the hotline as often and in as many ways as possible to ensure employees know of its existence. In some organizations, the hotline may be used for areas outside of compliance to report anything that just doesn't seem right within the organization. Such reports may relate to patient safety concerns, quality issues, harassment, accreditation concerns, human resources, or other issues related to organizational policies and procedures.

Whatever the purpose, the OIG has made clear its position that a key feature of an effective compliance program is a well-publicized reporting or communications mechanism that is a practical option for employees to report any compliance-related concerns. Additionally, it must be capable of rapid response while maintaining confidentiality and be transparent and consistent with its responses. Finally, if any compliance issues are reported to the compliance officer, via hotline or otherwise, the organization must carefully investigate the matter and take appropriate corrective action, as necessary.

The False Claims Act

The most potent tool available to the government in enforcing what it considers to be fraud and abuse, and one that can create major financial liabilities for health-care providers, is the False Claims Act (FCA) (31 USC §§ 3729–33). The FCA was originally adopted in 1863 during the Civil War to discourage suppliers of the Union Army from overcharging the federal government. The FCA states that any person who knowingly presents, or causes to be presented, to the US government a false or fraudulent claim for payment or approval; knowingly makes, uses, or causes to be made or used a false record or statement to get a false or fraudulent claim paid or approved by the government; or conspires to defraud the government by getting a false or fraudulent claim allowed or paid, violates the Act. No proof of actual damages, such as payment or approval of the claim, is needed to prove a violation of the FCA.[22]

The FCA's definition of *knowingly* was intended to establish liability of, for example, corporate officers who consciously avoid knowledge of false claims filed by their subordinates. The definition also applies to corporate employees who follow orders of superiors or even ignore the activities of coworkers. Both corporate officers and lower level employees may be liable under the FCA for improper claims for which they are aware or should have been aware.[23]

Qui Tam or Whistle-Blower Suits

The FCA allows a private person, often referred to as a *qui tam relator*, to bring a civil action in the name of the United States. The purpose of the *qui tam* provisions is to give an incentive to whistle-blowers to come forward and help the government discover and prosecute fraudulent claims by awarding them a percentage of the amount recovered. Over the past 5 years, *qui tam* suits filed under the FCA have accounted for the majority of civil fraud cases pursued by the government. Recoveries under the FCA topped $1 billion each year between 2000 and 2002. Of the more than $1.2 billion recovered for the 2002 fiscal year, almost $1.1 billion was derived from *qui tam* lawsuits.[24]

Billing Compliance

The greatest area of risk and exposure in health-care regulatory compliance is billing, specifically billing related to documentation and coding. The rules, regulations, and requirements related to coding and documentation are voluminous, often complex, and very difficult to interpret without assistance from governmental guidance or legal counsel. The most common types of so called billing frauds that the government frequently targets are: medically unnecessary services; billing for services not rendered; duplicate billing; teaching physician or PATH-related issues; upcoding; unbundling and separately charging for services; and false cost reports. Physicians and other practitioners must be appropriately educated and trained to be certain that medical documentation supports the medical necessity of all services and activities provided. Additionally, the accuracy of coding rests with the quality, legibility, and completeness of the physician's documentation in the medical record.

Compliance Program Challenges

Once the elements of a compliance program have been assembled and adopted by an institution, the challenge becomes one of implementing an effective program that can also be responsive to changing needs. The regulatory landscape is dynamic and always shifting. New rules or the revision of old rules are a constant challenge and can be a confusing factor for physicians, administrators, and other employees of AHSCs. As an institution works through the process of constructing, implementing, and maintaining a compliance program, there will be different areas of focus at different points in time.

Conclusion

In 2004, The Institute of Medicine (IOM) published a book entitled *Academic Health Centers: Leading Change in the 21st Century*.[25] The authors recognized the many accomplishments of AHSCs during the twentieth century but they also anticipated the need for significant change going forward. They called for change in each of the key components of the AHSC mission including: patient care, research, and education. Change is necessary if AHSCs are to continue to play their traditional role in a new era of health care. To accomplish this change, the report called for an even more fundamental reorganization in the governance structure of the AHSC itself to maximize interaction and communication across disciplines and components.

The IOM recommendations encompassed all levels of the AHSC multifaceted mission and anticipated a very different future for them, recognizing that conventional strategies will be less effective in that future. Today, AHSCs are facing the trends anticipated by the report and a host of unanticipated challenges. These challenges include areas in which AHSCs have developed particular expertise, such as regulation, accreditation, and compliance.

AHSCs must lead the way in each of these areas. The transitions envisioned by the IOM report are upon us. The environment we are in, one of process, measurement, and external audit, is part of our commitment to the public. There has never been a time more in need of leadership and accountability.

Besides content experts, training, measurement, and line authority to the CEO and Board, AHSCs need to establish good working relationships with various regulatory bodies. Developing a habit of self-reporting and calling the appropriate agency for questions even when the call reveals an area of concern, is an approach that can benefit any institution.

Author's Personal Reflections

At Rush University Medical Center, all of the components, including research education, patient care, and community relations, report up to a single management team. There is one CEO and one board of trustees, and we review research regulation issues, educational accreditation, as well as billing and financial requirements. In academic health centers, regulation and compliance is very complex, and involves many different parts. At Rush, we have federally sponsored research, regulation issues pertaining to private industry, accreditation requirements of four colleges, 700 in-house officers with residency and fellowship training in every specialty, and 800 physicians with a mixed model of private and salaried doctors. Rush is a large institution that has over 50% government payers, including the Medicare and Medicaid programs.

The most important part in building a compliance program is education. People need to be constantly aware of changes in regulation, and ideally, compliance methods need to be easy to use and easy to document. All departments and practices have a role to play. We also have a very active board of trustees that brings excellent ideas to the table. We make sure we share data with everyone. Everybody in the medical center is responsible, and we have a separate internal audit team that overlaps with our compliance efforts.

The agencies we report to also have a role to play. About 10 years ago, we had a research compliance issue, and as we identified and worked through it, we realized that there was some ambiguity to the language in the federal rules concerning the issue. As we tried to develop a solution, we worried that it would not satisfy the ambiguous language. So we reviewed this with federal authorities at several levels to see if our solution was acceptable, and the response we received was very positive. The regulatory bodies we've dealt with have generally been very reasonable and accommodating. Sometimes there can be challenges, and those can be frustrating, but when we have asked for clarification, or for suggestions about the proper methodology to use to meet both the letter and spirit of the law, while still providing badly needed services, nearly everyone we've dealt with has been very responsive.

It's always satisfying to see how the people at Rush respond to challenges, whether they pertain to compliance, finances, clinical care, education, or research. Our team has always rallied around solutions that were in the best interests of the people we serve and the larger institution. Academic health centers are the most exciting places to be in health care. There is nothing more stimulating than to be surrounded by medical students and other individuals at various stages in their training, because incredibly smart people are constantly questioning you, and that keeps everyone at the peak of their performance. We have the opportunity to see new treatments developed through research. Leaders of academic health centers are in a position where they get to understand the culture of an organization, and they can see how an institution can evolve, which reinforces the need for us all to evolve, so we can provide opportunities for better training and higher quality of care.

It's a tremendous privilege to be in a leadership position at an institution like Rush. Each person does this job his or her own way, and every organization is different. But at every academic health center, there are people who have tremendous ideas, and the leader's job is to figure out ways to listen to those people, and incorporate as many of those ideas as possible. With all the excitement and challenges that academic health centers like Rush face, and with all discussion nationally about reining in the escalating cost of health care, our main challenge is access to health care. It is conceivable that we will significantly improve quality and possibly address cost, but the resolution of access will not be achieved just by providing Medicaid coverage to the uninsured. The challenge is developing an appropriate health-care system for all people, so everyone can take advantage of the amazing discoveries and innovations that are being generated around the world.

—*LJG*

References

1. US Department of Justice. *Dept. of Justice Health Care Fraud Report, Fiscal Year 1994, Introduction*. §III (A)(1). Washington, DC. March 2, 1995.

2. US General Accounting Office. *Report to Chairman, Subcommittee on Human Resources and Intergovernmental Operations, U.S. House of representatives, Health Insurance: vulnerable payers lose billions to fraud and abuse*. (GAO/HRD-92-69; p.1). Washington, DC. May 1992.

3 US Department of Justice. *Health Care Fraud Report: fiscal years 1995 & 1996*. Washington, DC. August 1997.

4. Reno J. Statement by Attorney General Janet Reno on Health Care Fraud. Press Release. Washington, DC: Attorney General; March 6, 1997. Available at: www.usdoj.gov/opa/pr/1997/March97/095ag.htm (accessed February 21, 2011).

5. Brown JG. Inspector General, Department of Health and Human Services. Open Letter to Healthcare Providers. February 1997.

6. Bartrum TE, Bryant LE, Jr. The brave new world of health care compliance programs. *Ann Health Law*. 1997; **6**: 51–75.

7. Withrow SC. *Managing Healthcare Compliance*. Chicago, IL: Health Administration Press; 1999.

8. Brown JG. Inspector General, Department of Health and Human Services. Open Letter to All Healthcare Providers. March 3, 1997. Available at: http://oig.hhs.gov/fraud/docs/openletters/ltrhcp.htm (accessed February 21, 2011).

9. Withrow SC. *Managing Healthcare Compliance*. Chicago, IL: Health Administration Press; 1999.

10. Federal Register. Vol. 63, No. 35. Monday, February 23, 1998. Notices, p. 8988.

11. United States Sentencing Commission Guidelines. *Guidelines Manual*. 8A1.2, comment. (n.3(k)).

12. Federal Register. Vol. 63, No. 35. Monday, February 23, 1998. Notices.

13. United States Sentencing Commission. Proceedings of the Second Symposium on Crime and Punishment in the United States. *Corporate Crime in America: Strengthening the "Good Citizen" Corporation*. "A Presentation of Empirical Research on Compliance Practices: What Companies Say They Are Doing-What Employees Hear, A Study of Organizational Practices and Their Effect on Compliance." September 8–9, 1995.

14. Boyd E. Deputy Inspector General, US Department of Health and Human Services, as quoted, "Hot new job in health care: in-house cop." *Wall Street Journal*. September 18, 1997, p. B1.

15. Federal Sentencing Guidelines, Comment 3.(k) 95.

16. Federal Register. Vol. 63, No. 35. Monday, February 23, 1998. Notices, p. 8996.

17. US Department of Health and Human Services. *Office of Inspector General: work plan*. Available at: http://oig.hhs.gov/publications/workplan.asp (accessed February 21, 2011).

18. Federal Register. Vol. 63, No. 35. Monday, February 23, 1998. Notices.

19. *The Health Care Compliance Professional's Manual*. New York, NY: CCH Aspen Publishers; 2004.

20. Ibid.

21. Ibid.

22. Ibid. pp. 10, 130.

23. Serbaroli, FJ. Provider liabilities under the False Claims Act. *NYLJ*. September 29, 1994: 3.

24. Arent Fox. Whistleblowers in the driver's seat. *Health Care Alert*. January 3, 2003. Available at: www.arentfox.com/publications/index.cfm?fa=legalUpdateDisp&content_id=945 (accessed February 10, 2011).

25. Institute of Medicine. *Academic Health Centers: leading change in the 21st century*. Washington, DC: National Academies Press; 2003.

Human Resources and Personnel Management

*Harold L. Paz, Billie S. Willits,
Deirdre C. Weaver, and Sean Young*

> **From the Editor**
>
> Often underappreciated, the management of the individuals who work at academic health science centers is a vital function of these large institutions. This chapter presents fundamental information and management insights in an important area that all leaders of these institutions should understand.
>
> —*SAW*

In his book *Human Resource Champions*, Dave Ulrich notes that "human resource policies and practices should create organizations that are better able to execute strategy, operate efficiently, engage employees, and manage change."[1] While all four of these outcomes are important to any organization, they are particularly significant and challenging to complex and often large academic health science centers (AHSCs). By virtue of their role, AHSCs balance multiple educational, patient care, research, and community-service missions in a rapidly changing legal, regulatory, cultural, and technological climate. While few AHSCs are fully integrated in a single organization, a majority consist of a college of medicine, other health professions schools, a university teaching and research hospital, and a multispecialty physician practice, often with separate organizational structures. Given the complexity of AHSCs, effective strategy, operations, and employee engagement are required in order for the multi-faceted mission to be met. This chapter explores an approach to human resources management that begins with an organization's vision translated into a strategic plan and then operationalized through its budget and human resource policies to achieve the institutional mission, goals, and objectives.

Organizational Strategic Planning: The Penn State Hershey Model

At the Pennsylvania State University (Penn State) Hershey Medical Center, a fully integrated AHSC located in central Pennsylvania, planning is conducted year-round by four cross-campus teams, each made up of faculty and staff and supported by a vice dean or senior administrator, who are individually responsible for education, research, patient care, and community. Each mission team monitors and reviews institutional progress tied to defined goals and measured objectives against a backdrop of organizational culture and stated values. Meeting at least once a month and often weekly, the teams review institutional progress against defined metrics and changes in the environment. Both internal and external benchmarking is used to prioritize objectives that are translated into unified campus-wide operations, budget, and human resources policies. Each team leader reports quarterly to the campus executive council, made up of senior administrators and department chairs, which approves new initiatives, programs, and policies designed to advance the institution's strategic plan.

The unified strategic plan is brought to the medical center's governing board for review in November of each year and the operating budget is proposed for approval in May. This ongoing cyclical approach to developing an operating plan and budget that is derived from a constantly refreshed strategic plan serves to prioritize investment and resource utilization, focus decision making, and align human resource capital effectively. Finally, at the completion of each academic year, institutional leaders are rewarded financially for achieving institutional and individual goals with at-risk compensation. Similarly, all employees and house staff receive an annual bonus if the well-articulated organizational goals are met. This not only aligns individual performance with institutional success but also serves to reinforce the notion that employees need to be engaged in the strategic planning process.

While strategic planning is the central mechanism for achieving organizational advancement, several other processes operate in tandem. Like other AHSCs, Penn State Hershey has a culture of shared governance that is managed by the College Faculty Organization, Medical Group Board of Governors, Medical Center Medical Staff Physician Advisory Council, and senior management team. The bodies work in various ways to advance the strategic plan through approval of the curriculum, standing academic policies for students, promotion and tenure for faculty, and human resources policies for faculty and staff. In effect, these policies and procedures reflect the institutional culture embodied in the campus-wide strategic plan while at the same time shaping the actions and behaviors of the AHSC community going into the future.

As leaders and stakeholders set the strategic direction for the AHSC, it is the effective use of policies and procedures, in addition to resource allocation, that allows "human capital" to be engaged effectively in achieving the institutional vision. The participation of members of the four mission teams as stakeholders brings creativity, diversity, and expertise to bear on problems faced by the organization. This involvement encourages the stakeholders to be part of the organization's accomplishments and empowers them to knowledgeably discuss, in their respective work areas, the "why" of the results. Institutional knowledge of this kind provides the insight that others in the organization require to achieve success. Importantly, it can also contribute to timelier acceptance of institutional change.

When strategic planning is truly used in decision making throughout the organization, one can see that personnel and human resource policies become guideposts. That is, the strategy is set and policies to support the strategy are then established or modified. Reversing this approach and establishing policy with no link to strategy can lead to unintended negative results.

As an illustration of this point, consider a human resource policy that focuses on the appointment of a tenure-track researcher. Historically, research is conducted within a single discipline. Faculty members are hired into a specific academic department or clinical concentration. That department pays the salary and applicable benefits. Salaries in the organization are not public. It is not unusual for the salary to be known only to the department chair and the dean. Indeed, the payroll system might be set up to allow only the department and college to contribute to the salary and to know its amount.

To continue the illustration, in its strategic planning the organization establishes the goal to "Strengthen Our Research Portfolio to Promote Institutional Growth." Objectives will need to be designated to achieve this goal. An objective such as "optimize the use of intramural research resources" may be written. If "research resources" includes tenure-track faculty, and one practice to be incorporated is recruiting and hiring multidiscipline faculty, a human resource policy that limits hiring to one department may be inhibiting. Further, it may limit or work against facilitating collaboration between departments or colleges. The payroll system may not be able to accommodate a "dual" or "triple" department designation and may need to be redesigned. Once the strategic goal and the objectives have been endorsed by the organization, various operational changes may need to be made. In the future, as one reads the modified human resources policy, one will see that dual and triple department appointments can be made. That acknowledgment may, over time, lead to a cultural change in the way the curriculum is designed for multidepartment collaboration and may change the way recruitment and hiring occurs. The integration of research, education, and even clinical procedures may be influenced. The link between strategy and objective with operational change can lead to the desired organization change.

Organizational Response to Opportunities

In addition to the strategic planning process currently in place at Penn State Hershey Medical Center, ongoing issues that are articulated in policies and procedures are reviewed. Determining whether an issue needs to be dealt with in a policy, what the policy should say, how it will be disseminated, how it will be managed, and when it needs to be reassessed are all ongoing activities for an AHSC. These policies have wide-ranging applications. They may speak to faculty, physician, and support-staff issues. They may encompass legal issues, patient issues, and even issues that impact the general public. How to identify the needed policies, assess whether they work, and anticipate difficulties can be illustrated through examples, such as the "no tobacco use" policy.

There are times when an organization is confronted with a problem or opportunity that demands a rapid response, and for which existing plans and processes do not suffice. Said another way, there may be no opportunity for the organization's leadership to wait for its membership to identify an issue, establish a process for approaching the issue, and implement the process. Yet, even in these times when a problem or opportunity is identified by organizational leadership, the "top down" initiative can and does need to incorporate organizational collaboration in planning a process for addressing the issue.

An example of a leadership-identified opportunity presented to an organization for consideration can illustrate key elements of process planning that are similar to process planning used in a highly formal change management environment. The scenario for this example is an organization with a new senior vice president for health affairs and chief executive officer of the medical center. Shortly after the appointment, the American Lung Association and other health-care leaders of neighboring facilities approach this leader about the potential to establish tobacco-free grounds and campuses. As a practicing pulmonologist, the leader is well versed in the negative health impacts of smoking and tobacco use.

The change is important for the health and wellness of the more than 9000 employees and students, as well as the thousands of patients and visitors each year to the medical center. Further, there is a keen desire for the medical center, as the only AHSC in a region of 4.5 million people, to take a leadership role in this important health issue. For these two important reasons, the leader committed to a policy prohibiting tobacco use in the buildings and on the grounds of all medical center facilities. The timeframe for announcing the decision and the implementation of the tobacco-free campus is short but not immediate. The leader joins with the leadership of other local health-care facilities in making a commitment to go "Tobacco Free Together" at a public press event. The entities pledge to implement tobacco-free policies between the Great American Smokeout in November and New Year's Day, when many people make their traditional new year's resolutions.

In order for the implementation to occur on schedule, the leader asks that a coordinated educational campaign for employees, visitors, and patients be developed, and calls for increased emphasis on smoking cessation programs to assist those who wish to quit tobacco use. In addition, new human resource policies to address counseling and progressive discipline of employees who violate the new policy are instituted. All policies are to be in place by January 1.

Given that the timeframe is quite brief and the initiative is determined by the leadership rather than being faculty and staff identified, at least two dynamics are imperative. First, the message needs to be clear, and secondly, as much faculty and staff involvement in the planning and implementation of the change has to be generated given the short timeframe. The policy change could either be met with enthusiastic participation or with noncompliance. The former would result in a healthier population that could serve as a model for non-health-care employers in the area. The latter could result in an environment plagued with meting out disciplinary actions and charges of unilateral decision making in an organization that prides itself on a shared governance model.

In a joint announcement the participating organizations identify three key reasons for the policy change:

1. *As health-care organizations*, we have a responsibility to model healthy behaviors.
2. *As employers*, we want to do the right thing by encouraging our employees to choose a healthy, tobacco-free lifestyle and providing opportunities to quit.
3. *As care providers*, we want to protect our patients, visitors, and employees from the risks associated with second-hand smoke.

In addition, a number of secondary messages are noted:
- *Because we feel strongly about these issues, our health-care organizations have made a mutual commitment to each other and our community.* Between the date of the annual Great American Smokeout and January 1, when most people make their new year's resolutions, we are going "Tobacco-Free Together."
- *Our decision has the potential to impact hundreds of thousands of lives annually,* if you consider the total number of employees in our respective organizations and the number of patients and visitors to our facilities.
- Health statistics:
  - Deaths and illness caused by tobacco are significant. Cigarette smoking

causes about one in every five deaths in the United States each year.[2] Secondhand smoke is a known human carcinogen, responsible for at least 3400 lung cancer deaths each year, as well as more than 46 000 (range of 22 700–69 600) cardiovascular deaths and hundreds of thousands of asthma episodes. Smoking harms nearly every organ of the body, causing many diseases and reducing the health of smokers in general.[3]

▶ Results from decreased smoking include reductions in sick time, increased productivity among tobacco-free workers.

● In an era when hotels, restaurants and government buildings have gone tobacco-free, how can any health-care organization justify not doing so?

A committee of facilities, communications, and health and wellness staff, as well as representatives from the medical center's physicians and two unions (Teamsters and SEIU), is created. The group develops strategies and policies designed to support the January 1 tobacco-free goal:

● policy review and endorsement by department chairs and the senior management team

● town meetings for all interested employees; content of the meetings includes a review of new tobacco-free policies as well as details of support for employees who wish to quit smoking

● financial incentives, full coverage of smoking cessation programs, and discounts for nicotine replacement therapies

● communications plans, such as "on-hold" messages on the medical center's phone system, new signage, notices in patient appointment letters, advertising and public relations efforts conducted jointly with the other "Tobacco-Free Together" partners to educate patients and visitors of the pending change to the tobacco policy.

Assessing the Policy Change Process

As is the case with any organizational change, an assessment of the results of the change needs to be made after a reasonable period of time. This assessment aspect is often ignored. Too often the organization has moved on to other issues. Additionally, acknowledging that the change did not occur or did not occur as intended is difficult because it may be seen as an error, mistake, or failure, a perception that can challenge a leader's stature or authority. However, to refrain from the assessment may have an even more deleterious effect. It may be a "lost opportunity" to bring about a significant change. Further, it may be a "lost opportunity" to learn which factors in the process were not effective in the organization; this is vitally important to ensure that the same error is not made again in future actions. Beyond the "lost opportunities," and equally devastating, is the reality known to the faculty and staff but unacknowledged by the leadership. Lack of attention to the assessment may begin to establish a culture of noncompliance that will manifest itself in unpredictable behaviors in the future.

Both possibilities – that the organization has moved on and that the failure of the policy change is too "risky" to document – can be addressed. As the intent to change is shared with the organization, the announcement should also note why, how, and when the change will be assessed. In explaining the "why," leadership should be transparent, noting the importance of progress and that assessing past changes can provide insight for future decisions. Also, in stating "why," leadership should be clear that errors may occur, that the change is for an important purpose, and that "getting it right" is a valuable result for the organization.

More challenging than the actual assessment is publicizing the assessment conclusions. As is the case with other leadership commitments that are made to the organization, they must be carried out and shared with the organization. Just as results of focus groups and surveys need to be "reported out" to participants in order to maintain credibility for future inquiries, so must the outcomes of the policy assessment. Prudent leaders engage faculty and staff to review the outcomes, identify the cause of any results deemed "errors," and articulate possible solutions and/or different processes that may lend themselves to remedying the error. The entire assessment aspect of the process lends itself to continuous improvement. At the same time, the outcomes can help shape future directions for the institutional strategic plan.

The key points of the change process in the above scenario are: (1) clear articulation of the desired change; (2) definitive actions with timeframes and clearly identified roles; (3) use of easily accessed educational and awareness tools; (4) assessment to ascertain aspects of success and opportunities for improvement; and (5) communication of the assessment with "thank you's" for participation in the process.

Linking Strategies to Processes

Multiple authors and consultants have researched and published processes for change. Selecting one that fits the culture of an organization and consistently using it is the important point. Organizational change is imperative in our AHSCs today, yet substituting alternative process models too often can be counterproductive. It distracts from the essence of the change itself. It is helpful to observe the change process, as distinct from the specific changes being implemented. If the process continues to give good results, maintain it. If the process is no longer getting results of value for the organization, look for a new process. If research illustrates a more effective approach or if the nomenclature in the literature has changed so significantly that it renders the model "antiquated," then the AHSC should jettison the process and look for a new one. Changing the process too often is distracting; not changing when needed adds less value to an organization than could otherwise be achieved.

As the examples illustrate, and as noted earlier, there are various change processes available to an organization. Similarly, there are various strategic planning processes that are effective. The key is to link strategies with a change process, engage stakeholders, make the changes in policy, and then assess the changes to discern if modifications are necessary. Ensuring that strategy guides policy, rather than the reverse, can support the long-term strength of an AHSC. Engagement of stakeholders throughout the process encourages commitment to the change.

A number of trends have emerged recently that focus on strategic planning and change processes that facilitate organizational change. Many of these trends focus on faculty who, then, must be engaged as key stakeholders in order to address these trends. Engagement of stakeholders is vital to the initial development of appropriate policies, as well as to successful implementation, revision, or adaptation in response to changing circumstances.

Table 7.1 provides an overview of typical human resources and personnel policies of an AHSC. A majority of the policies cover all employees while some are specific to faculty and/or health-care providers. Several policies are relatively new and reflect emerging trends in academic medicine or health care in general. In a few cases, these policies have been developed in response to new regulations required for accreditation, certification, or reimbursement, including Americans with Disabilities Act policies, background checks, pre-employment drug testing, and worker's compensation reporting of work-related injuries.

Other policies are developed in response to institutional strategic priorities. Examples include lactation support, international medical aid missions, educational leave, and tobacco-free campus policies. Policies developed in response to external accreditation or regulatory requirements are typically led by human resources administration with the support of AHSC leadership, including legal counsel. These policies are reviewed with stakeholders as described earlier.

At Penn State College of Medicine and Penn State Hershey Medical Center, as throughout the University, affirmative action policies emphasize the responsibility of the institutional leadership to not only ensure nondiscrimination but to actively support and enhance diversity. Specific responsibilities outlined in the policy promote recruitment efforts that reach appropriate sources of job candidates to ensure a diverse pool, offer faculty and staff opportunities to enhance their skills and advance in accordance with their abilities, and provide training and guidance to managers to ensure consistent understanding and implementation of affirmative action plans.

TABLE 7.1 Policies for Human Resources and Personnel Management

Equity and Protection	Affirmative Action in Employment
	Americans with Disabilities Act
	Conflict resolution and complaints of unlawful discrimination and harassment
	Employee assistance
	Lactation support
	Medical missions
	Military leave
	Sexual harassment
	Tobacco-free campus
Evaluation and Supervision	Attendance
	Performance evaluations
	Excessive overtime
	Substance abuse
	Timekeeping guidelines
	Jury duty
	Leave of absence
	Bereavement
	Family and medical leave
	Employee performance improvement
	Physician sanctions due to delinquent medical records
	Disclosure of confidential patient information
	Personal appearance guidelines
Hiring	Background checks
	Employee orientation
	Employment
	Employment of relatives
	Pre-employment drug testing
	Search firm usage
	Relocation assistance
Compensation and Benefits	Salary scales
	Worker's compensation
	Timekeeping guidelines
	Educational privileges
	On-call policies
	Overtime compensation
	Paid time off
	Personal holiday and vacation
	Shift differential

However, a strong affirmative action policy is not always in itself sufficient to enable an AHSC to attract and retain diverse faculty and staff; policy is most effective when backed by programmatic initiatives, a strong commitment of resources, and the creation of an institutional culture that prioritizes such efforts. In addition to the university-wide affirmative action policy, the Penn State Hershey Medical Center and College of Medicine have created faculty development and retention initiatives including a Junior Faculty Development Program, pairing junior faculty with more senior mentors and offering workshops aimed at increasing the successful development of junior faculty members' careers. Though open to all faculty members, such programs, and the opportunities for networking and mentorship that they entail, can be particularly valuable to women and minority faculty. The recent establishment of a new associate dean for diversity position further emphasizes the commitment of institutional resources to enhance the recruitment of diverse faculty, staff, and students.

Response to Trends in Academic Medicine

Effective human resource policies and personnel management practices are vital as AHSCs respond to trends and challenges in academic medicine. While some of these issues cannot be viewed solely as human resource issues and are ultimately much broader in scope, human resource policies guided by a strong and responsive strategic plan can play a key role in successfully addressing such diverse challenges as faculty retention, conflict of interest reporting, industry relations, and the use of electronic medical records.

Faculty Retention

One trend that has remained relatively consistent is the retention rate of academic medical school faculty. The Association of American Medical Colleges (AAMC) indicates that the average faculty retention rate among AAMC member institutions remains at about 60% over 10 years, with turnover at roughly 40%.[4] Replacing personnel can be expensive in both direct and indirect costs. While retention is primarily a faculty development issue, human resource policies and tools can serve as assets in supporting more effective retention. If an AHSC finds that the turnover rate of faculty is approaching or exceeds the average, a strategic goal might be set to increase the retention rate. The strategy can be established for academic and financial reasons. An institution that tends to react in timely fashion to financial situations might choose to estimate the direct cost of the recruiting and hiring process as well as the indirect costs of time-to-fill and supplemental pay for existing faculty.

Establishing the approximate cost to fill a position may seem to be useless time spent on the obvious. However, when an actual dollar amount is established it sets a concrete goal that teams of faculty can identify and strive for. The common metrics are the cost of a recruiting firm and the travel and accommodation expenses for candidates. Less direct, yet often more costly, are the dollar equivalents for support staff time and for faculty time spent interviewing and attending selection committee meetings. An even more indirect cost may be calculated if deans discuss the time-to-fill phenomenon with department heads. Department and division heads may be less satisfied with the time-to-fill metric. Possibly the disruption in the department due to the turnover is more dramatic than is realized outside of the department. Articulating this disruption is important to the goal. That is, it may not translate into a dollar amount; however, it is tangible for faculty in the department. Taking into account time-to-fill along with the financial metrics can serve to stimulate a team of faculty to work toward a goal of higher retention.

Once a goal has been established through metrics, the team can approach the goal through a change process. Normally this begins by determining the cause for change. Here, another type of metric can be helpful. Information gathered through exit surveys or exit interviews can provide valuable insight into why faculty are leaving the organization. These findings may be difficult to accept, and depending on the findings, they may also be difficult to address in the current culture. Yet, just as articulating the goal is important, sharing the results of the exit information is important. How such results are communicated and to whom are significant decisions for an organization.

Engaging the faculty as "stakeholders" in the discussion of the findings is imperative. Although some may deny the need for change, recalling the cost of turnover may be convincing in such cases. Brainstorming how change might occur can be helpful to generating ideas and engaging the stakeholders. Using a skilled facilitator to identify possible ways to impact the exit information may be advantageous. The point is that identifying the goal, the means to accomplish it, as well as the barriers requires engagement of the faculty in the department or division for a long-term solution to be effective.

In addition to engaging faculty to improve retention, academic administrators may need to review their role in supporting faculty. It is common for supervisors to directly impact employee satisfaction and their desire to stay or leave. A supervisor's interest in the orientation of staff to a new organization, currently referred to as "on boarding," and subsequent inquiry into employee adjustments expresses an interest in the employee's success. Transferring this approach to bringing new faculty into an AHSC can be equally beneficial. While faculty tend to be self-motivated, awareness of the support that they may need and providing that support can make the difference in faculty retention. It may also give the academic administrator insight into changes that can and should be made in the organization to better improve overall retention.

Appointing Department Chairs and Directors

Another trend in AHSC staffing is hiring new department chairs and center directors. In a 2009 study conducted by William T. Mallon, EdD, and April Corrice of the AAMC, it was noted that "[d]eans appear satisfied with many aspects of the leadership search process, but less so with outcomes in achieving a more diverse leadership team."[5] Deans for the most part are satisfied with the search process, performance of the committee, duration of the search, and quality of the pool and finalists. There appears to be less satisfaction with the number of finalists who were women or racial/ethnic minorities. In response to these data, an individual AHSC may find it valuable to review its own data and address the desire for a more diverse faculty and academic leadership through a strategic initiative with a change-process supported by specific human resources policies.

Generational and Institutional Trends

It is important to address at least one "elephant in the room" as retention rates are being studied – the "generation" phenomenon. Research has noted generational differences in values.[6,7] If AHSCs cannot identify ways to accommodate these values, talent may seek other alternatives where their values will be supported. Developing both an institutional culture and specific human resources policies aimed at responding to generational differences, including differences in attitudes toward such issues as work-life balance, telecommuting, and flexible scheduling, will be essential if AHSCs are to succeed in attracting and retaining talented and diverse faculty and staff.

Two growing and related trends within AHSCs that must be addressed through human resource policies are the need to monitor, report, and manage conflicts of interest; and the necessity of a clear and consistent policy on industry relations, primarily the pharmaceutical and medical device industries. These trends are being driven by more stringent regulatory requirements affecting research and clinical activities, ethical concerns regarding research integrity and patient protections, and scrutiny from a variety of external and internal groups. Conflict-of-interest issues are addressed in greater detail in Chapter 5.

At Penn State University, conflict-of-interest disclosure is managed electronically, with disclosed conflicts going to a review committee for consideration as needed. Clear policies define the individual faculty members' responsibilities for disclosing any potential conflicts, as well as the consequences of failure to disclose or properly manage conflicts. If necessary, progressive discipline can be used as needed to bring faculty members into compliance with the policy. As the scope of clinical research continues to grow at AHSCs, managing potential conflicts of interest while supporting research aimed at the development and testing of new devices and therapeutic agents will require increasing attention from a variety of perspectives, including human resource policies and personnel management.

At Penn State Hershey, the industry relations policy has been developed, implemented, and refined through a consultative process engaging stakeholders at the AHSC, including department chairs, senior management, and the Medical Center Physician Advisory Council. Once broad-based consensus was reached, a uniform policy was developed using individual department policies as a starting point; where department policies varied, the institutional policy in most cases adopted the most stringent restrictions. Interestingly, as the policy has been revised, it has become more specific and more stringent on the basis of feedback from stakeholders themselves.

As with conflict-of-interest policies, the issues surrounding industry relations can be complex, since some types of interactions with industry can be beneficial in advancing research, education, and patient care. The goal of the industry relations policy is to clearly define which types of interaction with industry are permitted or even encouraged, as well as what activities are prohibited or restricted. The policy addresses such issues as participation in industry-sponsored speakers' bureaus and educational conferences; acceptance of gifts, meals, honoraria, and travel expenses paid for by industry; the use of free samples provided by industry representatives; interactions with industry representatives; and the presence of industry marketing and educational materials in patient care settings.

Because the industry relations policy has broad-based support and "buy-in" from faculty, the need for active enforcement of the policy through punitive or disciplinary action is minimized. Department chairs are expected to clarify the policy to faculty members when needed. Cases requiring any sort of disciplinary action or administrator involvement beyond that level have been extremely rare.

Administration and Regulatory Compliance

A somewhat different situation emerges when one looks at the same institution's experiences with policies regarding timely documentation of patient encounters in the electronic medical record. Responding to regulatory concerns, Penn State Hershey has developed policies aimed at eliminating the problem of unsigned orders and patient notes. Physicians and providers are aware that violation of the policies can carry serious consequences, both for the individual and the institution. Despite the potentially serious consequences of violating these policies, enforcement has on some occasions required progressive disciplinary actions, including temporary suspension without pay and loss of privileges. This can occur despite the fact that mechanisms are in place to notify providers of any patient records that are overdue or nearing the overdue mark.

Why are disciplinary actions more frequent in compliance issues than industry relations? A number of possibilities present themselves, including the fact that the electronic records systems are simply more accurate in identifying violations, whereas non-compliance with aspects of the industry relations policy might escape detection more readily. Another possible explanation is that because the process of policy development has in the second case been, by necessity, driven by leadership and implemented more rapidly, physicians do not perceive themselves as stakeholders in the policy in the same way as with the industry relations policy.

Addressing Emerging Trends

Numerous other trends in academic medicine – and in health care more broadly – are likely to demand organizational responses that include the development and implementation of appropriate human resource policies and management tools. The rapidly evolving health-care system alone brings with it many challenges including changing reimbursement models, a growing trend toward integrated delivery systems, new models of care, and dramatic transformations in both medical and information technology. In the realm of information technology alone, such developments as the widespread adoption of electronic health records and the burgeoning use of social media require the development of human resource policies that establish clear expectations for employees regarding confidentiality, patient privacy, and professional ethics and responsibility. In addition to the challenges facing all health-care systems, AHSCs are also confronted by an equally complex array of issues relating to their educational and research missions.

As technology, research funding, reimbursement schedules, and patient demands change, these emerging issues will present challenges to AHSCs. Applying consistent, effective human resource management tools can play a critical role in enabling AHSCs to respond effectively to these and other issues.

Understanding the challenges, identifying appropriate goals, recognizing barriers, engaging participants who are stakeholders, applying change processes, assessing the results with metrics, communicating the results, and modifying the changes as needed will keep our institutions viable and sustainable for the future.

Author's Personal Reflections

We say that our greatest strength is our employees. It's extraordinarily important to identify ways to recruit and retain both faculty and staff, and to ensure their ongoing training and education as well. It's an enormous investment to get people on board, and to provide them resources to be continuously effective. We want to be sure they're successful as individuals, but also in teams and across the institution. Turnover is expensive, both in terms of direct and indirect costs. There's the basic cost of replacing these individuals in terms of search process, but there are also costs from the vacancy and training. More important, when someone leaves, they leave with institutional knowledge and history.

One lesson I've learned in my position is how important it is to get out of the dean's office or executive suite, and really go directly to the employees. I try to be very direct in asking for their viewpoint or feedback, which I find extraordinarily productive. Some of the most gratifying things I do are to meet with employees over breakfast and go to departmental meetings, where I can sit face to face with faculty and staff, and hear directly from them about where things are going well, and where we have opportunities for improvement. In numerous instances, terrific ideas have been generated in education, research, patient care, and community service. These are conversations where I can explain why certain institutional decisions have been made, but also where I can listen, and find out what the impact of those decisions has been upon the institution and the individuals that work in it, and find ways to refine and improve those policies. For example, we had a situation where a number of faculty members were very upset about an existing policy. We set up a series of meetings with the faculty, so they would have a chance to voice their concerns and offer suggestions. We collected all the data we could about the impact of the policy, and then we collected external data from other institutions. We put a group together to review the information, and we emphasized the need for transparency. As a group, we came to consensus on an approach that made the best sense for the institution. It built a tremendous amount of trust, and it made policy decisions much more acceptable. Most important, this process allowed the organization to move forward in an environment where everyone had a chance to be heard, everyone had a chance to see what we were doing, and why we were doing it, and how others were doing it. So they felt there was a general fairness in the process.

We've also embraced strategic planning in a way where it's not an obligation, but a tool for us to move the institution forward. We have a vision that's focused on education, research, patient care, and community service, and we consider how we can make a contribution in our region, at the national level, and beyond. We have unique attributes here because we're fully integrated as an academic institution. At the institutional level, we want to make a difference in terms of wellness, education, and the economy. We also want to develop and acquire new knowledge, because we don't just teach and provide health care. We also conduct research that translates to new patient care and services.

As a leader, it's gratifying to see all these elements come together and see the institution flourish, and to see the success of our programs, the quality of our service, and the intellectual legacy we've developed together. It's also satisfying to see the new physical structures that are here as a result of collaboration – the new buildings and facilities. If I were to offer advice to anyone entering a leadership position at an academic health center, it would be to remember to keep your focus on the big picture, and to do everything possible to support your employees so they can be successful in their work. You can't micromanage in this job; you have to make sure the people who work for you can be successful, because if that happens, you'll be successful, and so will your institution. Try to develop the best strategic plan you can, with the input of your faculty and staff. Recruit and hire the smartest people you can, and make sure they understand their role within that plan. Then go out and get the big resources those people need.

The challenges surrounding access, quality of care, and cost are enormous, but so are the opportunities. Ultimately, we have the ability to improve the health and well-being of all those that we serve. I can't think of a more exciting time to be doing what I do. We're truly taking basic research and translating it to patient care in ways we never imagined, and I really believe that we will have an incredible impact on health. We're improving our processes of care, so we can focus on preventing and maintaining health, and we are improving quality and access. I hope we'll get much more efficient, so we can lower the cost of care per individual as well.

Ultimately, it's all about people; it's about ensuring that the people we serve – our students, our patients, and the community – are touched in a positive way by our presence. I still see patients one afternoon a week, which is always a great reminder as to why we're doing these things. But it's also about the people who work here. It's important that they have an opportunity to make contributions, and also have job security and personal fulfillment through their work.

—HLP

Acknowledgments

Donald Martin, MD, Professor of Anesthesiology and Associate Dean for Administration at Penn State College of Medicine, contributed to this chapter.

References

1. Ulrich D. *Human Resource Champions*. Boston, MA: Harvard Business School Press; 1997. p. 233.
2. Centers for Disease Control and Prevention. *Tobacco Statistics*. Available at: www.cdc.gov/tobacco/data_statistics/fact_sheets/health_effects/effects_cig_smoking/index.htm (accessed April 11, 2011).
3. American Lung Association. *General Tobacco Facts*. Available at: www.lungusa.org/

stop-smoking/about-smoking/facts-figures/general-smoking-facts.html (accessed April 11, 2011).

4. www.aamc.org
5. Mallon WT, Corrice A. *Leadership Recruiting Practices in Academic Medicine: how medical schools and teaching hospitals search for new department chairs and center directors*. Washington, DC: Association of American Medical Colleges; 2009. p. 7.
6. Raines C. *Beyond Generation X*. Menlo Park, CA: Crisp Publications; 1997.
7. Zemke R, Raines C, Filapczak B. *Generations at Work: managing the clash of veterans, Boomers, Xers, and Nexters in your workplace*. New York: American Management Association; 2000.

Trainee and Student Policy

Wilsie S. Bishop and M. David Linville Jr.

From the Editor

The students and trainees at academic health science centers are arguably the most important – and most vulnerable – groups of individuals to oversee. This chapter focuses on policies that impact their well-being and strategies to enhance implementation.

—SAW

Policies are maps that allow one to navigate bureaucratic systems while providing structure and limits to broad-based practices and role expectations. While Chapter 7 has addressed human resource (HR) issues broadly, the focus here is on student and trainee issues specifically. Comprehensive policies for students and trainees provide parameters for safe clinical practice, consistency in educational oversight, and guidelines for acceptable standards of behavior. In other words, an institution's policies represent a consistent and logical framework for administrative action. Policies that have been developed with input from the affected constituents, reviewed, and revised as needed are extremely useful to an administrator for decision making. The course of action dictated by a policy is one that theoretically has been agreed to and endorsed. Policies assure actions within existing federal and state statutes. Further, carefully crafted policies should evidence a standard of practice that is reasonable and prudent as well as expected of thoughtful administrators.

Without policies, an administrator must use his/her own judgment and often decide what actions are to be taken on the cusp of a crisis without benefit of judicious discussion and alternatives. Carefully crafted policies provide students, residents, and other trainees with sets of expectations for normally acceptable behavior that guide conduct during training, and also set parameters that will support reasonable and prudent actions in professional practice.

Accrediting organizations for all professional health sciences programs have expectations for specific policies to achieve compliance with accreditation standards. Policies codify "ways of doing business" and provide protocols for consistency. Some standards, like those of the Commission on Collegiate Nursing Education, specifically point out that program and academic policies of the parent institution must be congruent. The Commission on Accreditation in Physical Therapy Education emphasizes policies that protect the rights, privileges, and safety of individuals within the program and also look for consistency with institutional policies of a like nature. The Liaison Committee on Medical Education describes the purpose and responsibility of accreditation as "a process of quality assurance in postsecondary education that determines whether an institution or program meets established standards for function, structure, and performance. The accreditation process also fosters institutional and program improvement."[1]

This chapter explores the types of trainee and student policies that are essential for academic health science centers (AHSCs), the process for policy development and dissemination, and offers some perspectives on how policies facilitate the academic and administrative enterprise.

Types of Policies

Policies for health profession trainees and students fall into two major types: those that are universally applied to all students/trainees at the institution, generally found in university policy manuals, and those that are discipline-specific. In turn, discipline-specific policies can usually be grouped into four basic categories: (1) academic policies that provide guidelines for student admission and progression through academic programs; (2) behavioral or conduct policies that offer oversight of student behavior and extramural activities, such as student organizations; (3) policies promoting trainee safety that include regulations mandated by state and federal laws; and (4) emerging policies that address societal trends and their implications for health professionals.

In most AHSCs, discipline-specific policies require review and approval at a level above the individual college. This review ascribes university and/or system sanction to actions that will later be taken at the college level. Because of the nature of clinical training in affiliated institutions, academic policies must also be consistent with policies promulgated by affiliated clinical institutions. There will be times when the affiliated institution's policy will inform the university's policy and/or take precedence over the university's policy.

A review of policies found across AHSCs reveals significant consistency for students and trainees. Student policies in large part focus on academic requirements, professionalism, and expected student behaviors; they also cover personal health and safety. Policies for residents must also incorporate employment rules and expectations. AHSC policies are readily found on existing websites and many have links to training programs or activities that teach the intent and reinforce the content of the policy. In the process of policy development, the old adage that it is not necessary to "reinvent the wheel" applies. AHSCs can draw upon a wealth of existing information, but before modifying a policy from another AHSC, the professional and appropriate action is to contact that institution and ask permission to use and/or modify a policy or technique.

Academic Policies

Academic policies are discipline-specific and provide guidelines for student admission and progression through the program to graduation. As such, these policies establish minimally acceptable standards for program enrollment and completion. Academic policies may consider academic probation, dismissal, and appeal processes; promotion requirements; class and clinical absences; withdrawals and leaves of absence from clinical training; general course and grading policies, proficiency evaluations and grade appeals; academic honors; and academic misconduct. Academic policies may also outline specific responsibilities for faculty members, setting appropriate levels of supervision for trainees with respect to education level and clinical setting. Such policies allow clear understanding of the responsibilities of the faculty member and trainee. Essentially, these policies provide students and faculty a roadmap for admission to, and successful graduation from, the program. It is important that academic policies reflect expectations of appropriate licensing boards and professional organizations that will impact student future prospects.

An essential component of admissions policy relates to compliance with the Americans with Disabilities Act (ADA). Title II of the Americans with Disabilities Act of 1990 (Public Law 101-336) expanded the Scope of Section 504 of the Rehabilitation Act of 1973 (Public Law 93-112) extending protection to individuals with disabilities. As a result, clinical programs identified technical standards or essential functions that formed a basis for defining reasonable accommodations for people with disabilities. Most medical schools, along with other clinical disciplines, have developed such standards that reflect the needs of their programs and include processes to manage admission to, and progression through, these clinical programs to graduation. Common to most highly clinical and hands-on programs such as medicine, dentistry, and nursing are the following essential functions: observation, communication, motor function and coordination, intellectual abilities (conceptual, integrative, and quantitative), and behavioral/social attributes. Some institutions require students to sign off on a sheet describing the technical standards with an assertion that they have "read and understand" and are in "compliance" with the standards. Policies often include information on how students may request accommodation for disabilities through the centralized college or university that deals directly with student disability services.

The ADA is one example of a regulatory policy with specific implications for professional clinical programs and requires, in part, a discipline-specific approach for a comprehensive policy. The comprehensive nature of the ADA means that the professional colleges are subject to other sections of the act that are under the control of the larger institution such as reasonable accommodation for employees and barrier-free accessibility issues.

Health and Safety Policies

These policies are established to promote personal safety and well-being, and are typically not limited in scope to students and trainees. Often, such policies are grounded in mandates from state and federal statutes. Occupational Exposure to Hazardous Chemicals, a US Department of Labor and Occupational Safety and Health Administration (OSHA) promulgated rule (29 CFR 1910.1450) released on January 31, 1990, addresses occupational exposure to chemicals in laboratories. This rule requires establishing standard operating procedures for handling and disposal of certain chemicals and appointing a chemical hygiene officer for departments using these chemicals. Likewise, OSHA's Bloodborne Pathogen Standard (29 CFR 1910.1030) requires the development of an Exposure Control Plan and appropriate education of all individuals with potential exposure to dangerous body fluids. States also have varying needle safety legislation that must be reflected in student policies.

In addition to having education programs for students and trainees, it is vital that the culture of the institution support strict adherence to these standards. It is unfortunate that students and employees often feel they are being treated in a dismissive manner for reporting exposures to bloodborne pathogens.

Examples of other federal and state laws and regulations include those that provide oversight of the research process, the protection of human subjects, and radiation safety. Similar policies related to safety include those specifying criminal background checks, health insurance requirements, and immunizations for students and faculty. Most institutions have an office of environmental health and safety, which provides some level of oversight to these policies; however, it is the responsibility of the health professions program to assure that the university policies are appropriately adapted to the needs of the profession and consistent with similar policies at clinical affiliates.

Duty hour policies also provide appropriate structure for student and resident trainees. Specific adherence to mandates for maximum work hours addresses trainee well-being and demonstrates commitment to patient safety and a supportive educational environment.

Additional health and safety policies for students can incorporate ways to address chemical impairment, crisis response, and intervention. Many institutions have policies that establish committees to assist students in dealing with impairment and crisis. Appropriate mechanisms for identification and intervention should be incorporated into policy. Careful consideration must be made to include adequate flexibility to address specific needs of individual students. Similar to academic policies, impairment and crisis policies should reflect expectations of appropriate licensing boards and professional organizations.

Policies built from federal and state regulations are a very important step in assuring compliance with laws focused on the protection of health, safety, and personal security. Students and trainees need to demonstrate awareness and understanding of these policies through completion of specialized training, successful testing on the subject matter, and the ability to function in a clinical setting in accord with the principles of the policies. While academic policies set parameters for program admission, retention, and graduation, and professional policies shape behavior and attitudes, safety-related policies protect the health and welfare of the students and their patients.

Professionalism Policies

Policies related to student conduct and the oversight of student behavior and extramural activities, such as student organizations, relate to professionalism. These policies are most often implemented and enforced through the offices of student affairs. Professionalism policies address student conduct, honor codes, dress codes, and expectations relating to professional behavior. In addition, student rights and responsibilities, mistreatment prevention, and grievance policies are usually grouped under the professionalism rubric. Most institutions will have sexual harassment prevention policies and training opportunities. Professional schools should assure that students, residents, and other trainees have appropriate training in sexual harassment prevention and know to whom they can report suspected abuse.

An institution has the opportunity to shape the culture and values of its students through the type and nature of policies that focus on professionalism. In discussing topics related to professional dress and conduct, humanism, professional service, and continuing education, values and expectations are communicated and reinforced as part of the training process. Institutions are able to "brand" their philosophies and values by describing and reinforcing specific professional behaviors.

Central to the philosophy of professional work within a health science discipline is confidentiality. The Health Insurance Portability and Accountability Act of 1996 (P.L.104-191) requires policies related to assurance of confidentiality for the security and privacy of health information. The Family Educational Rights and Privacy Act of 1974 (the Buckley Amendment) generates policies related to the confidentiality of student information.

While these conduct and behavior policies are very important in informing students and residents, they may be viewed as elementary and brushed aside by very busy clinicians focused on patient care. One particularly helpful and entertaining teaching device that draws attention to some of these policies can be found on the Virginia Commonwealth University's School of Medicine site for "Standards of Professional Attire." At that site, students and residents are given the opportunity to "Dress a Doc."[2] In paper doll fashion, the participant is able to add and subtract clothing and accessories and receive immediate feedback on the appropriateness for the clinical area. While such devices may be challenged for their simplicity, they do provide an effective way of providing generally accepted standards in a way that helps the student/resident internalize the intent of the policy.

Virginia Commonwealth uses other tools to help teach the policy content in areas that focus on professional and interpersonal behaviors. The "standards and policies" relating to "humanism," provide a series of case studies for teaching and discussion.[3] This independent learning opportunity allows students and residents to think through some critical issues in a hypothetical environment before dealing with them in the clinical setting. Faculty time does not have to be expended teaching the "obvious." However, there can be assurances that students and residents have had an opportunity to consider and internalize some important concepts related to their professional behavior. A professional culture can be maintained without mundane instruction in the "obvious."

It is important to realize that acceptance of policies may be very much dependent on an individual's ability to understand the tenets of the policy. With today's technology, the process of providing policies in a variety of formats to facilitate understanding can be easily achieved. Institutions might consider, in addition to providing a copy of the policy in a straightforward format, providing a document on frequently asked questions, a report from the current literature related to the topic, and a slide version of the policy with key points identified on each slide. This approach is based on a belief that there is certain information that can be taught and reinforced with a self-learning strategy. On the other end of the spectrum is the approach taken by Vanderbilt University for their Master of Public Health program. The academic policies are identified in essentially two pages of web documentation.[4] Policies are briefly stated, direct, and definitive. Should students desire further information they can contact faculty or staff for more details.

The University of California Davis applies a distributive approach to informing students, residents, and faculty about specific policies. This institution incorporates policies at a location on their website in a "need to know" format. For example, the policy related to the National Institutes of Health's (NIH) "Public Access Policy" is located at the university library website.[5] An "overview" of the policy is presented with Internet links to PubMed and the National Library of Medicine, as well as the "frequently asked questions" link from the NIH website to provide detailed information on the federal requirements. After the reader has the appropriate background information, the website then directs them to information on how to comply, how to submit a manuscript to NIH, and how to cite the article. Further information and help are provided by a series of links to related websites. The Virginia Commonwealth University "teaching" website provides the policy and ways to internalize it. The UC Davis point-of-information website approach provides the policy and significant supporting documentation and online resources. Both examples illustrate the importance of using technology to communicate a policy and the resources for understanding and complying with it.

Emerging Policies

The academic environment is in a constant state of change. While policies help to structure the environment, some issues emerge over time with the advent of new technology, development of new federal regulations, or in response to trends or patterns of activities that develop on a campus. As an example, in the early 1990s, AHSCs had to develop policies that responded to OSHA standards for bloodborne pathogen exposures as scientific evidence clearly determined that old ways of handling blood and body fluids were no longer safe for health-care workers. Chemical safety, radiation safety, and other environmentally based policies have also emerged over time as new information and standards of practice have evolved.

While new scientific knowledge has been the driver of health and safety policies, societal trends and the impact of technology are now bringing to light the need for policies to regulate the use of social media. Even as recently as 5 years ago, it would have been impossible to identify the impact that social networking would have on today's society. Emerging policies address such societal trends and their implications for health professionals, as well as respond to the changing environment within AHSCs.

Several institutions are now developing "social networking" policies. A study conducted by researchers at The George Washington University School of Medicine assessed all 132 accredited US medical schools for their presence on social media sites. This study revealed that 100% (n = 132) of US medical schools had websites and 126 (95.45%) of the schools had a Facebook presence. However, only 13 (10%) of the schools had guidelines or policies that explicitly mentioned social media.[6] The focus of the policies in these schools, as of March

2010, ranged from behaviors/comments that should be avoided, to confidentiality and protection of patient and student information, to how to use blogs and other media for health education and as a teaching tool. The predominant focus of these policies is on professionalism and controlling content. The growing use of blog sites by health-care institutions and the personal habits of students will undoubtedly result in a growing need to address standards of use for social media by all health professions.

Policy Development Process

Step One: Define the Issue or Problem

The development process begins with recognizing the need for a written policy. Often this occurs when a dean or vice president faces a decision that would be easier to make if a policy existed. Policies in this case provide authority for administrative actions. Policies that are developed as a result of state or federal mandates may not need to go through each step of the process, but questions of implementation, costs, and authority must still be answered. Other policies emerge to set behavior parameters which in turn define acceptable standards of behavior and practice for health professions students.

Step Two: Gather Necessary Information on the Issue

It is often helpful to identify a committee that will gather necessary information and serve as a writing team to create a new policy. Prior to writing, a careful search of available resources will provide facts to support the policy as well as examples of how others have approached the issue. Since accreditation agencies and professional associations are policy oriented, they may also be a source of sample policy language. The writing team should determine if other health professions colleges within their university have policies that address the issue. The team may also find appropriate policies at other health science centers; but looking first within one's own division of health sciences will provide policies that have been reviewed and deemed to be in compliance with the university's and its governing board's policies. The writing team should discuss the issue with the dean, colleagues, faculty, and students to solicit varying perspectives on the issue before drafting a policy for further review. The team should review state and federal laws and regulations that may pertain to the issue. Consultation with university counsel before the draft is circulated will help assure that the proposed policy is legally acceptable and conforms to all university and governing board guidelines.

Step Three: Discuss and Debate at the College Level

The input of affected parties and stakeholders early in the policy development process is critical to successful adoption and implementation. The writing committee should use student government or student professional associations or other student/resident governance models to obtain input from multiple perspectives about the proposed policy. Faculty and, at times, staff should be actively involved in reviewing and refining the policy as it makes its way to the point of approval. Questions that should be considered at this point in the process are:

- Is the content within the scope of the college's authority?
- Is it consistent with college, university, and, where applicable, existing policies of the governing board?
- Is it consistent with local, state, and federal law? The US and the state's constitution?
- Is it consistent with the mission of the college?
- Does it support the college's goals or objectives?
- Does the proposed policy represent good educational practice?
- Are any of the requirements or prohibitions stated in the policy arbitrary, discriminatory, or capricious?
- Does the policy adequately address the original issue/problem?
- Is the policy clearly focused on one issue/problem?
- Can the policy be reasonably administered within the current organizational structure?
- Will there be costs involved in implementation? If so, who is responsible for bearing the costs of implementation?

Step Four: Write the Policy

After reaching consensus on policy content, the new policy should be drafted in a format that is consistent with other policies for the college and university, as well as be written in a clear and succinct style. Jargon, acronyms, and legal terms should be avoided. Any embedded timelines for action or response should be clearly stated to avoid confusion. If exceptions to time lines based on school holidays and vacations are allowed, these should be clearly identified in the policy. Policy statements cannot address every nuance of situations that will arise in the future; therefore, they should be stated as broadly as possible to allow for adjustment to fit special circumstances as needed. If a university or governing board require a standard format, it should be followed. (Remember that a policy should be broad-based and avoid referring to specific individuals by name.) Guidelines that accompany a policy should provide details on specific processes and implementation. Guidelines translate a policy into action and will include specific process information and other information that may be subject to change.

Step Five: Circulate the Draft Policy for Review

Even the most comprehensive process of policy development may omit an obvious and needed component. If time permits, and good planning should provide adequate time for review, circulate the policy to those stakeholders who will be affected by it – faculty, students, residents, as well as higher levels of administration who must ultimately approve and support the implementation of the policy.

The policy should be revised based on the feedback received from the questions, comments, and suggestions garnered during this review.

Step Six: Adopt the Policy

The appropriate governing bodies within and outside of the college and the AHSC should formally adopt the policy. For some policies, it will be appropriate to have approval or endorsement by student governance organizations, faculty senates or other governing body, as well as administrative councils of the college. Policy statements should note when approval has been given and by whom.

After the policy is approved at the college level, it should be forwarded to the vice president for health affairs and/or president for institutional and subsequent governing board action. Again, the policy statement should note when and by whom approval has been given and an implementation date. Subsequent revisions of the policy should also be recorded with the date and level of approval.

Step Seven: Communicate the Policy

For a policy to be effective, it needs to be widely distributed among those who will be affected by it. Most accrediting organizations expect that policies are readily available and broadly disseminated to students, faculty, and others. At a minimum, policies should be included in both paper and electronic publications. Some health professions programs also compile and publish policies in a student handbook that is distributed to students during their initial orientation to the program. One further step that could prove very useful should a student appeal a policy decision is to include a final page in the policy manual that requires that the student sign a sheet indicating he/she has received and reviewed the policies provided by the program. For example, students matriculating to the radiography program at East Tennessee State University's College of Clinical and Rehabilitative Health Sciences sign a statement of understanding which includes specific references to policies and program expectations.[7] At the Louisiana State University Health Sciences Center's School of Allied Health Professionals, students sign a statement verifying they have read and understand the policy manual given to all entering students.[8] These forms serve as a checkpoint to ensure students are well informed and acknowledge review of necessary policies.

An additional advantage of wide distribution of the policy is ensured implementation. Faculty and students should be aware of policies to provide a guideline for action and instruction for situations addressed by the policies. An occupational blood exposure is both serious and, for the most part, outside of the norm. A faculty member needs to be able to respond immediately to the situation. The student or resident will need to know what actions to take in the event of such an incident. A clear policy that discusses immediate first-aid intervention and reporting responsibilities is essential. If the exposure occurs in an affiliated clinical setting, the responsibility of the clinical affiliate and that of the university should be distinguished so each institution is aware of the extent of its liability. A plan for follow-up interviews, serological testing (by whom and financial responsibility), follow-up to a positive or negative test, appropriate paperwork, and consent forms should all be included in a policy to guide action by the person with the exposure as well as the instructor. A blood exposure incident policy is one of the most complex policies for an institution to develop. In addition to applying the federal regulations that govern an institution's handling of bloodborne pathogens, the policy must identify immediate actions that provide for the health and mental well-being of the individual who has had the exposure, as well as management of the risk for the institution related to the exposure. This type of policy must have sections that specifically address risk management including appropriate serological testing, retention of records, and compliance with all Health Insurance Portability and Accountability Act standards. Policies such as this must also include information about fiscal responsibilities for any serological tests as well as any necessary follow-up.

Faculty who are functioning in a clinical situation with a fully developed policy that addresses an unanticipated blood exposure will be armed with specific guidance that enables them to respond in a consistent manner, providing immediate and long-term support for the exposed individual, and reducing the legal liabilities of the university. Without an adequate policy, decisions may be delayed and the institution becomes vulnerable. Additionally, a student or employee who may be in need of clinical and psychological intervention will be left without having adequate university resources made available.

Some policies require assurance that faculty and students are knowledgeable and aware of their obligations to fulfill it. In such instances, an institution may develop specific training programs for students, residents, and faculty. Certainly a bloodborne pathogens/biosafety policy requires training and evidence of understanding for all faculty and students prior to their being in situations that could result in an exposure. Other policies that require training include those related to safety, such as radiation safety and isotope usage, and chemical and laboratory hazards, as well as those that are federally or state mandated such as training policies on prevention of sexual harassment or other forms of discrimination.

If training is instituted, it will be necessary to develop a record-keeping system that monitors when it is completed and when it needs to be rescheduled. All individuals identified for training must be informed of the importance of the policy and given an adequate amount of time to complete it. If the training is done in a classroom setting, enough sessions should be scheduled at times that will accommodate all those who must attend. Responsibility for assuring training and maintaining training records should be assigned to the individual most directly in charge of the activity.

Training for some policies may be done in an online, self-tutorial format. Such training modules facilitate consistent training for all affected by the policy. Online training modules may also have the ability to monitor and confirm those who have successfully completed it with a "certificate of completion," sending reminders of the need for annual or subsequent retraining or updates.

Step Eight: Evaluation and Revision

Very few policies "get it right" the first time. In fact, policies are dynamic and should be evaluated on a regular basis to determine if they are accomplishing the desired goals that originally prompted their development. If policies do not have sunset provisions, a schedule for policy review should be established and an individual responsible for oversight named. When an individual has oversight responsibility, policies are reviewed on a regular basis and can be modified to improve future courses of action. Without proper review and oversight, policies can become out of date or contradictory to other policies within an institution over time.

If a policy is to be revised, many of the steps in the development phase of the policy should be retraced. All affected parties should be aware of changes and have input into modifications. Revised policies should be annotated and include dates of modification and by whom the modifications have been approved. Historical data with the original dates of approval should be retained. Obviously, it is imperative to disseminate the revised policy to all whom it impacts. Policy handbooks and training modules will need to be updated.

Step Nine: Policy Implementation, Enforcement, and Exceptions

Policies should have an identified date as to when they become effective. In the policy development process, it is important to allow adequate time for discussion and full review by the various approving authorities. Those responsible for implementing the policy should consider when it would be most logical to introduce it – for example, at the beginning of a new semester or new fiscal year. Implementation should also take into account when and how the policy will be distributed. If an institution does not use electronic media for policy distribution, implementation may need to be delayed until the next edition of a catalog, student handbook, or policy manual. Consultation with university counsel concerning any contractual or legal considerations related to implementation is advisable.

Policies must be consistently and uniformly administered. Actions taken that are inconsistent or arbitrarily applied may create precedent that will impact future administration of the policy and will also put the institution at risk. In other words, institutions sometimes bring lawsuits upon themselves simply by not following their own policies – those that have been written and developed by the institution. For example, the *New York Times* reported the filing of a wrongful death lawsuit in Alabama against a provost in which it is claimed he did not follow a life-safety policy he helped develop for early detection of individuals experiencing emotional, mental, or psychological instability.[9]

While recognizing the importance of consistency in policy implementation, administrators must have the flexibility to consider exceptions in specific cases. A sage administrator once said that if all one did was administering policy as written, there would be no need for the administrator. While the statement may be a bit of hyperbole, it should be noted that there are times when it is more important to make an exception to policy than to blindly follow it. Exceptions to policy, when they occur, should be based on sound and rational review of the situation involved. Decisions at higher levels of administration that are contrary to those made by faculty or other administrators in the chain of command must be communicated back down the chain so that those involved in enforcement are aware that the exception was made and why. Exceptions to policy then can become "teaching points" and catalysts for policy revision, as appropriate. Exceptions to policies for students and trainees most often occur when the vice president or president must review a decision related to admission, retention, and progression in the program. In such cases, the administrative chain should be aware that the decisions are being made in response to carefully developed policies that should be consistently applied to all students. Those most knowledgeable and most directly involved in program administration are making substantive decisions in relation to implementation of policies for students and trainees. Administrative review of policy decisions being made by the vice president and/ or institutional president will most often be only for procedural due process. Due process assures that (1) the policy has been followed and (2) the student's rights have been protected. Written policies should include information on whether or not a decision can be appealed, to whom, the type of appeal (substantive or due process), and the procedure.

Policy Maintenance
• •

As noted throughout this chapter, policies emerge to respond to issues, provide for personal safety, meet federal or state laws and regulations, and set parameters for the academic process and professionalism. Policies are also driven and created by strategy to provide administrative guidance and a framework for consistent, objective responses to regularly occurring events in academia.

When a new school or college is established, the process for development and review is generally comprehensive and systematic, building on existing policies within an institution, accreditation guidelines, and a vision for professional culture consistent with the college's mission and values. For colleges with a foundation of policies already published and available to students and faculty, development often emerges out of necessity to address new federal regulations, aberrant behavior, or standardized practice across disciplinary lines.

It is useful to have a senior administrative officer assigned the responsibility for maintenance of all policies for the college. This officer, often an assistant or associate dean, will ensure that discipline-specific policies are in place and consistent with institutional policies, policies are developed to address all appropriate federal and state requirements, and policies are reviewed, updated, revised, and/or discontinued on a regular review cycle. An additional responsibility for this officer is to ensure that each student has received a copy of all policies for the college and has acknowledged receipt of the policies with a signed affidavit. The officer should maintain a file of the signed affidavits as they may be needed to document that a student was aware of a policy should enforcement of penalties at some future time be necessary.

Box 8.1 Characteristics of Effective Policy for Students and Trainees

✓ Responds to an identified issue or state/federal regulation and is consistent with good academic and professional practice as well as the mission and goals of the health sciences center.

✓ Is consistent with expectations of accrediting bodies.

✓ Is consistent with the authority delegated to the institution by its board of trustees or governing body.

✓ Is reviewed and adopted through proper channels, including those stakeholders directly affected by its implementation.

✓ Conforms to all legal and constitutional rights and requirements.

✓ Is communicated to the persons responsible for its implementation and to those who will be affected by it.

✓ Is reviewed and modified as needed on a periodic basis.

Conclusion

Policies are useful to an institution in so much as they reflect the corporate sense of how the institution does its business, and the extent to which key stakeholders are involved in their development and approval. As noted in Box 8.1, effective policies share key characteristics, and they should be widely communicated and available to all of those affected by them. Equally important, as policies are implemented, they should be consistently applied, revised, and updated.

Author's Personal Reflections

Effective policies are developed by engaging the people who will be affected by them. You bring together people with diverse points of view, particularly in an academic health center, because you have to represent all the various interests at stake. You have to create a culture of consensus. You want people to buy into the concept, and how it might be useful to them in their day-to-day lives. Policies aren't meant to be prohibitive; they're supposed to allow you to give the authority to work better.

At East Tennessee State University, we developed a Crisis Intervention Policy in a very constructive way. We brought together the people we believed needed to be part of decision making and problem solving in a time of crisis. And through the process of developing the policy, we were able to anticipate potential problems, develop useful protocols, and perform environmental scanning and risk management. We actually took several steps toward preventing crises from occurring in the first place. For instance, we decided that we needed to install siren towers around campus that could issue voice instructions in times of crisis or danger. When tornadoes tore through Tennessee, we already had a protocol in place, and we set off the sirens minutes before a tornado hit our medical campus. We would not have been prepared to do that if we had not developed the Crisis Intervention Policy. We anticipated problems, and we authorized the right people to act, and as a result, nobody was harmed when disaster struck.

Our policies have helped our students become more aware of their own personal responsibility and accountability in a crisis situation. Students realize that they're part of a larger university community, and when they see a potential danger situation, they understand their obligation, and they know how to report their concerns. We're preventing situations from getting out of control. For example, we have something called a "Gold Alert," where we can send out text messages and e-mails, to alert everyone on campus of a particular situation.

Policy development might not excite everyone, but I love to get the right people around a table working together on solving problems. When you get people clicking, and when they're all focused on the same problem, and working from the same mission-frame of reference, you can generate a lot of excitement. People have to feel that they have the ability to take action, and that they have authority, freedom, and resources to do their jobs. When I can get capable, passionate people together who have the necessary authority and adequate resources, I have a pretty good day at the office. I feed on other people's energy and focus. I work with deans of public health, pharmacy, nursing, medicine, and clinical and rehabilitative health sciences. These are all accomplished people in their own right, and each has a significant amount of responsibility. When you get that kind of capability, power, and energy together focused on one topic, such as interprofessional education, you can accomplish a great deal. That's what I find most satisfying about leading an academic health center. I have the opportunity to work with some very bright, high-achieving individuals who are really committed to the work that they're doing. I also get to work with students, and I help to shape the next generation of health-care providers. Together, we can envision a better way to deliver health care, and we can provide our students with the skills, knowledge, and values that they need to practice their professions in a better way. Not many people have that kind of opportunity in life.

In this kind of environment, you have to check your ego at the door. As a leader of an academic health center, you do a lot of coordinating and bringing people together. You have to be able to persuade, empower, and instill the sense of our common mission. I used to be a dean, and I had to let go of some of the characteristics that were so important to me as a dean. You have to realize that somebody else is doing those things now, and you're doing something different. Your job is to help empower people to use those skills that you once used in a more discrete unit. You're working with a much broader palate. Health care is going to evolve and change significantly in the lifetimes of our students. Team-based care is becoming increasingly important as a way to improve outcomes and reduce cost. I believe we will end up with a better patient experience, and health-care providers will be able to practice their craft at maximum level.

—*WSB*

References

1. Liaison Committee on Medical Education (LCME). *Functions and Structure of a Medical School: standards for accreditation of medical education programs leading to the M.D. degree.* LCME; June 2010. Available at: www.lcme.org/overview.htm (accessed January 23, 2011).
2. Virginia Commonwealth University School of Medicine. *Standards and Policies: who needs a dress code?* Available at: www.medschool.vcu.edu/professionalism/standards/dress_a_doc.html (accessed January 23, 2011).

3. Virginia Commonwealth University School of Medicine. *Standards and Policies: humanism*. Available at: www.medschool.vcu.edu/professionalism/standards/humanism.html (accessed January 23, 2011).

4. School of Medicine, Vanderbilt University. *Master of Public Health: academic policies*. Available at: https://medschool.vanderbilt.edu/mph/policies (accessed January 23, 2011).

5. Health Sciences Library, University of California Davis. *NIH Public Access Policy: how to comply*. Available at: www.lib.ucdavis.edu/dept/hsl/resources/other/nihmandate/ (accessed January 23, 2011).

6. Kind T, Genrich G, Sodhi A, *et al.* Social media policies at US medical schools. *Med Educ Online*. 2010; **15**: 10.3402/meo.v15i0.5324.

7. College of Clinical and Rehabilitative Health Sciences. *Radiography Program Student Handbook*. Johnson City: East Tennessee State University; 2010.

8. Department of Clinical Laboratory Sciences. *Student Policies and Procedures: 2011–2012*. Louisiana State University Health Sciences Center, School of Allied Health Professionals; 2011. Available at: http://alliedhealth.lsuhsc.edu/clinicallaboratory/PoliciesAndProcedures.pdf (accessed April 16, 2011).

9. Severson K. University provost is sued over faculty shootings. *New York Times*. January 18, 2011. Available at: www.nytimes.com/2011/01/19/us/19bishop.html?_r=3 (accessed January 23, 2011).

Faculty Accountability

Stephen Smith and Peter Davies

From the Editor

The faculty of academic health science centers are highly educated, independent-thinking professionals. Holding them accountable for their performance, therefore, is no small task. This chapter discusses an approach to faculty accountability that spans a wide range of essential parameters.

—*SAW*

Although academic health science centers (AHSCs) are founded on common principles in different countries, multiple organizational models may be in place resulting in varying faculty accountability emphases. This chapter identifies the common organization models and reviews the key principles that should be addressed by faculties of medicine that are part of any AHSC. Before exploring what those key principles are, it is important to clarify the meaning of the term "faculty accountability."

This chapter uses the term faculty to mean the whole of the academic medicine organization, which might comprise a number of separate schools or institutes. In different models, the accountable person might also oversee the health-care delivery function. In this chapter, the term "faculty accountability" is used to cover the breadth of responsibilities for which the head of a faculty of medicine might be held responsible by his or her superiors, board, or those who appointed him or her. The accountability also extends to a wide range of external bodies such as funders, donors, regulators, and professional organizations whose standards must be adhered to. It also extends to other stakeholders, such as the students who pay for their education, and to the wider community.

The principal element for which the head of the faculty will be responsible is the performance of the organization. That performance is principally measured by: quality (and quantity) of academic output; generation of income to support research activities; and, quality (and quantity) of teaching. In an AHSC, the translation of research and teaching for the benefit of patients, especially in the hospital partner within the AHSC, adds an additional critical dimension to those faculties. This chapter will examine the key components for which the Head of faculty is responsible and must oversee (or delegate) in order to be able to discharge overall accountability.

As noted earlier, depending on the degree of integration between the AHSC and other faculties within the university, different complexities come into play. In terms of faculty accountability, all the faculties – including medicine – should be held to account for ensuring that these links are in place, both at a management level and, crucially, at a practical level where real collaboration takes place for the ultimate benefit of human health.

Dimensions of Faculty Accountability

Accountability can be in a number of directions, or dimensions. It is certainly upward to the university center or the body or board that governs the faculty's activities. It is also downward to those who work within the organization, such as investigators or teaching staff, to provide the necessary leadership and direction. It is also outward to donors and academic or commercial partners, to regulators, to the public, and to those volunteers who participate in trials run by the faculty either on its own or in partnership with its associated hospital(s). Increasingly, it is also to the students who undertake courses at the faculty, who are rightly concerned about the quality of education they receive and pay for.

Faculty accountability can be divided along a continuum of dimensions as shown in Table 9.1.

The remainder of this chapter explores each of these dimensions in turn. The accountable officer will need to bring his or her skills to bear at times in each of them individually, but especially in bringing them together in a complex organization, and across internal and external organizational boundaries to ensure the goals are achieved.

Accountability: Internal Dimensions

Strategic Direction and Leadership

The head of faculty is responsible for providing strategic direction and leadership in the organization. Strategic direction for their division needs to fit with

TABLE 9.1 Dimensions of Faculty Accountability

Internal

Strategic direction and leadership of the faculty, and contributing to the strategic direction and leadership of the wider organization of which it is a part (AHSC, university, and so forth)

Performance management

Risk management

Financial accountability (accounting, regularity, proper use of funds, Accountable Officer)

Staff/human resources

Students

Infrastructure, estates, information technology and so forth, health and safety

Relationships with hospital partner(s) inside the AHSC*

External

Relationships with hospital partner(s) inside and outside the AHSC*

Relationships with other academic institutions

Relationships with donors and commercial partners

Contributing to health policy and health service development – regionally, nationally, and internationally

Regulatory and professional bodies

Reputation/communications

* The relationship with the hospital partner within the AHSC could be external or internal, depending on the nature of the AHSC's structure (AHSC = academic health science center).

the broader or parent organization's goals and strategic aims and plans. The head of faculty needs to ensure that its contribution is also consistent with the plans of other faculties. While the parent organization leads on the wider aspects of ensuring that all the constituent parts cooperate in their shared endeavor, the head of faculty needs to contribute to the collective development of the organization's overall goals. This, in particular, should center on determining the organization's overall strategic goals in health-related research and education, and, where appropriate, patient care services. It should also include how other faculties – such as those in natural and social sciences, engineering, computing and mathematics, the business school, and so forth – contribute to health-related goals. Finally, the head of faculty needs to ensure that mechanisms are in place to coordinate both management activity and practical collaborations between academics across faculties.

A key component of that strategic development is periodic assessments of the faculty's relative strengths and weaknesses, and whether current performance is delivering the necessary progress toward the strategic goals. The periodic assessment should consider whether there are areas where increased resources or attention should be paid to deliver on the strategic goal, or to seek to change its direction. This might be necessary because of inadequate resources available to achieve the goal in absolute terms, or because other opportunities that would have been foregone are more highly valued to the faculty, or to the parent organization. These decisions about where to invest and disinvest need to be taken in the awareness and, where appropriate, agreement of the parent organization and the health-service provider of the organization or external partner.

A further element that requires periodic review is the balance between basic and medical science, and applied, or translational, medical research. The degree to which the academic partner (whether in the medical faculty or non-medical such as engineering or the business school) also supports service-focused or service-driven innovations should also be an important consideration. And, as with other faculties, the degree of focus placed on research activities, as opposed to education, teaching, and personnel development of staff and students, needs to be actively understood and managed.

The amount of research that is undertaken for the benefit of the AHSC's patient population, as opposed to research that might have its principal application elsewhere in the world, can bring about tension within the faculty. Each school, institute, or division within the faculty may have different strengths and interests, which can create tensions between them and with the faculty overall. These tensions need to be actively managed and addressed as there will quite likely be some inherent difference of view at times between the research interests of existing researchers who are generating research income and the future strategic intent of the faculty or college. While this tension might exist in all academic institutions without a health focus, the tension can be more acute between parts of the research community that interface most closely with patients in the health-provider arm or partner, and those whose research interests might be in populations elsewhere in the world, or those whose research is not yet at a stage to have an impact on patients.

Two further aspects merit discussion: those which relate to the amount of activity that is research-driven resulting in high-quality academic impact, and those activities, including innovations, that might lead to commercial success. A faculty administrator may have to make decisions regarding the degree of effort and attention required, either by the institution or the lead academic, to establish a start-up that might lead to a successful spin-out company. In a similar vein, there may be commercially attractive propositions (in education or training or running services at home or overseas) that generate useful income to the institution, but in themselves do not push forward the boundaries of knowledge in a particular area. Again, striking the appropriate balance and acknowledging the opportunity costs involved require both periodic review and management of performance of those activities already underway.

In discharging all these responsibilities, the head of the faculty should deploy a leadership style focused on building consensus and setting direction. The head should delegate effectively and hold subordinates to account, recognizing that academic freedom and autonomy can make aspects of managing performance particularly challenging.

Performance Management

All aspects of organization and staff performance need to be managed in some way to ensure that actual activity undertaken supports the organization in achieving its strategic goals. Common management usages such as "you only get what you measure" or "you don't get what you want, but what you measure" clearly illustrate the importance of performance measures but are hotly contested in academic circles. Nonetheless, having the means to measure performance (or appropriate proxies) within the organizational models set out in Tables 9.2 and 9.3 is also required. Some of this will be through informal means, such as

TABLE 9.2 Degrees of Organizational Integration Models

Confederated/Cluster Models

University Board	{relationships}	Hospital Board
Principal	{relationships}	CEO
Medical School	{relationships}	Hospital

University Board		Hospital Board
Principal	"Partners" Board	CEO
Medical School	Partners supporting organization	Hospital

Integrated Models

University Board		Hospital Board
	President of Health System	
Medical School		Hospital

Fully Integrated Models

University Board	
Principal of Medical School and CEO of Hospital	
Medical School	Hospital

Academic Health Science Center Supervisory Board	
Executive Director/Dean	
Chairs/Board of Executive Directors	
Medical Faculty	Hospital

Adapted from: http://journals.lww.com/academicmedicine/Fulltext/2009/02000/Organizational_Models_for_Medical_School_Clinical.15.aspx

TABLE 9.3 Examples of Institutional Organization Models

Relative Degree of Institutional Integration					
Confederated/Cluster		**Integrated**		**Fully Integrated**	
Separate Leadership, Separate Institutions		**Integrated Leadership Roles and Governance, Separate Legal Entities**		**Hospital and University as a Single Legal Entity**	
Harvard Medicine	*Stanford University Medical Center*	*Duke Medicine*	*Johns Hopkins Medicine*	*Singapore University Health System*	*Amsterdam University Medical Center*
Cluster of hospitals connected with university	Separate entities with close relationships	Separate legal entities conceptually integrated through Duke Medicine	Separate legal entities but powers devolved to Johns Hopkins Medicine	One legal entity	One legal entity between faculty of medicine and hospital
Separate governance, balance sheets	Extensive university membership on hospital board with powers to nominate	Chancellor of health affairs at university is chief executive officer of Duke University Health System	President of university is chair of Johns Hopkins Medicine	Comprehensive single site infrastructure	Single executive board
Some shared posts			Dean of medical school is chief executive officer	One board oversees operation of university and hospital	Chairman is dean of the faculty
					Supervisory board appointed by Minister of Education

routine meetings with direct reports and other staff to discuss performance and personal development. Other functions of performance management will need to be more formal to ensure objectives are met. The wider organization might mandate a particular framework through which organizational goals are assessed using particular performance indicators as well as progress toward milestones. Regular performance monitoring and holding accountable those to whom that task has been delegated requires a degree of discipline and rigor if progress is to be made toward the faculty's and the greater organization's goals.

While performance indicators (such as research or other income generated per time period, quality of research undertaken, or feedback from student surveys) might be the same across all faculties within the university or college, the faculty of medicine in an AHSC has some additional aspects of performance that need to be monitored and managed. These include the regulatory environment in which it operates and the relationship with its hospital partner, particularly focused on the contribution that the faculty makes to translational medicine, education, and service delivery. This is covered in more detail under Risk Management in the following section of this chapter.

One aspect required in the performance regime is the balance between short-term priorities and activities, and those objectives with a longer-term focus, including future building capacity in relation to personnel. Performance monitoring also needs to ensure appropriate attention is paid to compliance with the regulatory frameworks in force, such as in relation to health and safety, and environmental protection.

Combining all these dimensions of performance, management should also take into consideration the context of academic freedom. Chairs, or heads of department, and their primary investigators are likely to have their own views about priorities – in particular, their research interest and bringing in income to fund it. While this is the essence of the academic endeavor, it needs to be executed within the context of broader strategic aims and priorities of the academic institution, as well as the shared endeavors with the hospital partner.

Risk Management

Allied closely to performance management is the need to manage risks that might threaten achievement of faculty objectives. Again, the parent organization may have mandated a particular framework or methodology to undertake this activity (there are many models available and discussed in management literature). In a faculty context, an important factor that needs periodic appraisal is the relationship with hospital partners where translational medicine takes place. The nature of the relationship across the spectrum of integration may mean those risks are judged differently, and the steps that might be taken to mitigate, remove, or lessen a risk could have a different complexion. For example, in a fully integrated model with the faculty and hospital as a single legal entity, resolving or managing a risk will be an internal matter; whereas, in a partners or federated model, the relationship and risk management dynamic would be external.

Financial Accountability

Financial affairs should be managed in such a way as to account for use of funds to the parent organization. Systems should be in place and enable accountability to external funders or donors, such as charities, government, or industry, for funds received, and showing that the agreed conditions or purposes to which those funds were meant to be used have been complied with.

In the federated model and across the integrated spectrum where the faculty and hospital(s) are separate legal entities, the faculty should account for the funds it might receive from the hospital as it does with other external sources of income. Even where the two entities are working together in a shared endeavor, there are likely to be constraints on how contributions can be used, or prohibitions to mix funds, requiring ultimately two sets of accounts to be managed. In the middle of the integrated spectrum, where there is shared leadership but separate legal entities, this requires an additional level of overhead to manage the moneys of a shared endeavor in two separate ways. In the fully integrated model with a single entity, the faculty needs to adhere to the internal rules governing the use of funds across the component parts of the organization.

Staff/Human Resources

As in any faculty or organization, staffing issues require a particular approach since it is ultimately individuals and teams that actually deliver the performance required of the organization. Again the head of faculty will need to ensure that those employed by faculty are treated in accordance with the parent organization's policies. Within a medical faculty, care needs to be taken that appropriate arrangements are in place for the selection and development of staff across all staff groups: academic staff (clinical and nonclinical), administrators/managers, and professional scientific and support staff.

Clinical scientists and others who undertake both academic activity in the academic partner, as well as clinical activity in the hospital partner, will require appropriate contractual and human resource arrangements that enable them to fulfill their responsibilities. In the fully integrated model, there is a single employer so these matters are internal to the AHSC (although even in this case, appropriate links to the parent university may be needed, such as for the conferring of degrees). In all other integrated or federated models, arrangements will need to be in place within the separate organizations to enable effective functioning within both organizations. Mechanisms will need to be in place at the management and HR level to ensure that new clinical or academic posts established in the faculty or hospital contain the appropriate mix of research, service, and teaching. This could also extend to taking a shared approach to selecting individuals who will be able to make the appropriate contributions to the overall AHSC mission, and fit with its ethos.

Managing staff with positions in separate organizations brings additional challenges, particularly in ensuring that incentives and reward systems are aligned. This is not necessarily straightforward since the pressures and objectives between academic and clinical priorities for an individual and organization may not always be congruent. For example, the academic priority might be generating research income and producing high-quality research, whereas clinical service may be more focused on meeting clinical and separate financial targets. These might not be fully reconcilable all of the time, so potential conflicts and tensions for an individual and for the organizations should be actively managed. In the UK context, where universities and hospitals are separate entities, those individuals who straddle academic and clinical practice and wish to excel and further their careers along twin paths may feel that they need to choose a dominant path as it may not be possible to devote the time necessary to excel at both. The head of faculty will have a particular role in career management, mentoring, and guiding such staff.

Students

The "education" pillar within an AHSC comprises both the continuing professional development of all staff employed within the organization, and the students who undertake courses of all types of study within the academic institution (part-time, full-time, executive education, undergraduate and postgraduate, and so forth). The provision of high-quality teaching and facilities to fee-paying students is of increasing importance due to the competitive and international nature of education. Students can now rate their courses and other factors. These results are used internally and externally to guide decisions, such as the level of income from other contributors. They can also be used to gauge internal promotions for staff with teaching responsibilities.

Both the caliber of students selected and their views on the quality of education they receive are important factors in influencing the institution's reputation, which in turn influences the ability of the institution to attract future students. While administration over teaching components is likely to be delegated, it should not be overlooked by the head of faculty, not just because of these factors, but because a proportion of these students will become the next generation of researchers, educators, and clinicians within the AHSC.

Education is also an important dimension of the relationship between the academic institution and the hospital since most of the clinical training is undertaken by staff usually, and in the main, funded by the health-care provider. Not only might this generate income for the hospital, but appropriate management arrangements should be in place to ensure that the outcomes sought are being achieved. For example, students may well be rating hospital staff on the quality of their tutoring, which needs to be properly acted upon to ensure standards are maintained or improved, even if the staff who conduct the training are not directly employed by the academic partner.

Broader Governance and Accountability

In addition to the financial aspects of accountability, the head of the faculty is likely to have specific responsibilities in all aspects of the broader AHSC's policies or delegated responsibilities, such as the proper management and husbandry of the facilities, infrastructure, or information technology. These areas can involve significant resources and capital expenditures and are essential to the execution of the institution's core activities. Employing the right professional or specialist staff (or a third party) to manage and conduct these activities is critical in order to provide the right strategic direction and management to ensure their contribution aligns with, and supports, the core mission.

Relationship with Other Faculty

The faculty/school of medicine needs to maintain close relationships with other faculty who have a role in health-based research to ensure synergies are identified and developed. This should be at an institutional level, as well as between heads of department and principal investigators across faculties. Fostering and maintaining these relationships requires effort, as different disciplines operating under different management arrangements may not necessarily encourage such cooperation.

In those AHSCs where the faculty of medicine has merged with a hospital to create an integrated model, maintaining relations with other faculty becomes a matter more of an external nature, even if the hospital remains affiliated with, or owned by, the university.

Relationship with Hospital Partner(s) Within the Academic Health Science Center

Where the clinical service delivery component is conducted within the same legal entity, the relationship to those more devoted to research is internal. Irrespective of whether the hospital is a peer of the academic component under separate leadership, or subordinate to it where the head of faculty also oversees the hospital, the critical component is the same: ensuring short- and long-term goals remain appropriately aligned and managed through operational pressures and changing priorities for either. Maintaining and nurturing this relationship requires a commitment of time and resources by not only the senior management team(s), but throughout the organization.

Accountability: External Dimensions

Hospital Partner(s) Within the Academic Health Science Center

The previous section considered the situation where the hospital partner was in an integrated model. This section considers the relationship between the hospital partner(s) and the academic institution where they are within a single AHSC, but are separate legal entities. The key point remains the same: ensuring that short- and long-term goals remain appropriately aligned and managed through operational pressures and changing priorities for either. In this instance, however, that relationship needs to be nurtured and maintained across an external divide. This presents different challenges, as not only the executive teams in both organizations need to agree on a course of action, but their respective separate boards must also concur. The execution then needs to take place within the two organizations and monitored by each party, who also need the means to hold each side to account for fulfilling its side of a commitment (through formal and informal means).

Hospital Partner(s) Outside the Academic Health Science Center

The academic partner might also have relationships with other hospitals that are not part of the AHSC. This might exist, for example, to train medical students or conduct clinical trials because of insufficient capacity in the hospital partner; or because the precise specialists are not otherwise provided; or for purposes of a general practice. In these circumstances, the relationship and activity require co-managing with that partner. In addition, the academic institution needs to be sensitive to the potential challenges this may bring with the hospital partner(s) within the AHSC, and manage these proactively.

There are a number of examples where universities have forged links overseas to design and deliver health services, or to conduct research and clinical trials. Additional complexities may arise with challenges of managing international and local staff, as well as sustaining the commitment of resources to ensure success over the long term. Such initiatives can take up significant amounts of senior management time and the opportunity costs of the endeavor need to be taken into account at the outset.

Relationships with Other Academic Institutions

While individual academics might have a wide range of opportunities in research collaborations with academics in other institutions and require little, if any, involvement at the head of faculty level, interinstitutional arrangements can require considerable engagement of management time and attention. Arrangements will need to be made to hold each other accountable in ensuring any commitments are delivered. In addition, attention will be required to ensure that the appropriate balance is struck between meeting one's own institutional priorities and the priorities shared with the partner. Before such institutional agreements are undertaken, the opportunity costs, as well as the risks involved, need to be properly evaluated. The additional complexities of overseas collaborations are similar to the issues outlined in the previous section on external hospitals.

Entering institutional relationships with other academic partners can take many forms. They might be bilateral, or through broader collaborations, or they might be on an exclusive or non-exclusive basis. Whatever form they take, the head of faculty will need to be alert to the challenges and potential conflicts of interest, as a partner might be a competitor in some circumstances and a collaborator in others.

Relationships with Funders, Donors, and Commercial Partners

Funders, whether charitable foundations, government grant income or subsidies, or other commercial sources, will all expect their resources to be spent and accounted for in line with the specific terms of the contract. In addition, maintaining broader relationships with actual and potential funders is a key component of senior faculty attention. Where arrangements are put in place that require closer partnership work (as opposed to that of a more transactional nature), greater effort is required to ensure that the shared endeavor is meeting its objectives for both the academic institution and the commercial partner.

Where research leads to opportunities to spin off innovations into commercial success, the faculty (or broader university) needs to ensure that it has the mechanisms in place to support such endeavors. The effort required to turn an idea into a successful product or company can be very substantial, and the lead academic and faculty will need to decide how this might best be met, while balancing commercial and academic interests. The academic who has made the discovery may or may not have the necessary skills, interest, or capacity to develop the commercialization of their innovation. Again, making sure these competing priorities are handled effectively falls to the head of the faculty.

In an AHSC context in particular, where improved health and contributing to the economy of a region (or nation) are interrelated objectives, the faculty needs to ensure the potential for application of an innovation to a wider population is pursued alongside academic and scientific excellence, and that it is done quickly. Ensuring that skills are in place to facilitate both, and that greater translation is encouraged, nurtured, and actually delivered is a responsibility that should not be overlooked.

Contributing to Health Policy and Services Development, Regionally, Nationally, and Internationally

Some departments in many institutions have a particular focus on sustainable development and improved health globally, and conduct research programs in developing countries. In faculties of medicine, much of the research will ultimately benefit all mankind and not just local populations. Irrespective of whether the faculty has a health policy department, senior leaders in the health system, including heads of faculty, have a (moral) responsibility to support the development of health policy and services in their region and further afield.

A faculty head within an AHSC may need to consider how individual academics might respond or seek to influence policy as part of their academic freedom and their research activities. In addition, the faculty will need to consider how it differentiates and sends consistent messages through the various bodies to which it might belong. In the United Kingdom, for example, faculty within an AHSC might belong to a grouping of medical schools and/or universities who seek to work together to influence public policy. Their hospital partner might also be a member of a network of university hospitals, or of large health service employers (the National Health Service Confederation or the Foundation Trust Network). Both might also be seeking to operate in a regional as well as national grouping. The AHSC might also be part of a wider network of AHSCs. Deciding on which and how these networks might be engaged (and to ensure that the most effective messages are given) falls within the wider responsibilities of the faculty head who could be held accountable for such activities.

Regulatory and Professional Standards

The head of faculty will need to ensure that an appropriate compliance framework is in place for their organization (or the wider university's framework is being utilized properly). In each country, licensing standards will need to be applied, and are subject to internal and external audit, spot-checks, and scrutiny. The head needs to be satisfied that the organization meets all the laws and regulations, conducting appropriate periodic reviews.

Reputation/Communications

All of the dimensions of faculty accountability – internal and external – can have a reputational impact. The head of faculty needs to be mindful of both the positive impact (and the opportunities to support it) of much of the work undertaken by the faculty and the potential negative impact where issues have not gone according to plan. Working with communications across the university and with any partners involved, such as the hospital partner or arm, the head of faculty needs to play a particular role in bolstering positive and handling negative communications.

Author's Personal Reflections

The rewarding part of leading an academic health center is that you have the ability to conduct the triple missions of research, education, and service. The challenge is to create a single governing entity that can move efficiently and rapidly toward fulfilling those missions.

We created a board in which the chairman of the National Health Services Trust sits on the council of the university, and the vice chancellor of the university sits on the board of the hospital. This is unprecedented. Every senior appointment at the medical level had to be agreed upon by both departments, and each party had a veto over the other. We also created a single office to deal with the licensing and management issues presented by clinical trials. This special-purpose vehicle essentially created a one-stop shop for dealing with clinical trials.

You have to be exceedingly patient in a leadership role. You have to understand that the different parties involved are coming from different parts of the biomedical spectrum. They all have unique challenges and perspectives, and they all have an important role in fulfilling the larger objective. The different parties involved also have different interests, and they are sincerely trying to maximize and achieve their own goals. They don't always appreciate the goals of the other parts of the team. As a leader, your job is to emphasize the bigger picture at all times, and bridge those divides with understanding and patience.

The practice of biology is undergoing a profound change. An activity that used to transpire between a small group in a laboratory has been transformed into very big science that occurs across huge institutions and industry. It now requires massive infrastructure to support it, including huge sequencing machines and large physical plants. But it also involves multiple disciplines such as physics, chemistry, and management. We're in the midst of a tremendous renaissance of scientific understanding that involves every branch of the sciences. We're redefining medicine in the new context of interdisciplinary innovation. It's very exciting to be involved at this stage. Almost every day there are developments and changes that are improving things on a large scale. For example, 7 years ago, my institution did not have any specialist stroke units. Today, we are saving 1000 lives a year through these new units. That is amazingly rapid and positive change.

When you lead an academic health center, you see both ends of the research spectrum. You see the basic scientific research being conducted at its infancy, and at the same time, you're translating discoveries from 10 to 15 years ago into meaningful, practical treatments. That's a very empowering and hopeful experience.

—SS

Bibliography

- Behn RD. *Rethinking Democratic Accountability*. Washington, DC: Brookings Institution Press; 2001.
- Hafner G. Can international organizations be controlled? Accountability and responsibility. 97 *Am Soc Int Law Proc* 236. 2003. Available at: www.ilsa.org/jessup/jessup07/basicmats/asilproc_hafner_article.pdf (accessed March 30, 2011).
- Wietecha M, Lipstein SH, Rabkin MT. Governance of the academic health center: striking the balance between service and scholarship. *Acad Med*. 2009; **84**(2): 170–6.

Developing and Implementing a Communications Philosophy and Supporting Policies

William F. Owen Jr. and Lee Miller

From the Editor

Regardless of how outstanding an academic health science center may be, it is only through effective communication that achievements are fully recognized, difficulties explained, and institutional vision understood. This chapter presents the need and strategies for effective communication as vital to the overall success of the institution.

—SAW

An academic health science center's (AHSC) communications philosophy, and supporting policies, govern the methods of conveying information to faculty, students, employees, alumni, the community they serve, press, government agencies, and other stakeholders. When it comes to communications at an AHSC, a careful balance needs to be struck between encouraging free and open dialogue on issues and the need to reinforce the AHSC's public image.

Uniform messaging is especially critical in stating official positions. A well-crafted uniform message can be informative, reassuring, and positive, even if delivering unwelcome news. On the other hand, failure to manage the messages being conveyed by members of the AHSC community can result in confusion and may cause reputational damage. In addition, poor messaging can be quickly and widely spread through electronic media. The descriptor "manage" rather than "control" is more applicable in an AHSC setting, because it is impossible to control messages conveyed by individuals, who may view themselves as speaking on behalf of the institution. In the event that misinformation is leading to reputational damage, it is important to take action to preserve the AHSC's standing and to promote its image.

External and Internal Communications Require Thoughtful Leadership

Even if legally permissible to limit what is said by members of the AHSC community, only speech that is threatening or harassing can and sometimes should be terminated. Otherwise, censorship of speech may be viewed as an impingement of the free exchange of ideas – a sacrosanct principle at the heart of universities. Members of the AHSC community should be encouraged to speak freely about their work and offer their personal opinions, but care needs to be exercised in distinguishing between speech that represents the AHSC and that which is private and individual. Although what is said by members of the AHSC cannot be controlled, AHSC leaders can create management policies that offer a clear understanding about who can speak on its behalf, the circumstances under which it occurs, how the AHSC logos and other identifying marks can be used, and the AHSC's obligation to oversee the commercial uses of its name and images.

For both external and internal communications, AHSC leaders should establish:

- procedures that allow members of the community to obtain approval before making statements on behalf of the AHSC
- guidelines for dealing with inquiries from government and similar agencies
- rules for dealing with confidential information
- operating procedures for how and when the AHSC will provide communications.

In this context, it is wise to have a designated clearinghouse where individuals can seek guidance and, if necessary, authorization to deal with various communication issues.

Equally important in managing the messages that emanate from the AHSC community is creating a culture in which all its members understand the organization's shared mission and values – that is, "what it stands for." Having the right rules governing AHSC communications is important, but it is not enough to simply promulgate policies and rules. Creating an environment where members of the community share a sense of mission and values increases the likelihood that its members will offer constructive and consistent messages.

Without guidelines, AHSC community members may innocently make statements that are inconsistent with the messages the leadership is seeking to convey on behalf of the institution. With the advent of the Internet, confusion caused by such unauthorized statements can quickly spread. Accordingly, it is important to spell out who is authorized to speak on behalf of the AHSC, under what circumstances, and the extent of their authority to do so. A good policy might indicate a statement to the effect that employees and administrators are free to express their own opinions on matters of interest, but when doing so they should indicate, "the opinions expressed are [their] own and should not purport to be speaking on behalf of the academic health center."

Similarly, while use of the AHSC name and/or logo on communications can promote allegiance and camaraderie among members of the community, the criteria for when the AHSC logo can be used needs to be clearly spelled out. Internal or external communications on AHSC stationery, or which include an AHSC logo or identification (e.g., institutional e-mail), give the impression that the message represents the position of the AHSC. Standards for when AHSC logos or e-mails can be used for noncommercial purposes need to be spelled out and enforced. Placing banners and signage on and off campus also needs to be regulated. Procedures for seeking and obtaining such approvals should equally be spelled out.

Communicating Shared Mission and Values Can Guide the Academic Health Science Center Community's Conduct

Organizational alignment among leadership and within the institution can be achieved by identifying and vigorously promulgating a common set of AHSC values and goals. A well-formulated and vigorously championed mission and values statement can provide uniformly accepted goals as well as a definition of unacceptable behavior. However, merely writing and distributing a mission and values statement is not enough. To ensure its members project the values of the AHSC requires a concerted effort to build an institutional culture or shared value system that embodies those values. By what is said and how AHSC leadership behaves, examples of desired values are set and reinforced. The AHSC community looks at and to its leadership for examples of acceptable and unacceptable behaviors.

An example of how an organization can do this can be drawn from Johnson & Johnson (J & J), which developed a simple four paragraph statement of values it refers to as the "Credo."[1] The J & J Credo is based on the idea that a corporation has certain social responsibilities to its customers, employees, the community, and its shareholders. The basic premise of the Credo is that by being responsible to the other constituencies, the company will attract customers and create value for its shareholders. To reinforce the Credo, J & J surveys its employees regularly, asking how well its top and local management are living up to its values. In turn, managers are required to develop and implement plans to address concerns and issues raised by the aforementioned surveys. Another way that J & J reinforces the values of its Credo is through a daylong training session devoted to the Credo that is also part of the annual, weeklong training for senior management. The Credo is highlighted during training for all managers. In a large and extraordinarily successful company that prides itself on a distributive management model, the Credo aligns J & J's values across its many parts and constituents.[2,3]

As part of establishing a communications philosophy and supporting policies, an AHSC should include a plan to develop, promulgate, and promote its mission and values so that there is a shared understanding of what the AHSC stands for. If properly inculcated, these values will serve as guideposts for individuals when they are communicating in ways that may reflect on the AHSC.

Communicating a Strategic and Forward-Looking Mission and Values Statement

The mission and values of the AHSC need to be timeless and enduring but also should reflect organizational realities, current foci, and needs. High-minded statements of values, which do not reflect the operations of the AHSC, will have little impact on people's behavior or their communications. Rather, the desired values need to be embedded in the AHSC culture. The AHSC leadership should operate transparently, sustaining these values – not simply espousing them.

For example, when faced with a need to provide greater accountability, a large, geographically distributed, state AHSC sought to consolidate selected services that had been dispersed among the schools, such as financial management, ethics and compliance oversight, investigations, legal services, contracting, advancement activities, and publications. Historically, the AHSC was managed by a small central administration that oversaw other functions such as campus security, utilities management, debt services, and labor negotiations. With support from the AHSC's board of trustees, the new AHSC president sought to better align the community through the development of a mission and values statement modeled after one that had been successfully promulgated at another AHSC.

A broad-based group comprising staff, faculty, and administrators came together and developed a mission and values statement that was readily accepted. In anticipation of its dissemination inside and outside the AHSC, the new mission and values statement was reviewed by an outside executive, who was previously responsible for messaging and corporate conduct under a mission and values statement. The former executive noted that while inspirational and reflective of the AHSC's values, the new mission and values statement was more effective for an institution with a distributive management model and contrary to a more centralized management model. Therefore, what was successful elsewhere was only superficially transferrable to the current AHSC. Because of this input, a revised mission and values statement was developed that better reflected the aspirational culture and the new operational model being sought.

A communications philosophy must be consistent with a common set of AHSC values and goals and/or align with aspirational goals that are vigorously promulgated and accepted throughout the institution. A mission and values statement should articulate a common boundary for attainment as well as a definition of unacceptable behavior, which accurately reflect the way the institution actually operates or seeks to operate.

Academic Health Science Center Leadership Must Communicate with a Unified Voice Prior to Major Announcements

A shared culture requires the alignment of senior leadership, around the AHSC's mission and values, and also with regard to messages about important issues. The AHSC's communication philosophy and supporting policies should ensure that senior management speaks with a "single voice." Otherwise, leaders run the risk of undermining the AHSC's communications through inadvertent mixed messages.

While a position is being developed on an issue of import, disagreement among the senior management team is expected. Consultation and input is important, not only to insure that the best decision is reached but also so that everyone is afforded the opportunity to participate in the decision. In the end, a consensus must ultimately be reached. Once a decision is made, as long as the decision does not involve unethical or illegal conduct, everyone on the senior management team needs to support that decision and espouse the same message to the community.

As an example, a large public AHSC needed to appoint a new dean to oversee one of its many campuses. A popular internal candidate had made his interest widely known. The provost and chancellor, to whom the deans reported, were charged with initiating the search process by which the dean would be selected. The internal candidate was well liked and a high performer in his current role. However, the chancellor expressed concerns that the candidate lacked the prerequisite advanced degree. The provost agreed but felt it important that the faculty and the candidate be aware of their appreciation for this candidate and permit his application for the deanship to go forward.

A search committee was established and a wide-ranging search was undertaken. As anticipated, the internal candidate applied for the dean's position.

Believing that the internal candidate would not be chosen, neither the chancellor nor provost communicated the fact that the lack of the requisite degree would be a problem. Surprisingly, the search committee recommended the internal candidate as the preferred finalist. Once the faculty heard word of his selection by the search committee, the chancellor and provost were placed in a difficult position. The chancellor and provost took a position without adequate internal conversation with key stakeholders, especially the search committee. There was understandable confusion that undermined the legitimacy of the final candidate's selection.

It is critical that senior management agree on a position and the inclusive messaging plan. An institution's communication philosophy and supporting policies should encourage a thorough vetting of controversial matters in a manner that allows disagreement among the management team to be explored without fear. Once a decision is reached, however, a procedure should be in place to ensure that it is communicated uniformly and consistently to all stakeholders. If situational changes require the AHSC to modify its position, members of the senior management team should come together to agree on a new position and approach to communicate the revised position.

Members of the Academic Health Science Center Community Should be Routinely Kept Informed of Matters of Import

The frequent and routine communication of even bad news to an organization eliminates the risk that misinformation may be innocently disseminated in a way that actually makes matters appear worse. This approach to communication reassures the members of the AHSC that their leaders are aware of the situation and have matters under control.

For example, upon receipt of a whistle-blower complaint accusing an institution of misuse of federal funds, the US Attorney opened a full-scale investigation resulting in the institution being placed under a federal deferred prosecution agreement (DPA). A DPA is a voluntary alternative to adjudication in which the government agrees to grant prosecutorial immunity in exchange for the defendant agreeing to fulfill certain agreed-upon terms. In this case, there was an agreement to pay fines, implement corporate reforms, and fully cooperate with the investigation. In exchange for fulfilling the specified requirements, the charges were to be dismissed.

During the several years when the DPA was in force, the institution was under the oversight of a federal monitor appointed by the US Attorney. As part of the agreement, the board of trustees and senior management team were replaced.

Many staff, faculty, administrators, and students felt that the AHSC was being run by the federal monitor, rather than by the board and president. The breadth of the investigation into wrongdoing, new ethics and compliance reforms, extraordinary and frequent negative publicity, and compliance costs running into the tens of millions of dollars contributed to community morale reaching an unprecedented low. As a result, many talented faculty and staff left the AHSC, which only served to compound the situation.

After the minimum time possible, the DPA was concluded and the charges against the institution were dismissed with prejudice; that is, the case was dismissed for good reason and the plaintiff barred from bringing an action on the same claim. The US Attorney who originally brought the charges against the institution shared publicly his view that it was now "transformed" and on the proper course. Notwithstanding the termination of the DPA, and even though the individuals guilty of the crimes had been prosecuted and left the institution years before, the US Department of Justice sought to have substantial monetary penalties levied against the AHSC. Moreover, the government insisted that in order to be eligible for participation in future federal health-care programs, the AHSC must agree to comply with the terms of a corporate integrity agreement for a period of 5 years.

The board of trustees and president felt that the corporate integrity agreement could readily be misinterpreted internally and externally, implying that the institution was again in trouble, thereby continuing to raise concerns within the AHSC community. To head off any potential problems, the AHSC initiated an extensive communications campaign across all sectors designed to explain what the corporate integrity agreement was, its impact on operations, and how other organizations had fared when they had operated under one. In addition, statements were released to the public as well as meetings held with the local media outlets seeking their assistance in educating the public about the corporate integrity agreement. A month after the campaign's initiation, a trustee noted that the institution's messaging almost made a corporate integrity agreement seem desirable for an AHSC![4]

Communications to the Academic Health Science Center Community Should be Strategic, Positive, Thoughtful, and Always Forthright
• •

Information that is delivered forthrightly with a rationale and sufficient explanation as to how a difficult decision was rendered, can make even unpleasant news acceptable, often with a surprising level of understanding by those adversely affected. Difficult messages should not be delayed. Candor and genuine sensitivity engenders trust, thereby enhancing, rather than distracting, the willingness of affected parties to cooperate for the benefit of the AHSC.

As an example, faced with declining state appropriations, and an inability to increase revenue elsewhere, a large public AHSC with heavy state subsidies forecasts a major revenue shortfall. As with most AHSCs, the majority of recurrent expenses are for salaries and benefits, and most of that expense is for faculty. The AHSC is highly unionized with employees represented by several unions, each on a different contract negotiation cycle. The union representing the faculty is the American Association of University Professors (AAUP). However, the AAUP's collective bargaining agreement was originally negotiated when the AHSC's finances were much stronger, and was not up for renegotiation for several years despite challenging financial times. Moreover, AAUP members were contractually obliged to receive at least two significant wage increases during a time when the majority of other union contracts lapsed with frozen salaries.

Financial forecasts to balance the AHSC's budget required layoffs with hundreds likely to be displaced. In response, the AHSC's board of trustees, president, and deans developed a restructuring plan for the workforce, but were anxious about how it would be perceived. They were concerned over the need to pursue layoffs, while the faculty enjoyed raises.

A decision was made to forthrightly communicate the nature of the financial situation with members of the AHSC community and the public. First, invitations were extended to every union leader to participate in individual and group meetings to review the AHSC's finances and to seek their help in constructing solutions. Most of the union leaders accepted. The AHSC community was made aware that these meetings were ongoing, and pressure built from the rank and file members in the unions whose leaders refused to attend. A plan to put the AHSC on sound financial footing that was realistic, understandable, and offered hope for the future was outlined and communicated to the AHSC community.

The workforce restructuring was announced but only after other approaches to reduce costs were communicated to the AHSC's employees. These approaches included elimination of pay raises for senior management, a partial hiring freeze, travel prohibition, reduction of organizational memberships, elimination of some print publications, implementation of energy efficiency measures, and even the elimination of bottled water purchases. Union leadership responded by working with the administration to find ways to reduce costs and advocating with the state government for a larger appropriation to the AHSC in future years.

The Communication Philosophy Should Celebrate Successes Within the Academic Health Science Center Community

AHSCs can often be resource constrained, which makes attracting and retaining top talent difficult. High performing individuals within an organization are often more accepting of compensation limitations if they are openly acknowledged and celebrated for their contribution to the AHSC. Non-monetary expressions of gratitude and accolades are a relatively inexpensive reward and can help to mitigate the impact of resource constraints.

For example, after years of active discouragement from the external research community, peers, and even the head of his academic unit, 10 years of research came to fruition for one AHSC researcher. He successfully developed a novel medical technology that displaced a century-old, "gold standard" test for a potentially life-threatening disease. Word of this discovery spread rapidly in the global scientific and public health communities, as well as in the lay press. The new technology was selected by the World Health Organization to replace the widely accepted standard test and received special mention by the Bill and Melinda Gates Foundation. ABC Weekly World News did a feature story on the new technology and used it for their inaugural story in a new segment on positive global activism.

The faculty member was celebrated by the AHSC at a special reception in his honor hosted by the university president. Invitations were extended to luminaries inside and outside the AHSC. The speeches, letters of congratulations, and legislative citations presented before the audience focused on the faculty member, rather than on his discovery. After the event, the AHSC president received several unsolicited calls and e-mails from faculty and staff remarking on the impact this event had on the AHSC and noting that this type of celebration and focus on the individual's efforts, rather than exclusively on nature of his work, should occur more often. Many attendees remarked that focusing on the value of an individual in difficult financial times was more important than financial rewards.

Establishing Appropriate Policies and Procedures Governing Communications

As noted above, creating a strong culture which reflects the AHSC's values is the best way to ensure that statements emanating from the AHSC are consistent with its mission and values. Notwithstanding, AHSC leaders should develop rules and procedures to provide guidance for members of the community further delineating what is appropriate. This assistance protects the AHSC from unauthorized communications that can place it in uncomfortably negative or inappropriate light, as well as provides informed notice of best conduct.

Privacy and Confidentiality

AHSC employees often have access to data, including personal information about members of the AHSC community, the institution's financial information, and medical information about patients. As accessibility to various electronic means of rapidly disseminating information increases, it is important to ensure that confidential information collected or generated by the AHSC is maintained in a manner that does not allow public dissemination. In addition to the legal requirements for maintaining the confidentiality of protected information, the AHSC should set forth a standard operating procedure to ensure that information of this nature is only used for legitimate purposes. This requires establishing standards to determine confidentiality, and procedures for maintaining and responding to violations of confidentiality.

Access to Communications Devices

AHSCs generally make available to their faculty, students, and employees access to electronic communications such as computers, e-mail, mobile devices, phones, and so forth. Guidelines and, if possible, rules as to when and how these devices may be used should be set forth. Policies governing who is eligible to use various communications devices and their appropriate use need to be clearly spelled out. Policies governing personal use, protection of passwords, spam, retention policies, pornographic materials, and so forth also need to be addressed.

Use of Identifying Marks

The AHSC's name, logos, or other identifying marks are property of the institution, have value, and need to be protected; trademarks are an appropriate means for such protection. Additionally, procedures for licensing should be set along with assigning responsibility for their implementation. A single clearinghouse is recommended, which can be housed within the AHSC or handled by a contracted external agency. Procedures should be in place to govern filming on AHSC property in addition to commercial use of photos of AHSC buildings and grounds. The AHSC should be vigilant in protecting both its reputation and the commercial value of its name.

Authorized AHSC Spokespersons

Policies should clearly state that only authorized individuals can purport to speak on behalf of the AHSC. Policies should clearly spell out that no one else should respond on behalf of the AHSC to inquiries from the press, government, or the community at large. The policy should spell out specifically to whom such inquiries should be referred. A single central clearinghouse for all inquiries is recommended to avoid confusion among the AHSC community as to where inquiries should be directed.

Conclusion

Managing AHSC communications when statements that purport to represent the institution can be disseminated around the world almost instantaneously requires a well thought-out communications philosophy and policies to support it. Those philosophies and policies should be designed to reflect and protect the mission, values, and reputation of the university and encourage the free interchange of ideas within the AHSC community.

Author's Personal Reflections

When I first came to the University of Medicine and Dentistry, the organization was involved in an environmental scan. Within the first couple of weeks, I kept hearing people share their desire to come together. I was confused because we were all one university, even though we were spread out all over the state, so I didn't know why we couldn't come together. And I discovered that the institution was operating under something called "The Bergen Line." Bergen was the name of the founding president of the university. He felt that the way to drive growth in an organization was to have people compete against one another, and so there was literally a geographical line of latitude, above and below which no collaborations could occur. If you were above the Bergen Line, you could not collaborate with people below the Bergen Line. As a result, we ended up with an exaggerated siloed culture, where people were forced to manage their own challenges without the input of peers. They were not even allowed to leverage the knowledge, assets, or opportunities across the line. The line forced us to essentially become independent schools, so rather than having eight schools under one university, we became eight schools under a holding company, almost like J & J.

My first job was to eliminate the Bergen Line. We focused on leadership across the institution, and we gave the leadership the mandate, the authority, and the tools to collaborate with each other. It started with the leadership, but what's important to the line worker is important to the boss. First the deans and vice presidents began meeting together, simply to talk about what they were doing. Within a year, I disappeared from the process because they started coming together on their own, and soon initiatives began to develop across campuses. We really started to see people come

---

together, and now that's a theme that animates our entire institution.

We've protected our image as an institution by being transparent. In the past, people tended to hide some misbehavior. Some of it was innocent, and some of it was genuinely out of malice. What we found in our organization is that the public trust is enhanced by being open and communicative. So I have been more visible, more open, and more communicative. We're geographically distributed throughout the state, but I've made it a point to distribute information to all campuses personally and repeat the same messages across the campuses. We have really tried to enhance transparency and communications as our way of engendering greater trust.

To create trust and open communication, we used a three-step process. First, we conducted an environmental scan, which was genuinely intended to take the conversation back up to 10 000 feet – to understand how the different constituencies viewed themselves and the organization. We wanted to check the pulse of the organization, to find out what various people thought about the institution, and to ask how they saw their roles. The second step was to distribute that information in an open way, to say, "here is what you and your peers say about what we're doing." Then we examined how we were doing in terms of the component parts. Were we going in the direction we wanted to go in? Was Campus A helping Campus B achieve what they believed to be greatness? Out of that, we developed a strong and simple sentiment, which has become a tagline: loud and clear, people wanted the organization to be viewed as a statewide asset. The third part of this process was to go back to the first step, and to ask our people what they thought a "statewide asset" is, and what role they believed they could play toward the organizational vision of becoming a statewide asset.

I'm a recurrent entrepreneur. I enjoy the journey and I like to build things. So the most rewarding part of this job is to see the success of the faculty and the students. I enjoy contributing to their growth. Leaders of academic health centers shouldn't ignore the spectacular lessons that are learned from enterprise organizations. We often have derogatory views of for-profit organizations, but they face and solve organizational challenges just like we do. There are wonderful examples of processes and best practices that come out of private industry. There are really three things that historically give us hope: faith, family, and education. For people who are in health care, the ability to educate the next generation of health providers or improve human health is such a wonderful and spectacular way of writing history rather than being a bystander. Humans are addicted to improving their own health and the next generation's health. The best way to do that is through education.

—WFO

Acknowledgment

Gratitude is expressed to Roger Fine, Esq., former general counsel of J & J for his insightful historical perspectives on the J & J Credo and its positive impact on management behavior and organizational communications.

References

1. Johnson & Johnson. *Our Credo*. Available at: www.jnj.com/connect/about-jnj/jnj-credo (accessed August 1, 2012).
2. Kaplan T. *The Tylenol Crisis: how effective public relations saved Johnson & Johnson*. Pennsylvania State University. Available at: www.aerobiologicalengineering.com/wxk116/TylenolMurders/crisis.html (accessed May 22, 2011).
3. Weldon WC. Johnson & Johnson: living up to its Credo. *Metropolitan Corporate Counsel*. December 1, 2008. Available at: www.metrocorpcounsel.com/articles/10790/johnson-johnson-living-its-credo (accessed May 22, 2011).
4. University of Medicine and Dentistry of New Jersey. *The Investigations Group: an important part of our ethics & compliance efforts*. Available at: http://investigations.umdnj.edu/eth_compl.htm (accessed May 22, 2011).

Community Relations

Barbara Atkinson, C.J. Janovy, and Marcia Nielsen

From the Editor

Academic health science centers are embedded in communities for which they take responsibility. In this chapter, the authors present a frank and coherent approach to community relations that should underpin the management of these institutions.

—SAW

Educating Policy Makers on a Controversial Issue, Building an Advancement Board, and Earning Taxpayer Trust: Three Community Relations Success Stories

Academic health science centers (AHSCs) provide important educational, health-care, and economic benefits to the communities they serve, but they also rely on community support in significant and unique ways. Their many initiatives could not move forward without wide-ranging philanthropic support. For publicly supported institutions, in order to maintain state appropriations – indeed, to exist – policy makers must support the AHSC mission. And, if the public supports that mission, policy makers will more likely follow.

For both public and private AHSCs, building and maintaining support requires consistent outreach, creativity, and long-term commitment. This is especially so for an AHSC whose community is defined across localities and counties. It is certainly the case for the University of Kansas Medical Center (KUMC), which literally sits on a state border, located in the heart of Greater Kansas City. The Kansas-Missouri state line divides the sprawling Kansas City metropolitan area.

Although leaders from both states often speak of, and aspire to, cooperation across the region, tensions are often readily apparent. Policy makers express frustration when one state offers tax incentives to entice a major company to move its headquarters across the state line. There is a long history of tension between these neighboring states.

Further complicating matters in defining community, a metropolitan area can consist of many cities across multiple counties. As is true for many other AHSCs, the KUMC is located in a poor urban area. AHSCs are often located in underserved areas, be they urban or rural.

A final challenge of note is that, like the KUMC, AHSCs can be a state's only academic health center. The KUMC is as close to Missouri as it could possibly be – the campus' eastern boundary is State Line Road. How the medical center came to be located 40 miles east of the university's main campus in Lawrence is better saved for history books; however, the campus location has added to community relations challenges from the beginning, as noted by Robert P. Hudson, MD, Professor Emeritus of the Department of History and Philosophy of Medicine, University of Kansas School of Medicine[1]:

> The two decades after the four-year [medical] school began operating in 1905 were not blanketed by tranquility … Bitter criticism persisted that the new school was more Missouri than Kansas because so many faculty lived and practiced east of the state line.

Today, the medical center operates programs in every county in Kansas, but some of the state's rural residents have expressed geographic concerns about KUMC's urban location. In spite of this, the AHSC works hard to maintain its valuable and productive relationships with many scientists, donors, and business, political, and civic supporters throughout our region, on both sides of the state line.

The KU School of Medicine consists of campuses in Kansas City and Wichita, Kansas, and has recently added a third campus in Salina, a community of 50000 in central Kansas, as part of its plan to address the country's critical shortage of rural physicians by training students who have a specific interest in this specialty. The first 4-year class began in 2011.

This chapter describes some community relations successes as the past decade has unfolded. As outlined by the several cases provided here, an AHSC can benefit greatly from exponential growth in community support for its priorities.

The Time is Right: Setting a Research Agenda that Excites a Region
• • • • • • • • • • • •

In 2005, the Greater Kansas City Community Foundation commissioned a Blue Ribbon Task Force of nationally recognized leaders to recommend ways the metropolitan region could transform itself to become competitive in the new, global knowledge economy. The foundation's leaders acknowledged that Kansas City's future was threatened by a host of serious urban problems and they wanted to craft a thoughtful plan to do something about it.

The Blue Ribbon Task Force, led by Dr. Benno Schmidt Jr., chairman of the City University of New York and of the Edison Schools Board, and a former president of Yale University, was joined by a diverse group of national thought leaders. The group embarked on an exhaustive study, meeting with more than 500 people from the community, reading dozens of reports, and drilling deeply into the structure and finances of the region's colleges, universities, and statehouses.

The AHSC leadership informed the task force about the progress the medical center had made in previous years and shared with them its ambitious goals – raise the standards for basic, translational, and clinical research, with a goal of becoming a top-25 medical center in basic life science and a top-50 center in research and development. In addition there was a plan to quadruple the medical center's external research funding from the National Institutes of Health (NIH) and private organizations to approximately $340 million annually in 10 years.

The task force's unflinching report, *Time To Get It Right*,[2] concluded that the KUMC could play a crucial role in saving the life of a city. After working on the goals that had been set, community leaders began to pay attention.

Although it recognized that KUMC had already been transforming itself into a research leader and economic engine for the community, the Blue Ribbon report came with very specific instructions for the institution, mirroring the goals that were shared with the task force. For example, the AHSC committed to "recruit an additional 30 senior faculty and 50 junior faculty over the next five years" and "add 20 senior faculty and 60 junior faculty in years 6–10." Other goals included building a new basic science or cancer research center of roughly 255 000 square feet at a cost of $90 million, and aiming to "work with" several other universities and research institutions in the area "to create [a] top 25 bioinformatics research and PhD program." This strategy involved "eleven major elements" that were "divided into two phases of roughly six and four years."

To help the AHSC carry out its mission, the Blue Ribbon panelists enlisted Kansas City's philanthropic and civic community along with Kansas and Missouri's political leaders. Panelists recommended $175 million in philanthropic support, over a 10-year period, just for KUMC. They instructed the state of Kansas to add $1 million a year for 10 years to the school of medicine's operating budget and channel $150 million from the state's $500 million, 10-year life sciences investment fund to KUMC facilities and faculty. In a period of increasing anti-tax sentiment, the panelists were so bold as to recommend passing a tax to support life science and medical research.

As is often the case, not all of the philanthropic support would materialize according to the instructions of the Blue Ribbon panel, but it was the first time that community leaders recognized the AHSC's invaluable contribution to the lifeblood of the community and stood strongly behind it.

Stem Cell 101: Building Community Relationships and Working with State Legislators to Prevent Harmful Legislation

The Blue Ribbon Report came out at a time when the area's civic and political leaders were acutely aware of the economic importance of creating a hospitable environment for scientific research. The city was just beginning to understand the significance of the Stowers Institute, established 5 years earlier with a $2 billion endowment and one of the country's largest privately endowed institutes for basic medical research.

Business leaders were also recognizing the threat from efforts to ban early stem cell research. That same year, they joined with scientists, religious leaders, medical professionals, and citizens to campaign for a constitutional amendment protecting such research in Missouri (that amendment passed in November 2006). Many of these same leaders were also joining efforts to defeat a House Bill (HB 2355) in the Kansas state legislature that would have banned early stem cell research and made criminals out of researchers, doctors, and even patients.[3] If the bill passed, those found in violation could be charged with a class five felony, facing 60 months in jail and civil penalties between $100000 and $250000.

AHSC leadership provided important testimony about what would happen if legislators passed the bill. As physicians, educators, researchers, and leaders in the health-care community, it is the responsibility of AHSC leaders as well as of all scientists and educators to be a resource, both to the public and to lawmakers who have a responsibility to decide such crucial issues. The critical problem with HB 2355 was that, while it aimed to outlaw human cloning, the specific language of the bill did so at the expense of criminalizing the exploration of an entire category of research that holds the potential to profoundly ease human suffering – research that will allow the study of the molecular basis of diseases as they develop from conception to death. This research holds the promise of discovering treatments and cures for such chronic diseases as Parkinson's, juvenile diabetes, amyotrophic lateral sclerosis, heart disease, cancer, spinal cord injuries, and Alzheimer's disease.

The opponents of stem cell research were not successful in passing the bill, but because of the numerous meetings and hearings, the AHSC was given multiple opportunities to educate Kansans about the value of our research. Between April and October that year, 50 talks on the science of stem cell research were offered to citizens throughout the state of Kansas. A series of seminars with Kansas legislators called Stem Cell Research 101 were conducted to educate them about the science and ethical considerations of this work. Depending on the audience, presentations could be tailored to a 10-minute or a 2-hour version.

Although it could be risky to speak to policy makers about these controversial issues, given that lawmakers control a significant portion of a publicly funded AHSC budget, it was a bigger risk not to. As the line between science and politics grows thinner, it is the unique responsibility of AHSCs to be a principled resource for policy makers, for the public, and for those who would benefit from these scientific endeavors.

Leaders across the community can appreciate a principled focus on the issues if leadership is careful to present itself as part of the community rather than as defensive scientists under attack. Leaders from the medical center, keeping the tone positive, understanding, and appreciating the deep moral and ethical considerations involved with the issue, were able to underscore the belief that it would be inappropriate to pass a law preventing and criminalizing the pursuit of research to discover life-saving cures and treatments. Medical center leaders also stressed that there would be unintended consequences of banning such research. They emphasized that the spirit of discovery that fuels scientific advancement in our society would be lost. They further pointed out that the community's population would face a risk of being deprived of the benefits of currently accepted treatments and the science behind those treatments. In addition, patients – and perhaps physicians – might leave the state to pursue the possibility of more innovative care elsewhere, resulting in a direct economic impact and an indirect loss of additional business growth.[4]

Community leaders stepped up and worked closely with the AHSC on this issue. Anticipating that some Kansas legislators would reintroduce an anti-human cloning bill in the 2006 session, the Greater Kansas City Chamber of Commerce made protecting research one of its top legislative agenda items. A group called the Kansas Coalition for Life Saving Cures campaigned to encourage Kansans to advocate for research to improve the quality of life for those suffering from debilitating disease. Educational efforts such as this can have tremendous collateral benefits throughout a community, the state, and the region. It can become an opportunity to teach new audiences, build new coalitions, and advance the mission of improving human health through research.

The sophistication of a thoughtful, systematic, grassroots effort can earn strong support in the legislature and from political leaders. At the beginning of the 2006 Kansas legislative session, when asked for an additional $5 million annual appropriation dedicated to earning the prestigious National Cancer Institute designation for the University of Kansas Cancer Center, that $5 million was included in the budget for fiscal year 2007. With significant bipartisan support, legislators approved the appropriation and have continued to do so every year since. Even during times of declining revenues and painful cuts elsewhere, lawmakers understand the enormous potential for return on investment in the knowledge economy.

The Advancement Board: Building Capacity for Community Relationships

An AHSC can establish strong community relations not just by fighting *against* harmful legislation, but also by fighting *for* something. In Kansas, this was a cancer center worthy of National Cancer Institute designation. In 2005, University of Kansas Chancellor Robert Hemenway announced that fighting cancer was the number-one priority of the entire university – not just the medical center.

The NCI's requirements are specific. The grant application lays out the "Six Essential Characteristics of an NCI-Designated Cancer Center." Adequate physical facilities are required, as well as proven ability to take "maximum advantage of institutional capabilities in cancer research and to appropriately plan and evaluate center strategies and activities." The AHSC has to show transdisciplinary collaboration and coordination, and a defined scientific focus on cancer research that is clear in all grants and contracts and in all formal programs. In addition, there must be demonstrated institutional commitment, as evidenced by space, positions, and resources. And, the center's director would have to be "a highly qualified scientist and administrator with leadership experience and institutional authority appropriate to manage the center and further its scientific mission and objectives."

It is a considerable challenge to meet these six essential requirements in addition to pricing out the costs of hiring researchers, building labs, and conducting clinical trials. The effort also requires enormous public and philanthropic investment.

Public support is vital and the stem cell debate demonstrated that lawmakers understood the benefits of investing in research. The state committed $581 million to create the Kansas Bioscience Authority (KBA),[5] an initiative designed to help build world-class research capacity, encourage bioscience start-ups, support the state's bioscience clusters, and expand and attract bioscience industries. The

KBA has committed more than $49 million over a 10-year period. This money has funded basic research and clinical trials, allowed investment in technologies that expand drug delivery capabilities, enhanced the ability to recruit talented researchers, and bankrolled major building renovations to create state-of-the-art laboratories. More evidence of public support was demonstrated in the creation of a state license plate to support the University of Kansas' breast cancer research and outreach efforts across the state.

Equally, it is vitally important to build upon a strong foundation of philanthropic support. For example, the cancer research component was renamed the Kansas Masonic Cancer Research Institute, recognizing more than 30 years of support from the Kansas Masonic Foundation and a new pledge of an additional $15 million to support cancer research over 5 years.

The Advancement Board of the University of Kansas Medical Center and the University of Kansas Hospital was formally convened. With the stem cell campaigns, new supporters and community relationships had been established on the basis of how the AHSC communicated concerns embedded in a controversial issue. These relationships could be further enhanced by communication focused on an issue that everyone could support: fighting cancer, a message that crosses all boundaries. Raising the financial support required enlisting the power of community advocacy.

The Advancement Board was conceived at the recommendation of a dedicated University of Kansas alumnus[*] who questioned why the KUMC didn't have a research advocacy board. In response, the AHSC leadership set about building one.

To build such a board, the AHSC began with a core group of 20 community members with clearly defined duties. Advancement Board members were to fulfill their roles by:

- spreading awareness of the mission and work of the academic health center
- attending board educational gatherings, orientations, committee meetings, and networking events
- making an annual contribution to the academic health center
- participating in fundraising and outreach events
- cultivating prospective board members through personal and/or professional networks.

---

[*] Forest Hoglund is an alumnus of the University of Kansas and a member of the KU Endowment Association Board of Trustees. In the early part of the decade, Forrest and Sally Hoglund's $4 million gift to establish a brain imaging center was the initial contribution to the KU First capital campaign and the largest for a building project in the history of the medical center. With the gift, the University of Kansas transformed a vacant lot into a place where 80 scientists at four regional universities use imaging to conduct pioneering brain health research.

The first Advancement Board meeting was held and early meetings focused on providing an orientation to the AHSC. AHSC leadership provided reports and presentations highlighting the important research and clinical aspects of an AHSC.

By design, board meetings were always hosted on campus so that community leaders could say they had been there. They were given tours of both the research and patient care environments so people could begin understanding the complexity of the organization as well as its breadth and depth.

Tours were given through neuroscience laboratories, laboratories where researchers were working to find cures for ovarian and breast cancer, the Center for Advanced Heart Care, and buildings that were being renovated for radiation oncology. Despite board member suggestions to hold meetings offsite due to restricted parking, those efforts were resisted to demonstrate the need for space in the event that zoning became an issue.

After the first 3 years, a solid foundation had been built and the Advancement Board determined that it was time to develop a strategic plan. This plan was launched with clear public policy objectives that involved government and community relations. According to the plan, "The primary focus of the Advancement Board will be to continue building a solid advocacy contingency that supports legislative initiatives which preserve state and federal resources and expand physician access."

The board's Governmental Affairs Committee would, among other things, "champion federal earmarks to support the academic medical center; host briefing events with city managers, directors and community leaders; host a caucus on health professions workforce supply with community influencers; and host Project Medical Education events for key legislators and community decision makers."

Meanwhile, the board's Community Affairs Committee was charged with sponsoring events "to educate the community on key health concerns and the academic medical center's approach to helping address these concerns, and lay out the groundwork for future fundraising." The members of this committee also pledged to find new ways to increase community awareness of the medical center's programs, successes, and priorities. Among other things, the Community Affairs Committee would "identify highly interested, engaged individuals who would prefer small group opportunities to take guided tours of the academic medical center; identify key community groups (Chambers, Rotary Clubs, Junior League, Central Exchange, and so forth) interested in having Advancement Board members or key academic medical center leaders on their meeting agenda and develop an action plan to present to these groups."

Over time, the now 80-member board had developed an extremely sophisticated infrastructure, such that it was clear it was not only meeting the needs of the academic medical center, but also addressing the personal passion felt by these individuals.

Putting Community Relationships to Work: The Johnson County Education and Research Triangle

In 2007, plans were announced for a research hub along with an intensive lobbying campaign for a tax to help pay for it. The Greater Kansas City Community Foundation and the Johnson County Education Research Triangle Advisory Council proposed to help Kansas State University, the University of Kansas, and the KUMC build three new facilities.

The proposed "research triangle" was to be anchored by a National Food Safety and Security Institute run by Kansas State University and additional facilities at the existing University of Kansas Edwards Campus (to offer science, math, and engineering degrees) in the southern part of Johnson County. The northern tip of the triangle would consist of a building where the KUMC would conduct clinical trials of all types, including those to test promising new cancer drugs. The initiative would be funded with a new, one-eighth-cent sales tax that was projected to generate about $15 million a year to be divided evenly among the three campuses.

Community leaders wanted to position their county to play a major role in the Kansas City area, becoming one of the country's top-20 life-science centers. Several of the community leaders backing this tax were members of the Advancement Board; however, the idea wasn't just an unprecedented show of support for the AHSC's work. As the sales tax campaign gathered momentum, the community recognized the fact that the University of Kansas and Kansas State University were partnering despite their reputations as cross-state rivals.

Any such proposal will have opposition. Well-known legislators were among the outspoken opponents arguing that the triangle was "nothing more than a government-subsidized personal dream project" that "ties the hands of county government."[6] However, community allies also spoke in favor of the project, noting that cancer patients will someday have more treatment options with tens of millions of dollars in private donations and new federal grants leveraged to the KU Cancer Clinical Research Center.[7] Community-wide education efforts can pay off. Still, passage can always be far from certain – especially in difficult economic times.

On November 1, 2008, the Saturday before the election, the *Kansas City Star* published an eloquent editorial urging readers to "Vote 'Yes' to expand research, treatments." More than anything, the editorial spotlighted the AHSC's work as a reason to support the tax.[8] With support from community and political leaders the tax increase passed. Revenues from the tax will generate $5 million a year – in perpetuity – for the University of Kansas Clinical Research Center.

Individual members of the Advancement Board had campaigned for the issue – making phone calls, donating money to the campaign, knocking on doors. Having 2 years to lay a strong foundation and work with these community leaders was invaluable. A diverse group of community leaders that was already exposed to and had a good understanding of the academic health center can be influential.

The Research Triangle vote was evidence of the Advancement Board's effectiveness. The Advancement Board will also work hard to promote the benefits of an NCI designation by hosting community awareness events, serving as spokespeople, and making financial contributions.

Summary Remarks

Good community relations are essential now more than ever, especially with the economic downturn depleting state revenues. The mood in the country favors smaller governments, translating into less support for state universities. With the country still engaged in a bitter policy debate over federal health-care reform, it is also crucial for us to continue to educate Advancement Boards about the long-term policy implications of the law so that they can reach out and educate the rest of the community.

The community that rallied around the KUMC is a broad one: from both sides of the state line and across the country; in urban, suburban, and rural areas; and inclusive of alumni, neighbors, students, faculty, and a wide array of friends. An AHSC is enhanced by their support for its priorities, and by their influence in achieving its goals. AHSCs can benefit from these resources and their time and talent, and can strive to not only demonstrate but achieve real and concrete progress.

At the same time, it is always important for AHSCs to invest the significant resources necessary – financial, human, energy – to deserve the community support they receive.

Author's Personal Reflections

Academic health centers provide important educational, health-care, and economic benefits to the communities they serve, but they also rely on community support in significant and unique ways. Our many initiatives could not move forward without wide-ranging philanthropic support. We are a state institution, and in order for us to maintain state appropriations – indeed, for us to exist – policy makers must support our mission. If the

---

public does not support that mission, then neither will policy makers.

Building and maintaining that support requires consistent outreach, creativity, and long-term commitment. This is especially so for an academic health center whose programs span multiple communities and counties. It is certainly the case for the KUMC, which literally sits on a state border, located in the heart of Greater Kansas City. The sprawling Kansas City metropolitan area covers 3800 square miles, with a population of about 1.8 million people. The Kansas-Missouri state line divides it. Although leaders from both states often speak of and aspire to cooperation across the region, tensions are often readily apparent. There's a long history of tension between these neighboring states. In a nod to early Civil War battles, the annual football game between the University of Kansas and the University of Missouri is popularly known as the "Border War."

My personal journey to Kansas came after spending 1996–99 as dean of the MCP Hahnemann School of Medicine in Philadelphia, Pennsylvania. I was recruited to chair the University of Kansas' School of Medicine Department of Pathology and Laboratory Medicine. Shortly thereafter, I was named executive dean of the school of medicine. When I came to Kansas City from Philadelphia, broad community support here seemed limited by comparison. We have benefitted greatly from exponential growth in community support for the KUMC and our priorities. The Blue Ribbon Task Force of nationally recognized leaders is a great example of how the metro area could transform itself to become competitive in the new, global knowledge economy. The foundation's leaders acknowledged that Kansas City's future was threatened by a host of serious urban problems and they wanted to craft a thoughtful plan to do something about it.

The task force embarked on an exhaustive study, meeting with more than 500 people from throughout the community, reading dozens of reports and drilling deeply into the structure and finances of the region's colleges, universities and statehouses. I was among the people they interviewed. I told them about the progress the medical center had made in the previous years and shared with them our ambitious goals. We wanted to raise our standards and quadruple our NIH funding. Therefore, I was not surprised when the task force's unflinching report, *Time To Get It Right*, concluded that the KUMC could play a crucial role in saving the life of a city. When we went to work on the goals we had set, community leaders began to pay attention.

Although it recognized that KUMC had already been transforming itself into a research leader and economic engine for the community, the Blue Ribbon report came with very specific instructions for us, mirroring the goals that we had shared with them. For example, we were to "recruit an additional 30 senior faculty and 50 junior faculty over the next five years" and "add 20 senior faculty and 60 junior faculty in years 6–10." We were to build a new basic science or cancer research center of roughly 255 000 square feet at a cost of $90 million. We were to "work with" several other universities and research institutions in the area "to create [a] top 25 bioinformatics research and PhD program." And so on. This strategy involved "eleven major elements" that were "divided into two phrases of roughly six and four years."

To help us carry out the mission, the Blue Ribbon panelists had specific marching orders for Kansas City's philanthropic and civic community and Kansas and Missouri's political leaders, too. Ultimately, not all of this philanthropic support would materialize according to the instructions of the Blue Ribbon panel, but our value was recognized.

As part of community support and outreach, it is important to have support from local news media. When a tax increase was proposed to pay for a research triangle, for which our Cancer Center was to be an anchor, the local paper came out in support of the tax increase with an eloquent editorial urging voters to vote yes to the increase:

> The KU Cancer Center, which is based at the teaching hospital in Kansas City, Kan., must continue to expand labs, hire doctors and scientists and demonstrate a strong commitment to cutting-edge treatment and research ... If Johnson County voters approve the research tax, the money will be returned many times over in good jobs, brain power, grants, scholarship funds and the amenities that come with a robust higher-education presence. But no benefit is more compelling than the opportunity to assist in a careful plan that should one day make the Kansas City region a more prominent destination for cutting-edge cancer treatments.

Community leaders and local media recognized our invaluable contribution to the lifeblood of the community and were strongly behind us. Establishing good community relations is vital to a vibrant and progressing academic health center.

—BA

References

1. Friesen SR, Hudson RP. *The Kansas School of Medicine: eyewitness reflections on its formative years.* Kansas City, KS: SR Friesen; 1996.
2. Greater Kansas City Community Foundation. *Time to Get It Right: a strategy for higher education in Kansas City.* Available at: www.gkccf.org/sites/default/files/resources/gkccf-p-time-to-get-it-right.pdf (accessed January 26, 2011).

3. House Bill No. 2355, Session of 2005. Available at: www.kansas.gov/government/legislative/bills/2006/2355.pdf (accessed January 26, 2011).

4. Atkinson B. When science and politics collide. In: Rice ML, editor. *The Interface of Science and Public Policy: Merrill Series on The Research Mission of Public Universities; a compilation of papers originally presented at a conference sponsored by The Merrill Advanced Studies Center, July 2005*. MASC Report No. 109. Kansas: The University of Kansas; 2005. pp. 69–72. Available at: www.merrill.ku.edu/publications/2005whitepaper.pdf (accessed January 26, 2011).

5. Kansas Economic Growth Act of 2004. Available at: www.kansasbio.org/info/section/kansas_economic_growth_act_overview.pdf (accessed January 26, 2011).

6. Research hub plan advances: Johnson County Commission must place the three-campus initiative before voters. *Kansas City Star*. Friday, April 20, 2007.

7. Campaigning for a research-boosting tax. *Kansas City Star*. Friday, August 15, 2008.

8. Vote "Yes" to expand research, treatments. *Kansas City Star*. Saturday, November 1, 2008.

Academic Health Science Centers and Global Medicine

D. Clay Ackerly, Krishna Udayakumar,
Alex Cho, and Victor J. Dzau

From the Editor

In our rapidly globalizing world, academic health science centers are becoming increasingly interconnected in education, research, and patient care. This chapter presents an important perspective based on direct experience that will prove useful to institutional leaders in navigating these complex waters.

—SAW

Academic Health Science Centers (AHSCs) should develop long-term strategies in global medicine.* In fulfilling their roles as global leaders in research, clinical care, and education, AHSCs should combine traditional activities with innovative public-private partnerships that facilitate international approaches to health-care, research, education, and entrepreneurial programs. This chapter describes the rationale for AHSCs to be key players in global medicine and examines factors contributing to success, applying experiences and examples of several academic centers. We also explore the risks of global medicine and discuss early lessons learned as well as implications for policy makers.

---

* *Global medicine* is used to describe all biomedical and health-care activities such as education and training, health-care delivery, research and development activities across the biomedical sciences and health-care industries in all economies.

Introduction

Health care has long played by different rules than the rest of the economy. For example, while other sectors of the US economy have looked abroad to reduce production costs or reach new customers, the traditional US health-care delivery enterprise (not including the biopharmaceutical and device industries) has been active only at the fringes of the global market. However, given the opportunities globalization presents, AHSCs are now beginning to engage more internationally.

While some of these activities have prompted skepticism or criticism, AHSCs can invest in global medicine through international public-private partnerships and should be supported in their efforts by forward-thinking public policy. In so doing, AHSCs will be better equipped to shape the global health-care system of tomorrow.

Academic Health Science Centers and Global Medicine

In much the same way that AHSCs have played a central role in biomedical sciences and health-care delivery in their own communities, these organizations can be critical drivers for medical care around the world, leveraging public-private partnerships to address critical global health needs and guiding development of the health systems of the future. The potency of the AHSC model is evidenced by the recent interest shown by many developed countries that are either creating (e.g., the United Kingdom and Singapore)[1,2] or strengthening (e.g., Canada, the Netherlands)[3,4] their own AHSC capacity, as well as the myriad partnerships that exist between AHSCs and communities in the developing world – communities that cannot afford their own AHSC infrastructure.

Within the health sector, AHSCs are unique in the breadth of activities encompassed within their tripartite missions of education, research, and clinical care. A plethora of opportunities to engage in globalization now exist for AHSCs across these missions.

Research

In biomedical research, AHSCs have achieved numerous breakthroughs in basic science as well as in translating and commercializing these discoveries.[5] However, progress has slowed and the costs of discovery and translation are increasing. Going forward, especially given limits on their support in the United States from state and federal government, AHSCs must support and leverage their expanding research capacity and infrastructure worldwide, such as that demonstrated by the growth of science parks and the biotechnology industry in many countries, including China,[6,7] India,[8] and Singapore.[9]

National governments in these and other countries are clearly becoming more engaged: public research spending in developing countries is estimated to be over $2 billion annually.[10] This international growth in capacity represents unique opportunities for collaborations that can increase the productivity of laboratories both at home and abroad. When expertise is shared, the volume and quality of technical understanding and innovation are accelerated, supporting improvements in human health and economic development.

Patient Care

Care delivery overseas presents numerous opportunities for AHSCs as well, including the establishment of hospitals, clinics, and other international clinical programs as well as providing advisory services related to clinical care. Despite the challenges besetting US health-care providers and the resource and infrastructure limitations of many other health-care systems, AHSCs can adapt their knowledge of integrated-delivery systems, evidence-based medicine, and state-of-the-art technologies to advise health systems in developing countries to meet the needs of diverse communities.

Education

AHSCs are already emerging as contributors to health-care improvements in under-resourced countries through research and commitment to alleviating global health disparities. The educational mission of AHSCs, in particular, has perhaps the greatest potential for achieving long-term improvements in health globally.

The opportunities range from partnering to establish new schools and programs in medicine, nursing, research, and allied health professions, to creating varied exchange and distance-learning programs. The health-care workforce shortage, already profound in many regions, is exacerbated in less developed nations by the lure of higher salaries and better working conditions in more developed nations.[11] Addressing this problem, however, requires an immense effort: the World Health Organization Global Health Workforce Alliance estimates that it would cost $2.6 billion per year for 10 years to train an additional 1.5 million workers to meet the needs of African countries alone.[12]

Clearly, the scope of this problem is beyond the capabilities of AHSCs alone. Nevertheless, AHSCs can play an important role in both the developing and the developed world. Lower-cost teaching methods are needed to reach far greater numbers of learners across the spectrum of the health-care workforce. Also, AHSCs have a history of developing innovative educational approaches, such as evidence-based and team-based methods, as well as distance learning.[13] This experience can be translated in culturally sensitive ways to strengthen and expand the number of global health-care workers, leveraging existing international partnerships to reach new learners.

In addition, global health-care human capital development should not be limited just to increasing the number of workers, but should seek to improve the quality of workers across the spectrum of training (e.g., undergraduate and graduate/residency medical training, nursing, research and allied health). This requires a transformative educational paradigm, one that incorporates new methods of knowledge acquisition, problem solving, teamwork, and multidisciplinary care.

Further, the impact of human capital development can be felt beyond care delivery as health-care administration and management, as well as biomedical and clinical research, will benefit from improved workforce development. One workforce innovation taking place at AHSCs is the development of Global Health residency programs, such as those at Brigham and Women's Hospital and Duke University.[14,15] These programs incorporate targeted didactics and applied international health experiences, typically providing a master's degree and access to international sites that provide care and engage in research. While these programs can produce only a limited number of graduates each year, they can (and are expected to) become part of the cadre of future leaders in global medicine necessary to promote and guide large-scale change.[16]

Rationale for Academic Health Science Centers to Become Global Leaders

AHSCs must engage in global activities in order to address global health disparities, increase productivity and amplify the impact of academic research, education, and clinical care missions, and prepare for the challenges of a rapidly changing world. In short, despite the real risks of globalization, AHSCs have the capability to assume a leading role in global medicine, as well as the moral and business imperatives to do so.

Meeting our Global Responsibilities

It no longer suffices for AHSCs to provide care to only those patients who come through their doors. AHSCs must accept responsibility and invest in the health of their communities by developing models of effective care-delivery that abate health disparities locally and nationally. Indeed, efforts are underway in the United States to explore financial models capable of supporting local investments, such as the evolving "medical home" and "accountable care organization" concepts.[17,18]

This responsibility may extend beyond domestic borders, as international health disparities can frequently be more severe in other countries. Deficiencies in environment, hygiene, economic development, and access to health care are at the root of dramatic disease burdens and shortened life expectancy in 5 billion of the world's 6 billion citizens.[19] The global health-care workforce is inadequate to meet these challenges – the World Health Organization estimates that an additional 4 million health-care workers are required to satisfy current needs.[20]

Even for AHSCs that focus on local or national missions, as leaders in medicine with world-class expertise, AHSCs can take steps to accept a measure of global responsibility. Further, such international efforts can yield many benefits at home. As articulated by the US Institute of Medicine's Board on International Health, "America has a vital and direct stake in the health of people around the globe, and this interest derives from both America's long and enduring tradition of humanitarian concern and compelling reasons of enlightened self-interest."[21] The importance of the latter should not be ignored, since national and global security can be enhanced by improved capacity to track and prevent pandemics, better economic and political stability among other nations, and medical diplomacy – leveraging international relationships to enhance a country's image abroad.[22,23]

It is also important to recognize the bidirectional potential of global medicine activities as innovations from abroad can be applied at home. Global medicine can foster mutual exchanges of talent, ideas, care models, and even technologies, in which developing economies provide creative solutions to be applied in developed economies, as well as the reverse.[24] For example, specialty care models are establishing themselves in low-resource environments, such as the Aravind Eye Care System in India.[25] These programs often incorporate novel approaches to patient outreach and creative use of human capital (e.g., community health workers) that may be applicable to US community-based projects.

Amplifying Impact

While the ambitions of AHSCs vary, engaging in global medicine promises to amplify the impact of their academic missions. As described earlier, global medicine can support the research enterprise through international collaborations and by increasing academic output and broadening audiences for research results. It can also advance the educational mission of AHSCs by reaching new groups of talented learners and increasing opportunities for exchange among existing groups of learners. In addition, new models of care can be shared and improved through international experience and collaboration.

Meeting New Challenges

Independent of the impact that AHSCs can achieve abroad, the extent to which globalization will drive change in a health-care system makes going global a strategic imperative, not simply an option. For example, US AHSCs historically have been major resources for specialty care and training worldwide, with many international patients traveling to them to receive care. This has changed since the events of September 11, 2001, with international patients increasingly seeking alternatives.[26] As pressures from reduced reimbursement by US payers and competition from other providers at home and abroad increase, it is not surprising that some AHSCs have turned to international activities to attract patients or develop other revenue opportunities.[27]

Importantly, the rise of "medical tourism" has increased competition among hospitals. Estimates of market size vary, but one conservative estimate puts the potential annual volume of US patients who could travel abroad to seek medical care at 500 000–700 000, representing $35 billion in clinical revenue.[26] Other estimates suggest that the size of the global medical tourism market is $60 billion or more.[28,29]

Regardless of the exact number, the threat is real, and the arrival and expansion of various international accrediting bodies signal that global health-care standards are emerging and the playing field is leveling. One such organization, the Joint Commission International, has grown substantially since its founding in 1997. In 2000, it accredited just three institutions, but by March 2008 it accredited over 170 institutions in more than 30 countries,[30] increasing to 300 institutions in 39 countries by 2010.[31] Other bodies, such as the International Society for Quality in Health Care and the Trent Accreditation Scheme in the United Kingdom, are also accrediting international provider groups.[28]

Further, the effects of foreign competition can be felt at home even if few patients travel overseas. For example, in 2008, one large employer in New England leveraged an agreement with a Singaporean hospital (where cost-sharing requirements for their employees would be waived if they sought care abroad) in order to negotiate lower prices from US providers.[32] In such an environment, if AHSCs are to remain competitive, they must deliver higher-quality, internationally cost-competitive health care.

AHSCs can also be threatened by emerging global competitors outside the arena of clinical care. For US AHSCs, research dollars are increasingly flowing overseas, due in part to lower costs of conducting research abroad.[33] The loss of domestic opportunities is not limited to basic science, as clinical research is experiencing tremendous international growth because of lower research costs, faster patient enrollment, and fewer regulatory hurdles abroad.[34] For example, while the United States represents nearly half of all global clinical trial sites, its market share has been decreasing.[35] Conversely, emerging economies are experiencing tremendous growth in clinical research, presenting both challenges and opportunities in workforce development and strengthening human subject research protections.[36]

Across all missions and activities, action carries risk, but inaction does too. For example, collaborations among emerging and developing economies are occurring (often termed "South-South" collaboration).[37] These efforts are to be applauded, but they are also a warning that other institutions could be left behind as future paradigms are established.

The State of Academic Health Science Centers' Global Medicine Activities

Given the range of potential global medicine activities, as well as their attendant benefits, many AHSCs have already taken steps to invest in global medicine. These efforts span the AHSC missions, from care delivery to education to research to health-systems design, and even include related business opportunities, such as managing foreign hospitals.

Many prominent global medicine programs appear, perhaps understandably, to have focused on partnerships with nations with resources, such as the United Arab Emirates, Qatar, Israel, Singapore, Korea, Spain, Italy, Ireland, and Canada; or with high-end health care in developing countries like India.[28] However, other experiments are under way in allied professions (such as nursing,[38] dentistry,[39] and public health[40]), medical school partnerships in countries such as Malaysia and Tanzania, and through the creation of interdisciplinary institutes or centers such as the Duke Global Health Institute[41] and many others. These efforts will undoubtedly continue to expand over the coming years.

Potential Risks of Global Medicine for Academic Health Science Centers

Global medicine activities require careful management of financial, organizational, politico-legal, and reputational risks by AHSC leadership. Profit should not be the primary goal of global medicine; but as with any other activity, engaging in global health care must be financially viable. This requires adequate capitalization and sustainable business models.

From an organizational perspective, there are concerns about bandwidth for faculty and staff, dilution of existing intellectual and institutional assets, and extra efforts needed to establish institutional buy-in at home for new activities. New personnel may be required abroad posing unique human resource challenges, including quality control and assurance that attitudes are consistent with institutional culture. Cultural differences may also lead to divergent expectations, both in terms of desired outcomes and the manner in which they are achieved.

The myriad legal and political risks vary according to national legal systems, political environments, and the relationship of AHSC activities with foreign interests. Foreign business practices may be incompatible with US standards, and managing political relationships can require significant effort from senior executives. Further, engaging in care delivery and human subjects research, where the potential for direct harm is highest and most visible, dramatically increases politico-legal risks.[42] The risks of global medicine are not limited to AHSCs; the activities undertaken may cause more harm than good if not implemented appropriately. Thus, AHSCs should recognize that "first do no harm" applies both to their own institutions and to their new global partners.

To accomplish this, AHSCs should develop robust organizational policies and support systems to address the multiple risks associated with global activities, including approaches to human resource management, banking and financial tracking, and approaches to financial and legal risk-management.

Early Lessons in Global Medicine for Academic Health Science Centers

Global medicine, still in its infancy, is quickly evolving and requires flexibility and mid-course corrections. However, two early lessons for AHSCs are already manifest: (1) keep activities mission-focused and (2) engage in durable public-private partnerships.

As self-evident as it may sound, staying mission-driven is critical, as it provides a sharp focus for strategic planning and evaluation of potential opportunities, as well as guidance once activities are underway. Since partnerships with foreign entities usually include financial arrangements, misalignment between mission and business practices can occur. Staying mission-focused is therefore critical to success, and a periodic reevaluation by AHSCs of their global medicine activities will help ensure mission-activity alignment, and, when necessary, can highlight the need for changes in organizational structure. The recent movement of Harvard Medical International from the university to Partners Healthcare is an example of such a realignment.[43,44]

The opportunities and challenges of global medicine are too large and the solutions too complicated to be addressed alone. Partnerships should be actively sought and established in a rigorous and deliberate fashion. Cultural differences loom large between many nations, and are best explored and overcome through personal interactions. An "on the ground" presence is critical to establishing trust and forging lasting relationships.[45] Such trusting relationships are critical to long-term success since initial outcomes may be at variance from original projections and several years may be needed to realize the full expectations.

Given the complexities of health care, the socio-legal and political issues in different countries, and the significant resources needed, public-private partnerships offer an emerging model of effective implementation.[46] In fact, public-private partnerships have succeeded in multiple settings and have increased in recent years.[47,48] When evaluating potential partners, issues such as a record of successful relationships, cultural compatibility and understanding, and alignment of goals must be considered, with each partner's needs corresponding to strengths offered by the other. Furthermore, as discussed earlier, it is important to remember that partnerships should be bidirectional. Capabilities are rapidly improving in many countries and partnering entities have strengths and experiences likely to prove valuable and portable to AHSCs. Conducting a public-private partnership correctly can be a daunting task, but progress is evident despite the challenges.

The Duke-Singapore Experience

Early global activities involving certain AHSCs have met with difficulties: conflicting expectations of the funding host and the AHSC[49] or the failure of a new medical school to gain recognition by accreditation bodies (e.g., the US Liaison Committee on Medical Education)[50] have led to suboptimal experiences.

These experiences helped inform the partnership between Duke and the Singapore Government in the creation of the Duke-NUS medical school and research center. In 2000, the Singaporean government launched their Biomedical Sciences Initiative, investing over $15 billion to support the development of a knowledge-based economy. The government recognized that they lacked the workforce necessary to develop effective translational research programs (a gap that requires physician-scientists and other professionals). Through a commitment of more than $400 million, Duke and the NUS founded a new graduate medical school (Duke-NUS Graduate Medical School), which matriculated its first class in 2007. The explicit goals of this partnership are increasing the supply of clinician-scientists and supporting Singapore's emerging translational research infrastructure.[51] Mindful of earlier examples, a central feature of this relationship included specific goals and timelines, using key performance indicators as metrics.

Thus far, the enterprise is considered successful by both partners, as measured by a trusting relationship between Duke and Singapore, the quality of the students enrolled, the curricular innovations implemented, the recruitment of outstanding faculty, and the establishment of signature research programs, among other key performance indicators that have been met successfully.[52] Reflecting the early success of the Duke-NUS GMS, Duke and NUS announced the signing of a "Phase Two" agreement in 2010 that further extends this collaboration.

Given the importance of global medicine activities and the early-stage nature of many of these programs, additional lessons from these efforts should be explored and shared widely.

Policy Implications of the Globalization of Academic Medicine

Health care remains one of the most heavily regulated sectors in developed economies. In order to facilitate global medicine and support organizations (including AHSCs) as global leaders in health care in the face of increasing global competition, several critical barriers affecting research, clinical care, and workforce development should be addressed.

Policies Affecting Research

Policies to improve international research efforts, particularly in the area of clinical research, have been well-characterized elsewhere and remain important.[33] Clinical research is rapidly expanding into developing economies, largely due to lower costs for conducting trials and access to treatment of native populations. This trend has been accompanied by inconsistent quality of research, questions related to data integrity, and instances of research fraud. In response to these concerns, the US Food and Drug Administration has established international offices and several public and private efforts are underway to better train the research workforce in these markets. AHSCs can play a central role in helping to improve regulatory frameworks for clinical research globally as well as developing and delivering training programs to improve the quality of research. In addition, AHSCs should provide thought leadership in ensuring that appropriate research studies are carried out internationally and that vulnerable international populations are protected and not "experimented upon" while providing access to new therapies.

Policies Affecting Clinical Care

Issues in international clinical care collaborations are beginning to emerge, as well. As the demand for cross-border care increases, so does the need for robust and meaningful accreditation, transparency in quality and outcomes, and effective means for supporting continuity of care. Providers both in the United States and abroad, accreditation bodies, and payors (including Medicare and private insurance companies in the United States) must ensure that foreign competition is robust and also healthy for patients.

Several AHSCs have engaged in international affiliations in areas of clinical care, from specific service lines to entire medical facilities. Consistent policies that articulate the expectations of such affiliations may be helpful in ensuring that these collaborations result in high-quality health-care services and may help clarify some of the liability risk that remains in such arrangements.

Policies related to reimbursement for provision of nondomestic health-care services also need to evolve. Technology and a highly trained international workforce now allow for fairly seamless "telemedicine" services with few technical challenges. For example, "Teleradiology" and "TeleICU" services sourced from diverse areas could be critical in providing high-quality radiology services during evening and weekend hours at rural hospitals and other facilities across the United States that struggle with staffing. These services could also provide real-time oversight for house staff at AHSCs who have little if any access to attending physicians during overnight hours.

Policies Affecting Education and Training

Workforce development and education are among the most urgent needs and intervention may be most beneficial in this arena, as current market forces have done little to meet current demand. Both targeted funding and improved standards and regulations could be of great help.

To develop and sustain a critical mass of global health workers and leaders, training programs must be established and funded. Workforce needs span the educational continuum, including the physician track (undergraduate, medical school, residency, and so forth) and beyond (nursing, allied health, and so forth). To date, programs have been supported largely by tuition and philanthropy. Additional funding is required, however, and given the importance of these activities to national priorities (e.g., medical diplomacy, international development, and global competitiveness of domestic health-care entities), government funding sources would be both helpful and appropriate. For example, while it represents only one component of the continuum of educational needs, the recent emergence of global health residency programs is currently threatened by a lack of sustainable financing. Residents trained in these programs comprise a critical component of the future global health workforce, but the costs of their more intensive training (e.g., course work and international rotations) are not covered by traditional means. In the United States, a federal model of support, such as an international public health corps, or an adjustment in Medicare graduate medical education payments, could improve the sustainability of such programs.

While some US accrediting organizations, such as the Joint Commission, have begun to accommodate international applicants, others, such as the Liaison Committee on Medical Education, which accredits US medical schools, have not. Each organization should approach globalization in its own way, but harmonizing highest-quality standards and accepting international institutions is important and should be encouraged. Otherwise, the efforts abroad to create high-quality programs may be undermined by an apparent "double standard" wherein location, not quality, matters. This is not a message that should be sent abroad, as it would undermine the ability of AHSCs to engage in partnerships that can promote welfare both locally and abroad.

Some may be concerned that such global accreditation could either exacerbate the "brain drain" in lower-income countries or, conversely, reduce the flow of international students to educational institutions in developed countries. The likely result is not entirely clear, and it requires analyzing the cross-national flows of both students and trained workers. The brain-drain concern is understandable since, in theory, the presence of global standards should make it easier for qualified workers to move across borders from low- to high-income countries (because high-income countries would have increased confidence in the quality of workers' training). It is possible that the reverse could occur, since the opportunity to receive accredited education may reduce the need to relocate, allowing students and educated workers to remain in their own countries. For example, the Duke-NUS Graduate Medical School permits students to obtain US-style and quality education (with a joint Duke-NUS degree) without having to travel to the United States. The final equilibrium or "trade-balance" of workers and students is presently unknowable; however, a "free trade" approach to workforce development is a positive step. Improvements in global health outcomes will be best supported through robust training unencumbered by cross-national restrictions and supported by common quality standards.

Conclusion

The world is changing rapidly. As threats to global population health increase, so do the opportunities to make a positive impact. Investing in global medicine has its pitfalls, but the risks of inaction can be far greater. By leveraging their myriad strengths through strategic partnerships, AHSCs can amplify the impact of their mission-based activities and reduce health disparities both at home and abroad.

Author's Personal Reflections

Globalization has affected Duke significantly. It makes us see the world in a different context. We understand that the medical center and medical school of the future must have a global perspective, and that we must confront health-care disparities as well as change the way we educate, conduct research, and develop public-private partnerships. Duke's culture is completely different in this global context. We have a lot to learn from others, but we can also teach others what we've learned. We have a large number of students who are spending a lot of time overseas through Duke Engage, which supports students overseas. We also have a partnership with McKenzie and the World Economic Forum through the International Partnership in Innovative Health Delivery. In order to develop more low-cost solutions for health-care delivery, we looked at innovators and entrepreneurs. We went around the globe to examine how people are using creative ideas. We can help innovators scale up and replicate their model in their own country or elsewhere. We brought together members of the World Economic Forum, leaders from business, the pharmaceutical and medical device industry, and other nonprofit organizations to help develop the concept. We identified more than 50 entrepreneurs. We looked at their needs and we tried to bring them business know-how, financing, and regulatory support. We created this organization to bring together innovators, investors, industry, and government. We can't simply go there and take some ideas and apply them. We can't just have our own perspective and think that we're doing good. We know we have to engage partners at the local level who understand many of the local issues. We need partners that may have the funding resources to actually make things happen. That's a very important part of the globalization effort. We also have a mentorship panel and conferences, and we have websites offering a place to learn, to share ideas, and to find out what's going on in India, China, and elsewhere.

Because we have embraced our global role, we have enhanced our reputation. As a world institution, we need a world reputation. Duke is involved in 64 countries. There's no question that being involved in other parts of the world brings significant new resources to Duke. We developed the Duke National University Singapore partnership with the Singapore government, in which we provided joint degrees for doctors. We've been in existence for 6 years, and we just graduated our first class. If you simply calculate how globalization adds to the bottom line, it's very difficult to quantify. But partnerships like this open up the possibility of exchange. Our students travel there, but their students also travel here. We made significant initial investments, but now money comes in from that partnership. Of course we are not doing this for the bottom line, or as a source of revenue, but we would not do these things if we had to substantially dilute our resources. We're also making a positive difference in the world, and providing life-changing experiences for our faculty, students, and staff. During the Haiti earthquake, we sent seven teams to work in Port-au-Prince and elsewhere – not just doctors, but nurses and physical therapists. They were working in very difficult conditions, but they were passionate, and they all come back saying that it was a life-changing experience. I went in with the second team, and it was very moving.

That's what's so rewarding about being in my position. I get to see committed and passionate people trying to do the right things in the United States and elsewhere. I always say what we do is "doing good, and doing well." It's so satisfying to see the full spectrum of things we do to help society and serve the community. We care for individual patients, but we also make an impact on population health, prevention, and wellness. We are so proud to educate the next generation of health-care providers and leaders, who are essential to health both locally and globally. It's not just about doctors, nurses, or social workers; it's about our whole team coming together to serve patients and the community. I just feel so privileged that I have the opportunity to do what I do. I'm a true immigrant. I was born in China, I left as a refugee, and I came to the United States to study on my own. I've seen amazing things in medicine, but I've also seen individuals who aspire to lead and make a difference, and that can be really impressive and inspiring.

—*VJD*

Acknowledgment
• •

The authors wish to thank Jonathan McCall for editorial assistance with this chapter.

References
• • • • • • • • • • • • • •

1. King's Health Partners Named as One of UK's First Academic Health Science Centres. *Medical News Today*. March 11, 2009. Available at: www.medicalnewstoday.com/articles/141823.php (accessed February 20, 2011).
2. Singapore National University Health System. *About Us*. Available at: www.nuhs.edu.sg/corporate/introduction.html (accessed February 20, 2011).
3. Academic Health Science Centre. National Task Force to Review the Future of Canada's Academic Health Sciences. Press Release. March 10, 2009. Available at: www.ahsc-ntf.org/?document&id=1&mp=83 (accessed February 20, 2011).
4. Erasmus Medical Center. *Heading for '013: Strategic View of Erasmus MC for 2013; 2009*. Available at: www.erasmusmc.nl/5663/162999/Koers-013-ENG-(totaal)-(def) (accessed February 20, 2011).
5. Association of University Technology Managers. *AUTM U.S. Licensing Activity Survey: FY2009*. Available at: www.autm.net/AM/Template.cfm?Section=Licensing_Surveys_AUTM&TEMPLATE=/CM/ContentDisplay.cfm&CONTENTID=5239 (accessed February 20, 2011).
6. Lai HC, Shyu JZ. A comparison of innovation capacity at science parks across the Taiwan Strait: the case of Zhangjiang High-Tech Park and Hsinchu Science-based Industrial Park. *Technovation*. 2005; **25**: 805–13.
7. Prevezer M, Tang H. Policy-induced clusters: the genesis of biotechnology clustering on the East Coast of China. In: Braunerhjelm P, Feldman MP, editors. *Cluster Genesis: technology-based industrial development*. Oxford: Oxford Scholarship Online Monographs; 2007. pp. 113–32. Available at: www.oxfordscholarship.com/oso/public/content/management/9780199207183/toc.html (accessed February 20, 2011).
8. Frew SE, Kettler HS, Singer PA. The Indian and Chinese health biotechnology industries: potential champions of global health? *Health Aff (Millwood)*. 2008; **27**(4): 1029–41.
9. Bharadwaj KV. Singapore makes room for biotech. *BioSpectrum Asia Edition*. March 1, 2007. Available at: www.biospectrumasia.com/content/080507SGP3548.asp (accessed February 20, 2011).
10. Gardner CA, Acharya T, Yach D. Technological and social innovation: a unifying new paradigm for global health. *Health Aff (Millwood)*. 2007; **26**(4): 1051–61.
11. Pang T, Lansang MA, Haines A. Brain drain and health professionals. *BMJ*. 2002; **324**(7336): 499–500.

12. World Health Organization. *Global Health Care Workforce Alliance Report*. Available at: www. who.int/workforcealliance/news/education-taskforce-report/en/index.html (accessed February 20, 2011).

13. Kolesnikov-Jessop S. Team program is an experiment in active learning. *New York Times*. April 29, 2009. Available at: www.nytimes.com/2009/04/29/education/29iht-riedmeduke. html (accessed February 20, 2011).

14. Brigham and Women's Hospital. *Residency in Global Health Equity*. Available at: www. brighamandwomens.org/Departments_and_Services/medicine/services/socialmedicine/ gheresidency.aspx (accessed February 20, 2011).

15. Duke Global Health Institute. *Global Health Residency/Fellowship Pathway*. Available at: http://globalhealth.duke.edu/education/postdoc-proff-programs-indiv/global-health-residency (accessed February 20, 2011).

16. McCannon CJ, Berwick DM, Massoud MR. The science of large-scale change in global health. *JAMA*. 2007; **298**(16): 1937–9.

17. *The Medical Home: a solution to chronic care management?* Washington, DC: Deloitte Center for Health Solutions; 2008. Available at: www.deloitte.com/us/medicalhome (accessed February 20, 2011).

18. Fisher ES, McClellan MB, Bertko J, *et al*. Fostering accountable health care: moving forward in Medicare. *Health Aff (Millwood)*. 2009; **28**(2): w219–31.

19. Lopez AD, Mathers CD, Ezatti M, *et al.*, editors; for the World Bank Group. *Global Burden of Disease and Risk Factors*. Oxford: Oxford University Press; 2006. Available at: www.dcp2. org/pubs/GBD (accessed February 20, 2011).

20. World Health Organization. *World Health Report 2006: working together for health*. Geneva, Switzerland: World Health Organization; 2006. Available at: www.who.int/whr/2006/en/ (accessed February 20, 2011).

21. Institute of Medicine. *America's Vital Interest in Global Health: protecting our people, enhancing our economy, and advancing our international interests*. Washington, DC: National Academies Press; 1997.

22. Iglehart JK. Advocating for medical diplomacy: a conversation with Tommy G. Thompson [interview]. *Health Aff (Millwood)*. 2004; Suppl. Web Exclusives; W4, 262–8.

23. Fauci AS. Lasker Public Service Award: the expanding global health agenda; a welcome development. *Nat Med*. 2007; **131**(10): 1169–71.

24. Richman BD, Udayakumar K, Mitchell W, *et al*. Lessons from India in organizational innovation: a tale of two heart hospitals. *Health Aff (Millwood)*. 2008; **27**(5): 1260–70.

25. Bhandari A, Dratler S, Raube K, *et al*. Specialty care systems: a pioneering vision for global health. *Health Aff (Millwood)*. 2008; **27**(4): 964–76.

26. Ehrbeck T, Guevara C, Mango P. Mapping the market for medical travel. *McKinsey Quarterly*. May 2008. Available at: www.mckinseyquarterly.com/Mapping_the_market_for_travel_2134 (accessed February 20, 2011).

27. Merritt MG, Railey CJ, Levin SA, *et al*. Involvement abroad of U.S. academic health centers and major teaching hospitals: the developing landscape. *Acad Med*. 2008; **83**(6): 541–9.

28. *Medical Tourism: consumers in search of value*. Deloitte Center for Health Solutions; December 2008. Available at: www.deloitte.com/view/en_HR/hr/industries/lifesciences healthcare/964710a8b410e110VgnVCM100000ba42f00aRCRD.htm (accessed February 20, 2011).

29. Crone RK. Flat medicine? Exploring trends in the globalization of health care. *Acad Med*. 2008; **83**(2): 117–21.

30. *Joint Commission International Annual Report*. Joint Commission International; 2007. Available at: www.jointcommissioninternational.org/Annual-Report/ (accessed February 20, 2011).

31. Joint Commission International. *About JCI*. Available at: www.jointcommissioninternational. org/about-jci/ (accessed February 20, 2011).

32. Einhorn B. Hannaford's medical-tourism experiment. *Business Week*. November 9, 2008. Available at: www.businessweek.com/globalbiz/content/nov2008/gb2008119_505319.htm (accessed February 20, 2011).

33. Clark DE, Newton CG. Outsourcing lead optimization: the quiet revolution. *Drug Discov Today*. 2004; **9**(11): 492–500.

34. Glickman SW, McHutchison JG, Peterson ED, *et al.* Made in the USA, tested overseas. *N Engl J Med*. 2009; **360**(8): 816–23.

35. Brower V. Going global in R&D. *EMBO Rep*. 2004; **5**(4): 333–5.

36. Bhalla V, Janssens B, Liao C, *et al. Looking Eastward: tapping China and India to reinvigorate the global biopharmaceutical industry*. Boston, MA: Boston Consulting Group; 2006.

37. Thorsteinsdottir H, Melon CC, Ray M, *et al.* South-South entrepreneurial collaboration in health biotech. *Nat Biotechnol*. 2010; **28**(5): 407–16.

38. University of Pennsylvania School of Nursing. *Global Health Affairs Program*. Available at: www.nursing.upenn.edu/gha/Pages/default.aspx (accessed February 20, 2011).

39. http://global.unc.edu/index.php?option=com_content&view=article&id=206&Itemid=79 and www.dentistry.unc.edu/ (accessed February 20, 2011).

40. Harvard Global Health Institute. *Population Health, Demography and Aging*. Available at: http://globalhealth.harvard.edu/population-health-demography-aging (accessed February 20, 2011).

41. Duke Global Health Institute. *Making a Difference in Global Health: strategic plan for the Duke Global Health Institute, 2007–2012*. Available at: http://globalhealth.duke.edu/documents/DGHI_Strategic_Plan_Executive_Summ_for_web1.pdf (accessed February 20, 2011).

42. Sleeboom M. The Harvard case of Xu Xiping: exploitation of the people, scientific advance, or genetic theft? *New Genet Soc*. 2005; **24**(1): 57–78.

43. Marks C. HMS spin-off will drop Harvard name. *Harvard Crimson*. February 4, 2008. Available at: www.thecrimson.com/article.aspx?ref=521684 (accessed February 20, 2011).

44. Baxter V. Brand on the run. *Arabian Business*. June 3, 2008. Available at: www.arabianbusiness.com/brand-on-run-49052.html (accessed February 20, 2011).

45. Kolars JC. Should U.S. academic health centers play a leadership role in global health initiatives? Observations from three years in China. *Acad Med*. 2000; **75**(4): 337–45.

46. Pécoul B. New drugs for neglected diseases: from pipeline to patients. *PLoS Med*. 2004; **1**(1): e6.

47. Lowry RC. Nonprofit organizations and public policy. *Rev Policy Res*. 2005; **14**(1–2): 107–16.

48. Hinnant CC. Nonprofit organizations as inter-regional actors: lessons from Southern growth. *Rev Policy Res*. 1995; **14**(1–2): 225–34.

49. Associated Press. Johns Hopkins' Singapore center to close. *Boston Globe*. July 25, 2006. Available at: www.boston.com/news/education/higher/articles/2006/07/25/johns_hopkins_singapore_center_to_close/ (accessed February 20, 2011).

50. Cornell News. Private Foundation in Qatar Commits $750 Million to Establish the Weill Cornell Medical College in Qatar. (April 9, 2001). Available at: www.news.cornell.edu/releases/April01/weill.qatar.html (accessed February 20, 2011).

51. Williams RS, Casey PJ, Kamei RK, *et al.* A global partnership in medical education between Duke University and the National University of Singapore. *Acad Med*. 2008; **83**(2): 122–7.

52. Duke-NUS Annual Report, November 19, 2008. Available at: www.duke-nus.edu.sg/sites/default/files/ourfirstreport.pdf (accessed February 20, 2011).

Afterword

"A Most Complex Invention"

Richard I. Levin and Steven A. Wartman

THIS VOLUME IS WRITTEN 100 YEARS AFTER THE CREATION OF THE modern Academic Health Science Center (AHSC) in the United States, an enterprise that, to articulate a common perception, can be described as one of the most complex organizational inventions. The development of the AHSC was impelled, according to a landmark report by the Institute of Medicine (IOM), by three seminal events: (1) the Flexner Report for the Carnegie Foundation of 1910; (2) the founding of the National Institutes of Health in 1930; and (3) the creation of Medicare and Medicaid in 1965.[1] Indeed, the IOM now has challenged AHSCs

> to recognize the interdependent and complementary nature of their traditionally individual roles ... [requiring] the purposeful linkage of these roles so that research develops the evidence base, patient care applies and refines the evidence base, and education teaches evidence-based and team-based approaches to care and prevention."[1, p.5]

Despite the persistence of the century-old tripartite mission of education, research, and patient care, the chapters of this book describe how the AHSC of today has many forms and traverses the full spectrum of organizational structure, from local and focused to multinational and conglomerated. In the face of unprecedented economic challenges in today's world, many have suggested that the AHSC cannot survive in its current form. What the authors of this volume suggest is that it *must* survive for the health and well-being of all, but that new leadership and transformational policies are necessary to answer both the IOM's challenge and the new economic realities.

In the past hundred years, the growth of AHSCs worldwide has been astounding. For example, in the United States in just the latter half of the last century, while the population grew by 54%, the mission components of AHSCs grew between 120% and 1000%, and National Institutes of Health funding to fuel research grew by 1500%.[2] In the United States, AHSCs conduct the bulk of biomedical research, and its growth has been a major contributor to the doubling of life expectancy.[2] The sum of those productive years of life have added some $70 trillion to the US gross domestic product with a minimum return on investment for the research portfolio of 20:1.[3,4] The experience in other developed countries has been no different. In the United Kingdom, the estimate for economic gains from cardiovascular disease research alone between 1985 and 2005 is $109.5 billion.[5] In Australia the return on investment from 1990 to 2007 is $54.2 billion,[6] and in Singapore, research contributed an estimated 2.3% of gross domestic product in 2007.[7] By any standard, these international estimates are the definition of a hugely successful enterprise. Yet, with anticipated economic challenges, globalization, and the maturing of the AHSC, even the best centers face uncertainty and need to seek new business models.[8]

The proposed causes of this seeming paradox – AHSC success, by any measure, from life extension to economic gain as contrasted with potential economic failure – are many and varied. The health economist Rashi Fein[9] suggests a combination of challenges and failures: external ones related to the disruptive innovations of new competitors, government inconstancy, and the strange market for health care in the United States; and internal ones related to a failure of leadership of the AHSCs themselves. The result contributes to an already inefficient and expensive system, whereby, for example, the United States spends a dollar to provide what other developed countries buy for 63 cents,[10] and achieves the same life expectancy as Chile at seven times the cost.[11] The United States also faces a novel set of challenges brought by the new Patient Protection and Affordable Care Act.[12] But the United States is not alone with these problems: new or modified health systems in the Netherlands, the United Kingdom, and many other countries will force consolidation and changes in each of the missions of AHSCs.

This book answers these challenges by providing a blueprint based on empirical data and personal observations from leaders of some of the foremost AHSCs. These challenges are intimately tied to the remarkable role of the leader of the AHSC as an agent of change with the responsibility to align the management of the enterprise in ways that have been described as both heroic and collaborative.[13] Also included are the roles of the many members of the senior management team as well as the range of issues raised by students, trainees, faculty, and staff. The intricacies and peculiarities of financing these institutions are discussed along with the unique need to actively manage the cross-subsidization of funds from clinic to classroom and research bench in the midst of growing, fragmented regulation and a strong focus on managing conflicts of interest and commitment. There is also the need for collaboration and successful engagement with political and community leaders at every level. Finally, we are reminded that success requires translation of what we accomplish into useful knowledge for our constituencies with a vigorous strategy for communication.

These chapters, individually and collectively, provide insight into the fundamental need to achieve the "virtuous cycle,"[14] such that each of the mission areas of education, research, and patient care support and enhance each other. In this way, a transformation to successful, mission-focused management can proceed, even in the face of long institutional histories with well-established traditions and policies.

What is described in this volume is neither easy nor simple,[15] and for more than two decades, leaders have been warning of impending crisis.[16,17] However, the AHSC is essential to the development of biomedical knowledge, technical innovation, knowledge translation, economic development, and health care throughout the world.[18] The information and insight provided here offer important guidance for the new generation of leaders who must sustain – and indeed advance – these critical institutions for the health of all mankind.

References

1. Committee on the Roles of Academic Health Centers in the 21st Century. *Academic Health Centers: leading change in the 21st century*. Kohn LT, editor. Washington, DC: National Academies Press; 2004.

2. Centers for Disease Control. Ten great public health achievements: United States, 1900–1999. *MMWR*. 1999; **48**(12): 241–3. Available at: www.cdc.gov/mmwr/preview/mmwrhtml/00056796.htm (accessed February 3, 2012).

3. Murphy KM, Topel RH. Diminishing returns? The costs and benefits of improving health. *Perspect Biol Med*. 2003; **46**(3 Suppl.): S108–28.

4. Hatfield M, Sonnenschein HF, Rosenberg LE. *Exceptional Returns: the economic value of America's investment in medical research*. New York, NY: Mary Woodard Lasker Charitable Trust; 2000. Available at: www.laskerfoundation.org/media/pdf/exceptional.pdf (accessed February 6, 2012).

5. Health Economics Research Group, Office of Health Economics, RAND Europe. *Medical Research: what's it worth? Estimating the economic benefits from medical research in the UK*. London: UK Evaluation Forum; 2008. Available at: www.brunel.ac.uk/385/other/TAP825EconomicBenefitsReportFULLWeb.pdf (accessed on February 6, 2012).

6. Lateral Economics; for Research Australia. *The Economic Value of Australia's Investment in Health and Medical Research: reinforcing the evidence for exceptional returns*. October 2010. Available at: http://researchaustralia.org/Publications%20Special%20Reports/The%20Economic%20Value%20of%20Australias%20Investment%20in%20Health%20and%20Medical%20Research%20October%202010.pdf (accessed on February 6, 2012).

7. Marjanovic S, Chonaill SN. *Health and Medical Research in Singapore: observatory on health research systems*. Cambridge: RAND Corporation; 2010. Available at: www.rand.org/pubs/documented_briefings/2010/RAND_DB591.pdf (accessed on February 6, 2012).

8. Desmond-Hellmann S. *Chancellor Proposes New Approach to Secure UCSF's Financial Future*. Available at: www.youtube.com/watch?v=ANbj3FXvjlc (accessed February 2, 2012).
9. Fein R. The academic health center: some policy reflections. *JAMA*. 2000; **283**(18): 2436–7.
10. Reinhardt U. Trends: the healthcare perplex. *Milken Institute Review*. 2009; Third Quarter: 8–15.
11. Weisenthal J. Forget Medicare, this is the chart that shows why America is doomed. *Business Insider*. March 6, 2011. Available at: www.businessinsider.com/us-most-inefficient-healthcare-system-in-the-world-2011-3 (accessed March 7, 2011).
12. Patient Protection and Affordable Care Act, 2010. Pub. L. No. 111-148, §2702, 124 Stat. 119, 318–19.
13. Gosling J, Mintzberg H. The five minds of a manager. *Harvard Business Review*. 2003; **81**: 54–63.
14. Wartman SA. Towards a virtuous cycle: the changing face of academic health centers [guest editorial]. *Acad Med*. 2008; **83**(9): 797–9.
15. Wietcha M, Lipstein SH, Rabkin MT. Governance of the academic health center: striking the balance between service and scholarship. *Acad Med*. 2009; **84**(2): 170–6.
16. Barondess JA. The academic health center and the public agenda: whose three-legged stool? *Ann Intern Med*. 1991; **115**(12): 962–7.
17. Burrow GN. Tensions within the academic health center. *Acad Med*. 1993; **68**(8): 585–7.
18. Anderson G, Steinberg E, Heyssel R. The pivotal role of the academic health center. *Health Aff (Millwood)*. 1994; **13**(3): 146–58.

Acknowledgments

I would like to acknowledge the outstanding work and efforts of Lynn Bentley, Administrative Coordinator at the Association of Academic Health Centers, for her detailed and comprehensive efforts to assist in the coordination and editing of this book. In addition, I would like to thank Richard I. Levin, MD, Senior Scholar in Residence at the Association of Academic Health Centers, for his most able proofreading and editorial assistance.

—SAW

Index

Entries in **bold** denote references to figures or tables.